THE LTR* MONEY BOOK

THE LTR* MONEY BOOK

The Personal Finance Guide
for Every Kind of
*Living Together Relationship

LINDA BURR HARDEN
and
GERALD HARDEN, JD, CPA

Everest House
Publishers New York

Copyright is not claimed on the U.S. Government Tax Form 1040, the California state divorce papers, and the official application for Social Security reproduced in this book.

Designed by Sam Gantt
ISBN: 0-89696-011-0
Library of Congress Catalog Card Number: 78-57415
Published simultaneously in Canada
by Beaverbooks, Pickering, Ontario
Printed in the United States of America by
The Book Press, Brattleboro, Vermont
First Edition

CONTENTS

II—FOR MARRIED COUPLES

III—DIVORCE

INTRODUCTION

LATE IN 1976, Lee Marvin lost the most important shoot-out of his entire career. It didn't happen at the OK Corral or any other Wild West setting, but at the State Supreme Court in Sacramento, California. There, in what was quickly hailed as a landmark decision, the court ruled in favor of Marvin's ex-roommate, Michelle Triola, and her suit for one-half of the property they had accumulated while living together for six years. Film rights, a Malibu home, an island in the South Seas—it all added up to approximately $2 million. Michelle wanted her half because she claimed that she and Lee had an oral agreement to share all community property; Marvin denied her claim and countersued.

When all the dust had settled, the court ruled that cohabitation without marriage still gives each party the right to share in all community property if there is a separation. Michelle, in her victory, opened the courtroom doors to all California couples living together, and they are considerable in number. A recent survey indicated that in the twenty-one to thirty age group, more people live together than get married.

You may be wondering, how does this affect me? Well, that depends. If you're living with someone in California and you're considering a split, it means that you (or your partner) have the ability to go into court to settle your differences, just the way divorcing couples do.

If you don't live in California, the Marvin case does not affect you directly, but keep in mind that, in 1970, California was the first state to pass a no-fault divorce law. Now, eight years later, almost every state in the union has some sort of no-fault law on its books. Widespread acceptance of the Marvin case may be just as inevitable.

Which was one of the reasons this book was written—one of the reasons, but not the only one. Actually, *The LTR Money Book* is three books in one, covering all stages of romantic involvement: living together, marriage, and divorce. If you're married, for example, you'll find practical advice here on how to avoid the marriage tax, how to save money on credit cards, tips on investments, insurance, retirement benefits, and other money matters.

If you're contemplating divorce, you are about to embark on a very costly procedure. You'll need help to save every dollar possible. In *The LTR Money Book,* you'll learn about predivorce strategies, get answers to your questions about lawyers and accountants, find out how to save money on alimony and child support, and more.

For both married and divorcing couples, there's an important chapter on the monetary hiding places in a tax return—and how to find them. If you suspect your partner is concealing income from you (for whatever reason), here's a step-by-step guide to discovering it. Don't worry about having to read a lot of tax and legal terms, though. *The LTR Money Book* was written in nontechnical language; you'll read about some of the problems people have had, and how the courts have resolved the issues, but that's about as close as you'll get to any tax or legal problems.

Ideally, you should read this book before you actually embark on a new romantic adventure. Once you become involved, it's often difficult to follow some of the suggestions or alter previous mistakes. Even if you never anticipate living with someone, or if you are happily married *forever,* you can still pick up some valuable financial advice which could easily save you a lot of money some day. Needless to say, if you're involved in a divorce (where so many things can, and often do, go wrong), even reading this book after you've started proceedings will prove to be a case of "better late than never."

Finally, keep in mind that all the advice in *The LTR Money Book*—including the tax and legal aspects—is of a general nature. It is impossible to cite a particular tax or legal reference and then say it applies in all cases. LTR laws vary widely from state to state, often being changed, refined, and/or rescinded by state legislatures on a yearly basis. In addition, the Federal courts are continually handing down decisions which affect us all, regardless of state boundaries. So a good rule to follow in this book is that the advice here will be applicable in about 90 percent of all cases. Even in the other 10 percent, it's better to have some general idea of the tax and legal consequences than none at all, because then at least you can ask your lawyer, or CPA, the correct questions.

With or without professional help, we hope the advice in this book will help you save money in any LTR problem you may encounter. After all, that's why it was written in the first place.

PART ONE

LIVING TOGETHER FOR FUN AND PROFIT

1

OF HEARTS AND DOLLARS

THERE'S NOTHING LIKE BEING IN LOVE, especially in the beginning. Those early feelings of euphoria, fulfillment, and "togetherness" simply cannot be rivaled at any other time in life. In songs, books, and movies, we celebrate romance —pure and simple, without a cloud in the sky.

Why, then, in the midst of all this passionate prose, do we insist on injecting a crass note about finances? Well, mostly because people who walk around in a romantic fog all day long have notorious disregard for their wallets. Even that would be all right if every love story had a happy ending, but most of them don't. The problem is that the euphoria and the glow eventually wear off, but the bill collector is forever at your door.

So, whether or not you consider this in the best of taste, the time to review your financial affairs is *before* you ever decide to live with another person. But before we get into the economics of living together, there is something even more basic to consider.

Stop, Look, and Listen

Before you pop the question to a potential roommate, you should be aware of some dangerous situations. Never, never discuss possible cohabitation with another person while you are imbibing alcohol, nursing a hangover, getting ready for bed, in bed, taking a bath together, making up from your last fight, or paying your bills.

Before you enter any such discussion, you should have given a great deal of thought to this move, and you should have at least a mental list of some pretty persuasive reasons for wanting to live together. If your reasons are things like "Why pay rent on two apartments?" or "I hate to sleep alone" or that the other person can cook or will do your laundry, you are in trouble. The absolute worst reason is "My divorce will never come through anyway." If that is *your* reason, stop right now, and rethink your decision, because you're playing with dynamite.

A Possible Tax Savings

Once you have come up with some solid reasons for living together, consider this financial one: In most cases you will probably be saving a substantial amount in tax dollars by not getting married. It is difficult to explain why our tax laws are written this way, to encourage divorce and cohabitation without marriage, but they are. Perhaps it's just a backlash against the times when our laws encouraged marriage, with one spouse staying at home to raise the family. This is underscored by the fact that Congress still allows tax deductions for dependent children and lower rates for married couples, provided only one spouse works. Unfortunately, more than 60 percent of all families consist of two working parents, and these are the people who pay what is commonly known as the "marriage tax." These are the people who can least afford it.

Even aside from the monetary considerations, a lot of

people consider marriage an unacceptable alternative. It is "permanent" in a way that living together never is, although we are now on our way toward building a separate body of law for unmarried couples which will probably be as large and complex as the one for married couples. Unmarried partners sometimes end up with alimony payments or huge property settlements, and that's why you must be careful when you begin one of these relationships.

Common-law-marriage States

Another point to remember is that if you live in a common-law-marriage state and you hold yourselves out to be married, you may be considered legally married even without a license. These states are Alabama, Colorado, Georgia, Idaho, Iowa, Kansas, Montana, Ohio, Oklahoma, Pennsylvania, Rhode Island, South Carolina, Texas, and the District of Columbia. How do you "hold yourselves out to be married"? By opening joint bank accounts, by using the same charge accounts, and, most damaging of all, by introducing your roommate as your spouse. Do not do these things in the above states unless you actually want to be considered legally married. There is a popular misconception that if you live together for seven years, you are "married" via common law. Not true. Common-law marriages are valid only in the states listed above and need no qualifying time period before they are considered to be in force. For example, if an unmarried couple were to register as "Mr. and Mrs." in a Texas motel—even for one night—that is enough to make them common-law husband and wife.

Joint vs. Separate Tax Returns

In a few instances, you may discover that you'll pay less in taxes if you both file one joint tax return. However, unless you are legally married (via ceremony or common-law marriage), *do not* file a joint return. The IRS takes a very dim view of people who do that.

Gay Couples, Take Note

A very large percentage of the gay couples who live together are not married. This may be for personal reasons, tax advantages, or because most states do not recognize homosexual marriages. However, all of the advice in this first section on living together applies as much to gay couples as to straights.

What's Ahead?

The following chapters were designed to help you in all the tricky areas of living-together relationships. To be honest, few people have any idea of the problems and sticky situations they will run into after they start living together. If you follow the suggestions step by step, you can cover all the preliminary planning in one session. The checklist in Chapter 13 was created to help you sort out various problems, run interference, and, in general, save you time. If you use it as an aid or handy guide, then you should have no trouble. Don't view it, however, as a series of tests and contracts which must be fulfilled. A Magna Carta it isn't. After all, people started living together to escape all of the hassles of marriage and divorce, not to create new ones.

Finally, one of the biggest problems in writing the first section of this book was how to refer to its audience. A compilation of likely candidates included the following:

- Roommates
- Swinging singles
- Unmarried liaisons
- LTRs (living-together relationships)
- Partners of the opposite sex sharing living quarters (the U. S. Census Board phrase)
- Consensual unions

Partners	Friends
De facto marriages	Meretricious relationships
Cohabitors	Old lady/old man (as in "my")
Lovers/mistresses	

You'll note that some of these appellations have a snide, sometimes downright nasty tone to them. Well, the times may be a–changing, but there's a little bit of John Calvin still left in most of us.

Anyway, after wrestling with this problem for over a year and discarding catchy acronyms like LIN (Lover in Residence ("How's your old Lin?") and distinctive, Bondian designators like SUSW (Shacking Up, So What?), we ended up writing the entire section without one catch-all word or phrase. Therefore, you will find a number of terms sprinkled throughout to denote living together. You'll find references to partners, roommates, friends, unmarrieds, LTR couples . . . in other words, something to irritate almost everyone.

2

SETTING UP THE GROUND RULES

Goods which are not shared are not goods.
—Fernando de Rojas

IT'S DOUBTFUL WHETHER SENOR ROJAS would have written those words had he lived with someone in an unstructured LTR. For one thing, those goods of yours which are not covered by some sort of an agreement can end up as the other person's property if you're not careful. It is in the beginning that your LTR is most fraught with peril and most susceptible to misunderstandings, so it is at this time that you should make a concerted effort to set up some ground rules. These will be the basic decisions you will both have to abide by during your relationships. For most people, it's a fairly easy job: Both of you worked before and you plan no dramatic changes after setting up housekeeping together. In this instance you both know beforehand what your income will be. Your income-tax withholding, exemptions, etc., will not change. Your ground rules will be relatively uncomplicated. Just decide who's going to pay for what. This may be no different from the situation you encountered when you had a previous same-sex roommate.

The Dutch-treat Method

You may decide the simplest course is just to split things down the middle: ½ on rent, ½ on food, ½ on utilities, pooling the costs of all incidentals. Or you may decide on some minor adjustments: equally splitting rent and utilities (such as electricity and heat), but separately buying your own food, etc. The problem in this case—and you will discover it rather quickly—is that this arrangement is best suited to same-sex roommates. Why? Well, when you live together in an LTR, somehow the rules change. Whether these are "human" instincts or not is a moot question; the tendency is to play traditional husband-and-wife roles. Should you decide on this sort of setup, you will have to agree *firmly* on certain rules, because it is in these situations that income distinctions become blurred and monetary disputes are common.

> *Very important note:* No matter what role definitions or income divisions you decide upon, we cannot stress too strongly the need to accomplish all of this planning *before* you start living together. To delay financial planning is to court disaster. You may believe this to be "calculated" and contrary to the nature of your free relationship, but the problems you'll run into later on are far greater. When you leave crucial matters like these up in the air, with nothing more than lazy verbal commitments like "We'll settle all the money stuff later," you run the risk of entering the relationship with conflicting expectations. This is almost inevitable when incomes are disparate. Don't expect the higher-salaried person to assume a higher proportion of the expenses

until it's actually been agreed to—either orally or in writing. And don't plan on quitting your job until you both sit down and work it out on paper.

When There's One Breadwinner—the Classic "Husband-Wife" Situation

Sally Smith, secretary, earns $8,400 a year. She is about to move to a new apartment with John Jones, ace executive, who earns $48,000. They have already decided against splitting all their expenses in half. Their reasons: If they had agreed to a 50/50 split, then, judging by Sally's salary, they could realistically afford only a $250-a-month apartment (¼ of Sally's monthly take-home pay, $162, less $40 for income taxes, equals $122—the standard calculation Sally should use when setting rent maximums). Needless to say, John, who could easily afford an apartment with rent at twice that amount, would prefer to live in more sumptuous surroundings.

So, to even things up a bit, John offers to pay ¾ of the expenses, since he is earning more than five times the money that Sally does. (Note: Remember that this take-home pay is not five times more than Sally's, since he is in a higher tax bracket and he may also have an ex-family to support.) In return for carrying more of the financial burden, Sally agrees to handle ¾ of the housekeeping, since John, as a result of his job requirements, must work longer hours. Therefore, they are working together in what can best be described as a "husband-wife" relationship. Under no circumstances should they move in together without a crystal-clear statement of their intensions. Called agreements or contracts, they can be of the simplest nature. You don't need a lawyer to help you draw it up—just sit down together and put on paper what you have already agreed to verbally.

Sample Contract

Sally Smith and John Jones hereby agree that:

1. They will share Apartment B at 2150 Johnson Street, San Francisco, and will be responsible for its monthly rent of $500 in this manner:

   Sally Smith—$150
   John Jones—$350

2. All other communal expenses (food, utilities, etc.) will be shared, with John paying 75 percent and Sally paying 25 percent.

3. They further agree that Sally Smith will be responsible for the following duties:

   Food shopping
   Cooking
   Laundry

4. All house cleaning and other maintenance will be split equally.

5. Neither will purchase linens, lamps, furniture, etc., without agreement from the other party.

Date _____________ Agreed __________________

Agreed __________________

Other Variations on This Theme

Now, suppose after four months of blissful harmony, John comes to the conclusion that Sally's talents are being wasted in her job. Sally has always wanted to be a sculptor but has never had the time or money to pursue this career. So, John offers to bankroll Sally's artistic effort in exchange for her total management of the household: cooking, cleaning, laundry, shopping, bill paying, etc. If Sally should accept this offer, then they ought to decide whether they want to get married in order to file jointly, since Sally will no longer have any immediate income. However, let's assume they still want to be single. In that case, they may want to draw up a more elaborate contract, such as the following:

Sample Contract

Sally Smith and John Jones hereby agree that:

1. They will share Apartment B at 2150 Johnson Street, San Francisco, and John Jones will be responsible for its monthly rent of $500.

2. All other expenses such as food, clothing incidentals, utilities, art supplies, and miscellaneous household items will be paid for by John Jones.

3. Sally Smith will be responsible for the following:

    Food shopping
    Laundry
    Preparing meals
    All cleaning
    All entertaining
    Bill paying
    All other household upkeep.

4. They further agree that they will keep separate bank accounts, with John reimbursing Sally for any expenditure under item 2.

5. Any proceeds from the sale of Sally Smith's sculpture will be divided in this manner: ¼ for John Jones, ¾ for Sally Smith.

Date ____________ Agreed ________________

Agreed ________________

Some Important Things to Remember

The above borders on contract cohabitation. To keep it from becoming such an arrangement, in which one partner must pay social security taxes for the other, John should not make any outright payments to Sally for her duties around the house. He can, however, make tax-free gifts to Sally of up to $3,000 a year for her personal support. After that point, John must file a gift-tax return and pay a tax on anything over $3,000. (Note: Any part of that $3,000 which Sally spends on John will not count as a taxable gift.)

To make sure things go smoothly, Sally should do three things before proceeding. First, she should make sure that she has a substantial balance in her checking or savings account. This will allow her to make household purchases whenever necessary and not worry about being immediately reimbursed by John. Sally's bill paying and reconciliation of all accounts should be limited to once, or at the most twice, a month. Second, she and John should agree upon a monthly sum to cover her incidental needs: small clothing, items, toiletries, etc. Third, Sally should purchase all of her major personal needs *before* she quits her job. For example, her wardrobe should be complete to her satisfaction. Once she embarks on her own career, the wardrobe will only need occasional maintenance.

In the situation described above, John can take a dependency deduction for Sally of $750 for federal income taxes. (Check the appendix to see if your state is one which has old laws on its books against two married people living together. If that is the case for Sally and John, then John cannot take Sally as a dependent on his tax return, as it violates state law.) He can also apply for certain benefits for state income taxes as well. Once Sally qualifies as a dependency deduction, within the limitations, her medical expenses may be deductible on John's return as well.

If Sally earns under $750 a year, John can use the more advantageous tax rate reserved for Head of Household. Remember, however, that if Sally has any gross income in excess of $750, then she may not be counted as a dependent whether or not John actually is supporting her.

If the person being supported has children who are also being supported by the taxpayer, such children should also qualify for the exemption deductions. They may also be covered under the taxpayer's existing health insurance as "foster children."

When the supporting person is the one with the children, it may be possible to pay the other person for taking care of the children. This will have the effect of transferring income to the other person, who will be taxed at a much lower rate, while at the same time giving deductions to the person paying for having the children watched.

When There Are Two Breadwinners

If your incomes are more closely aligned, then it is much easier, and less perilous, to adopt a "two breadwinners" stance in the relationship. In this way, you split everything 50/50—rent, food, housekeeping. Minor adjustments can be easily handled without specifically writing them into your agreement (e.g., he does all the cooking; she handles the laundry). Therefore, you really don't need a separate agreement if you utilize the checklist in Chapter 13. Tailoring an agreement exactly to your needs and specifications is really only necessary when one partner's income is reduced or curtailed.

One item to remember: Make sure the apartment you end up sharing follows the ¼-monthly-net formula of the person with the lower salary.

Advantages of a Two-breadwinners System

This kind of relationship is probably the best in terms of future harmony. Each of you is responsible for ½ your communal living expenses. Dividing any amount by two has never been a difficult calculation; there is much less chance for mistrust or misunderstanding. More important, with the equal footing you get from a 50/50 relationship, neither partner is in the position to bully the other economically. Financial independence can only strengthen your relationship and keep it honest. Your tax returns are simple, and you get the benefit of the "filing single" tax rate. It truly is the best of both worlds.

Possible Job Problems: What to Tell Your Boss

Considering that we are approaching the twenty-first century, you shouldn't have to tell your boss *anything* about your new roommate.

However, there always are exceptions. And if one of them could cost you your job, then it certainly seems worth the money to take a few precautions. For starters, if you are about to start living with someone with whom you also work, check out your company's policy on married couples working together. This is important because if they do have such policies, they will apply as much to LTR couples as marrieds. For example, many companies have policies against nepotism—that is, husbands or wives working in positions which allow them to promote their spouses over other workers. In most cases, these companies only restrict marrieds from working in the same department. If, as an LTR couple, this is the only restriction you face, nothing will probably happen to you, provided you both are not in the same department. However, if your company has harsher rules for married workers, be discreet among your fellow workers and company administration officials. Some companies with nepotism policies outlaw married couples completely. The nepotism policy will probably be particularly enforced when the couple, whether married or LTR, comprise a manager/worker relationship, such as boss/secretary or vice president/manager or other likely combinations. In these cases, the company is trying to protect itself from charges of favoritism by other workers. You should be very careful and very discreet in these situations.

Don't tell your coworkers about your new living arrangements and, by all means, make sure that administration doesn't find out.

Take Two Precautions and Call Me in the Morning

If your company has an outright ban on the employment of married couples, live by these two rules:

1. Keep your new relationship to yourself. Don't spread the news around, especially among coworkers.
2. Make sure that you have different mailing addresses as far as the company's administrative office is concerned. They need employee addresses for W-2 forms, bonus checks, and Christmas-card lists. If one partner's parents live nearby, use their address. Failing that, find a good friend who will let you put your name on his mailbox. Your last resort should be a post-office box, only because it looks so suspicious. Even if administration doesn't catch on, once that number appears on the company Christmas-card list, you'll be the subject of a gossipy guessing game among your coworkers.

If you should get caught living with someone and your company has rules against marrieds working together, you may very well be fired. Unless it's the federal government you're working for,[1] you really don't have any recourse—a private company can fire you for just about any reason it wants,[2] just as you can quit your job at any time. So, in certain cases, you will have to live together with the realiza-

---

[1] The ACLU has successfully prosecuted several cases like this. The employer in all cases was the federal government.

[2] If you have entered into an employment contract with your company, and they try to terminate you (without settlement) before the contract expires, then, of course, you have a case. Also, if you believe your firing was actually based on racial or sexual discrimination instead of just living with a coworker, then you also have a case.

tion that one of you may end up in the unemployment line. (You may also want to re-evaluate the whole idea of living together under these admittedly trying circumstances, especially if you and/or your roommate are pulling down a substantial salary.)

When It Seems Better to Be Married

In certain employment areas, you are more attractive to a prospective employer if you are married (family man, more stable, more bills, etc.). If you find yourself in this position, it is undeniably tempting to lie and say you are married. After all, you are living with someone, so what's the difference?

Well, if you're found to be single, you could stand a good chance of losing your job, especially if your employer holds very conservative views on these matters. (Fortunately, there aren't many such employers around any more.) A more likely problem is health and life insurance and the mess it can become when your "wife's" name is on all of your company's forms.

For example, take the case of Beatrice and Benedict. When they first started living together, Benedict was unemployed. Then he found a job opening in sales at a life insurance company. Because competition for the job was keen, Benedict indicated on his application that he was married, thinking this would make him a more attractive candidate for the position. He got the job, but was never sure if his marital status had anything to do with his success. So, to play it safe, he listed Beatrice as his wife on all company forms, including his health and life insurance policies.

Five years later, when they parted less than amicably, Beatrice asked for spousal support. When Benedict refused, Beatrice threatened a court action, stating she believed she was married to him all along.[3] She said she would cite the insurance policies as evidence and also inform Benedict's company of their domestic problems. With that, he capitulated and agreed to spousal support.

So, even when you don't lose your job, phony marital status can cost you plenty.

You may also notice that on the W-4 (withholding) form, which you must fill out when first starting to work, there is a section to indicate your marital status. The only time this could cause you any trouble is when the IRS audits your tax return and feels that you are really married, although filing as a single. One of the ways they might try to prove this is to check the W-4 form you filled out for your employer.

In any case, maybe all of these problems will make you think twice before you tell your future employer "I did," when in fact you never sang the wedding-bell blues in your life.

---

[3] This is called "putative spouse" in legal terms. In other words, Beatrice really believed she was married, but he didn't think he was.

3

PROPERTY: BUYING IT, SHARING IT, SPLITTING IT UP

He would be setting up as a man of property next,
with a place in the country.
—John Galsworthy

AND IF HE WANTED to remain a "man of property," he would be wise to list all of his belongings as "separate."

This is a step that many may feel is not necessary, but if you are an exceedingly cautious person, or the kind that likes to think several moves in advance, you may want to make up a list or an inventory of all the major or important items you bring into the relationship. It's difficult, at a time of great joy in a relationship, to think forward to the day when it all may end. But "divorces" do occur in partnerships, just as they do in marriages. When it ends on an acrimonious note, there may be some ownership fights over small, seemingly insignificant items—records, books, those chopsticks you lifted from a Chinese restaurant.

So, while you may not want to suggest this to your partner (it does seem a bit cold and calculating for someone head over heels in love), you might take a few minutes to make a complete inventory of the smaller items you really care about, especially those which will be mixed in with your partner's.

If you're using the checklist in Chapter 13, there is plenty of room to list your small valuables. If you just want to make one up by yourself, don't forget to add:

Records and/or tapes
Books
Silverware and/or crystal
Crockpots, food processors, etc. (in fact, just about anything in the kitchen)
Towels and sheets

To lend some authenticity to your list, have it notarized (cost is a nominal fee), or sign it in front of witnesses and have them notarize it, or date the list and then mail it to yourself. Don't open this letter after you receive it, as the sealed envelope's postmark provides your proof of date.

What about the larger items? You may think (sales receipts and lists notwithstanding) that if you come into a relationship with a king-sized waterbed and dining-room set, then you'll be leaving with them as well. Of course, this will probably be the case as long as hostilities do not escalate. However, when lovers want to play rough, they can be absolutely ingenious about it. Here's a true story. Two people, Dan and Susan, whose partnership was already on the skids, had a terrible fight one night, culminating with Dan storming out of their apartment. When he returned the next afternoon, he couldn't get back in because the lock had been changed. It wouldn't have mattered anyway, since Susan had already called a moving van and had all Dan's belongings put into storage *under her name*. Even when Dan finally found out where his things were, he couldn't get them out because he couldn't prove possession.

The last anyone heard, Dan was talking things over with a lawyer.

Calling In the Law

Granted, that was an extreme case. Most people don't have that much venom stored up. But what usually happens when there's a disagreement and your partner rips off your sofa? Can you call in the local sheriff to get it back for you? Not likely. (Remember the old adage "Possession is nine-tenths of the law.")

Can you retrieve something through small-claims court?[1] Well, that's always one course of action, although it takes a very long time to get a ruling, and even if it is in your favor, you've got to get the local sheriff to collect it and that's not one of his favorite jobs.

How to Deal with Community Property

Community property is that property acquired by either you or your roommate (other than property acquired by gift or inheritance) during the time you lived together. It is owned jointly by both of you during your partnership.

In general, the community property acquired by your partnership will fall into three general categories: consumables, small purchases, and large or time purchases.

Consumables

This is a subject that will probably be decided once you've settled the question of role definition. If you are going to split the food and other shopping chores 50/50,

---

[1] Small-claims court is just what the name implies; it's for claims no higher than $500 in value. There are no lawyers involved—you "prosecute" or "defend" yourself with no outside help, and the judge makes the final ruling.

say on a weekly or monthly basis, then the easiest solution is simply to pay for what you buy when you buy it. Alternatively, regardless of who does the shopping, each food bill can be split in half. Or, if all the shopping is done by one person, then each week's tally must be split. This third way is usually the best in terms of saving money, since one person becomes more expert at saving coupons, locating bargains, or finding special shops (dented-can stores, produce market, etc.). If only one of you drinks or smokes, then those purchases (booze, mixers, cigarettes, or similar items) should be accounted for separately.

If you have accumulated a large pantry and are now ready to split, the easiest way to deal with this is 50/50, or as close to it as possible.

Small Purchases

You will want to decide what items will go into a general "fund" for the both of you. If you buy wine glasses, for example, and then must replace broken ones, these can be listed as general community property, along with other glasses, silverware, linens, bedding, desk items, books, records, and the like.

Set up a petty-cash system for these purchases. It works this way: Each of you contributes a set amount to the fund each month ($20 each, for example) that's kept in a picturesque cigar box. Out of that amount, either of you can make purchases as long as you remember to leave a receipt for the money you take. At the end of each month, leftover cash plus receipts should equal the $40 you started out with. It's also an efficient way to keep track of those smaller purchases which are sometimes hard to account for after a day or two.

These purchases can all be easily split up later, on a 50/50 basis. You won't have many of these purchases in a typical partnership, unless you're both starting from scratch in setting up your household (not usually the case for most people). If you do buy a number of small purchases—say, to set up a kitchen—and later on you decide to go your separate ways, there may be some foolish agony in store when you try to split something like a drainboard. If it's a harmonious parting, you'll have no trouble with the odds and ends. But if bitterness abounds, you may find yourselves squabbling over trivial incidentals like wastepaper baskets and spice racks.

A word of advice: Give in to the other person's wishes before hostilities escalate. Sure, you may lose some money when you don't get your "fair share," but is it really worth the hassle? Usually, when you're generous in situations like this, it softens the hard edge of parting and lessens the chance of other fights.

However, some people are always ready to dig in and get what's *rightfully* theirs. They should be prepared for a pitched battle over that $3.00 drainboard and every other inconsequential item in the house.

Large or Time Purchases

If you find it necessary to purchase large items (furniture, appliances, etc.) as a couple, you would do best to follow this rule: If neither of you can afford to purchase the item separately, then you shouldn't buy it at all. Only one of you should make the purchase, or apply for the credit and make the subsequent time payments. There are two reasons for this. First, it's a lot easier to get credit this way. Second, if the item is so expensive that you can afford it only with your combined incomes, then you're probably to the limit of your budget already and should forget about it for the time being.

Credit is much harder to come by when an unmarried couple applies for it. The people who process the applications are understandably (if unfairly) suspicious about the stability of your relationship and your responsibility for the payments should you split up. For example, to buy a $2,500 dining-room set on time, you will each probably have to show the credit department enough earning power and credit rating to purchase that set by yourself. Then they might draw up a joint time plan for you. But don't count on it. Any store has the right to refuse any individual credit. Under these circumstances, it would not be unlikely for them to do just that.

Here's another way to look at the credit problem. If you both have limited incomes and you both are paying off other credit purchases, plus rent, food, utilities, and other monthly expenses, can you really afford another large time payment even if it's a joint one? Probably not.

You might be tempted to lie and say you're married to get the credit under "Mr. and Mrs." Don't do it. First, any sort of credit check will denote your single marital status and immediately put the creditors on guard. Second, there can be dire consequences later on if you do get credit from the store as Mr. and Mrs. when you're both actually single.

In the long run you can't go wrong with the rule that only one person buys and makes payments on any time purchases.

Tax Note

One money-saving reason for having only one person make the time purchases is to allow that person (usually the one with the larger income and the itemized tax return) another deduction: this one for interest paid on time purchases. Let's say that, for the purposes of this illustration, Jane Roe is going to make all of the large purchases in her partnership. Once this has been agreed to, she has two ways to go. The first is to retain sole possession of any item she buys and to draw up an agreement to that effect. This can be agreed to in a simple statement[2] like this:

> It is hereby noted that the $2,500 dining-room set (table, six chairs, and buffet) at 123 Brown Street, Lubbock, Texas, belongs solely to Jane Roe. It is also noted that Jane Roe will be responsible for all payments, charges, and interest on said dining-room furniture.
>
> ______________________________ Jane Roe
>
> ______________________________ John Doe
>
> ____________ Date

An alternative to this is for Jane to buy the dining-room furniture and then set up an agreement with John so that he is responsible for half of the time payments. In this situation, Jane is the only one responsible to the store, and if John reneges on his half of the payment, it is Jane who still must come up with the entire amount. Of course, she keeps the furniture, unless she cannot make the payments and her purchase is repossessed. If this is the alternative you use, then the agreement should also make some provision as to who keeps the furniture in case of a future split.

---

[2] It is not necessary to have these agreements notarized.

4

CONTRACT COHABITATION: CASH ON THE LINE

There is no fortress so strong that money cannot take it.
—Cicero

CONTRACT COHABITATION is not for everyone. The idea of "hiring" a live-in lover is repugnant to many people. However, for those people who are very wary, or "gun-shy" from a previous marriage, or who want to "control" a relationship, contract cohabitation has certain attractions.

Most of you have probably heard about this specific form of partnership. For those of you who are not familiar with contract cohabitation, a brief description is in order.

Contract cohabitation involves two people living together as employer and employee. The contract, whether written or oral, defines the terms of the relationship, including salary, vacation, days off, specific duties, sex requirements, fringe benefits, etc.

The question of love is never specifically outlined in most contracts. Employers are usually willing to let this "develop" according to their own needs. They can terminate an employee, for example, who falls in love. Or, conversely, they could dismiss an employee for not returning their love.

Of course it's possible to argue that employees have the same rights and power. In the abstract sense of contract cohabitation, they do. But in reality, the employer, the person who holds the pursestrings, controls the tempo and the emotions of the relationship.

The discussion here is not meant to center on the social, legal, or moral aspects of contract cohabitation. Rather, the focus is on the monetary aspects of such a contract and how it compares with just plain living together.

Employer Expenses

First, consider the expenses if you are the employer. Whatever and however you decide to pay your employee, it must meet the minimum-wage standard, which will eventually be $3.35 per hour. In most cases, you will probably be paying at least $500 a month, and above and beyond this amount, you will also have to pay an extra amount (currently 5.85 percent, and rising steadily) into the social security system. As an employer, you are required to keep the work area (your home) safe for the employee. This will require extra insurance. And in some states, you are required by law to carry workmen's compensation insurance to protect your employee. This could end up costing you an extra $20 per month.

Conversely, you might be able to deduct some of your employee's salary if you can prove that a portion of this employee's work was spent, say, entertaining clients. This would be a normal business expense. Proving it, however, is the difficult part. You shouldn't count on this deduction until you've discussed the situation with a good accountant.

Remember, if you're audited by the IRS, they will scrutinize your contract cohabitation agreement as closely as your other monetary dealings.

Employee Expenses

Obviously, you're going to have to pay tax on your earnings. Count on paying over $1,000 of that yearly $6,000 in federal taxes alone. State and city taxes will also have to be paid, plus your social security payments (also 5.85 percent of your wages).

Since it's highly unlikely that your employer will provide any retirement benefits, other than the required social security, you would be wise to start an IRA (Individual Retirement Account) as your own personal pension plan. You may contribute up to 15 percent (up to $1,500) of your salary to the IRA each year.

Make sure that you are in some way covered by insurance while you are working for your employer. And when you're negotiating the employment contract, see if you can't get some health insurance coverage from your employer. For example, a woman employee should hold out for abortion and maternity insurance just in case.

Which Is Cheaper?

You should be able to tell from the previous discussion that contract cohabitation costs money. Its main benefit, especially to previously married employers who may have been burned in their last divorce, is that everything is cut and dried and protected by the employment contract. If you are not paranoid about the consequences of living together and the consequences of possible split-ups, then don't pay the extra money in income and social security taxes and workmen's compensation insurance. Work it out your own way, draw up your own agreements, and save money.

Sample Contracts

You really do not need the help of a lawyer to draw up one of these contracts. You know better than anyone what you want (or expect) out of the agreement, and the contract should reflect that—stated in the simplest possible "plain English" terminology. However, if you are in a high tax bracket, or unsure of all the tax ramifications of such a contract, then by all means have your accountant review it with regards to your current tax situation.

John Jones, who resides at ____________________, wishes to employ ____________________ at $100 per month.

Condition:

____________________ specifically agrees to:

1. Perform normal household cleaning duties
2. Do all necessary shopping chores
3. Perform sexually, and sex shall not be unreasonably withheld
4. Be socially available when John entertains clients
5. Give thirty days notice before quitting

John agrees to:

1. Allow reasonable sick leave
2. Provide workman's compensation insurance
3. Permit reasonable denial of sex
4. Allow one day and two nights per week off
5. Perform the necessary accounting for payroll taxes, etc.
6. Give at least thirty days notice before dismissal
7. Allow two weeks per year as paid vacation

Signed ____________, 19__

____

John Jones

____

5

HOUSING: UNEXPECTED WAYS TWO PEOPLE CAN SAVE MONEY

What is more agreeable than one's home?
—Cicero

TWO OF THE MOST IMPORTANT decisions you'll face in a new relationship are whether to live together and where to live together.

By now you have answered the first question—presumably with a yes. The next step is to put a roof over your head. It's not as easy as it looks. Both rent checks, and house payments, are at all-time highs. If you want to save money *and* find a place to live, then you have to be prepared to spend some time investigating the various options open to you as well as putting a pencil to every option available. First of all, if you have little combined income (or if only one of you plans to work) and you have no savings, then your options are pretty much reduced to renting. You will also want to rent if you are unsure of the durability of your new relationship, or if you think there's a good chance of a job transfer, or if there are other uncertainties in your future. Compared to buying a house, you'll find that your first year of renting is much cheaper. It is only after the second year that owning begins to pay off. So if you have any doubts about short-term stability, by all means rent until you're more sure of the future.

There may be a special consideration if one partner has recently sold his or her home. This is usually the case after a divorce. The gain on the sale of a home must be reinvested (by buying another one) within eighteen months of the sale, or the tax bite becomes ferocious. But except for that, renting has many advantages: no high mortgage payments, no real estate taxes, no insurance (unless you want it), the landlord is responsible for maintenance, and you can move any time your lease is up.

Tips on Leases

Normally, you are much better off with a lease than without. Considering how costs are rising these days, and depending upon how long you want to live in your apartment, you may want a one- or two-year lease if you can get it. This is merely insurance against a landlord passing on increases to you (for example, his real estate taxes will almost always go up).

Some landlords will counter by requiring the first and *last* month's rent plus deposit before giving you a lease. At this point, you will have to weigh the security of a lease against giving up a month's rent without earning any interest on it. Also, once your original lease expires, try to negotiate a new one, but don't do this until your landlord raises your rent. Some will let the issue slide for months (even years), so don't provoke it. But as soon as an increase *is* passed along to you, try to get that rent stabilized via a new lease.

The only time you shouldn't have a long lease is if you are unsure about the stability of your new relationship. If your partner leaves after one month, sticking you with the balance of a two-year lease, you will have to find a new roommate, or pay the extra rent, or try to get out of the lease, or sublet. It can get expensive. In these cases, perhaps the safest bet is a sublease until you're more certain of the stability of your partnership.

Choosing the Right Apartment for Both of You

Next, consider some of the basics of renting an apartment for the two of you. First of all, do either of you presently live in an apartment big enough to accommodate both partners with little strain? This usually requires an extra room besides the standard single's arrangement of a living room/bedroom.

Now you're probably thinking that to really save money a studio or one-bedroom would be sufficient. But sometimes it's necessary to spend a little extra to make life more than just bearable. So if it's at all possible, try to find a place that will give you both a "separate" place to go to when you need to be alone (e.g., she in the study, he in the living room). The extra cost is definitely worth it, if for nothing more than breathing room.

Which brings us to another sticky problem. You, John Doe, and you, Jane Roe, have decided to live together and (coincidentally) Jane Roe now inhabits an inexpensive but spacious two-bedroom apartment. Since Jane now pays a rent far lower than anything you could hope to find together, you, John Doe, decide to move in with her. OK, Jane, pay attention, because there are some important things you should do. First, check the lease, if you have one. If there are instructions in the lease as to how many people may inhabit the apartment, you may have to pay more rent to have a roommate. Or, at the very least, you will have to notify the landlord. Do this one of two ways:

1. Tell your landlord orally. Be casual about it; just mention it "because you think he ought to know."
2. Notify him in writing. Make this a very simple letter. Just state that as of the beginning of next month, another person will be sharing the apartment with you. If it involves a rent increase, simply tell him that next month's rent check will reflect the increase. It's up to you whether you should tell the landlord that your new roommate is of the opposite sex. You know your landlord best, but the usual advice is to leave out the new roommate's name unless you are specifically asked for it.

The primary reason that notification is important is that you don't want your lover's car towed away from your apartment parking lot or to have him/her arrested for burglary by the police when your landlord spots "an intruder" sneaking into your apartment.

Once you have things straight with your landlord, then your new roommate is ready to move into *your apartment*, and it will always remain *your apartment* if you move nothing and do nothing but allow the new co–tenant to stick his or her possessions wherever they may fit. Here's a suggestion if you both have a number of belongings. Take some extra time and move all your things to one side or one corner of the room. Then, when new roomie appears on your doorstep with a favorite lamp or super stereo, *both of you* arrange the furniture in each room to your mutual satisfaction. This is not so much a money-saving idea as it is a "feelings saving" idea. If your new partner has to contend with the way you've arranged the bed and dresser, or has to leave a treasured painting in the hall closet because there's no wall space left, then there's a good chance your partner may always feel like a visitor (or worse, an intruder). It's an extra strain no one should have to bear because it's so easily overcome.

Apartment Hunting

The chances are good that you'll both be out looking for an apartment or house after you've decided to live together. Naturally, you'll each have specific needs and desires which you'll want the place to meet, but the standard rule (and it's a good one) is that your rent should be no higher than one week's take-home pay. That's rent plus incidentals like electricity, gas, and, in some areas, heat. You may also be responsible for certain repairs on the place or other extra costs like garages, etc. The lease or oral agreement with the landlord should spell out all these in detail before you move in.

New vs. Old

Some of the most expensive apartments you'll ever find are in some of the oldest buildings in existence. Renovated brownstones and Victorian houses are now as popular as the most modern of apartment buildings. They carry extra expenses, however. Most have hardwood floors, and you will want at least some throw rugs to absorb extra noise as well as add warmth. They will cost more to heat and will most likely have older, less efficient heating units (very important when you must pay this cost). They are harder to clean and in general will require more of your time in upkeep. They will also require extra purchases such as a stepladder (for your twelve-to-fifteen-foot ceilings), curtains and/or draperies, a shower curtain, and sometimes appliances—refrigerator, stove, and (for those of you can't rough it) dishwasher.

In general, modern "luxury" apartments will end up costing you less just in timesaving features alone. However, if you are hooked on older apartments, see if you can find one in need of repair and then do the painting, etc., on your own, in exchange for lower rent from the landlord.

House Hunting

You may be tempted to go the whole suburban married-couple route and rent a house. If so, you should be aware of some extra costs you wouldn't be faced with in an apartment. In a house, you will definitely have to pay for heat, plus water, plus garbage collection, plus yard maintenance (either you'll do it yourself or, if leisure time is precious to you, you'll pay someone else to do it). Also, when a water pipe breaks or something else goes wrong in a house, you'll probably have to fix it yourself. There's no building super to call and complain to when you're in a house of your own.

Renting a Condominium or Co-op

Whether it's a high-rise apartment or townhouse, a condominium or co-op can be rented in much the same manner as you would rent a house. You will have the same extra charges for heat, water, and garbage collection—plus you may also have a monthly maintenance fee to pay to the local homeowner's association. This, in turn, keeps the common-area grounds—pool, etc.—in good shape. Fees vary with each homeowner's association.

Special Problems of Unmarried Apartment Hunters

The problems of searching for an apartment or house are legendary. Combing the want ads, weekends spent pounding the pavement, dealings with real estate people—it can end up giving ulcers to even the most even-tempered of people. As unmarrieds, you'll face other, even more exasperating problems.

The Disapproving Landlord

You will sometimes run into landlords who frown on your life style and won't rent to you. You have two options:

trickery or another landlord.

If you've just started looking when you run into this problem, look for another place. Who needs the hassle? There are enough business-minded realtors around who are only interested in your cold cash to allow you to easily bypass the prudes.

However, if that superconservative landlord holds the key to your "dream" apartment, or if you're desperate, down to your last choice, and pressed for time, you may want to hold back certain details of your partnership from your prospective landlord. Use any of these means.

1. Try to have just one of you sign the lease (the one with the higher income). *However,* sometimes two signatures are required on a lease. In that case . . .
2. Ask to review the lease before signing, take it home, and have the other party sign with just the initials of his/her first name. In most cases, this should be enough. *However,* some landlords require full names signed in their presence with numerous credit references also supplied. In that case . . .
3. Lie. Tell him you're married and that the female partner, as a liberated woman, chooses to keep her own name and credit cards. Since this is becoming quite common, it should do the trick. *However,* if the landlord demands a wedding license as further proof . . .
4. Look elsewhere.

What About Tenants' "Rights"?

A good question. Just what are a single couple's "rights" under the law in this situation? Well, it depends on the state you live in and its laws concerning cohabitation and fornication. If you live in a state with strict laws against cohabitation and a landlord refuses to rent to you because you are unmarried, there is probably little you can do about it. After all, you are breaking the law.

In more liberal states (California and Colorado, for example), where there are no laws against cohabitation, you should have some grounds for litigation against a landlord who refuses to rent to you *solely* because you are an unmarried couple.

Should One Partner or Both Sign the Lease?

If there are no problems with the landlord, it is a good idea to have both signatures on the lease. This will protect each of you in case one party moves away and breaks the lease or leaves behind extensive damage to the apartment.

What About Lease Renewals?

Assuming that only one of you originally signed the lease, when renewal time rolls around you can do one of two things: Sign the renewal exactly as the first lease was signed (one signature) or sign with both names. If you choose the second, the landlord should be aware of your living arrangement before you return a new lease to him with two signatures. Otherwise, he's in for a surprise and perhaps an unpleasant one if you've misjudged him.

Renting Is Sometimes the Best Choice

Despite some pesky problems, renting does hold a number of advantages over buying, including the freedom to move easily. If you're just starting out in this relationship, give yourselves a period of adjustment. Don't rush into a major commitment like buying a house together until you're sure that this is it.

When you are sure, by all means grab the real estate section of the Sunday newspaper and start talking to agents, because buying a house is one of the best investments you'll ever make—especially when you're both single.

Buying a House

If you can afford it, *purchasing* that roof over your head will provide you with substantial tax savings, and for singles living together, the savings are even bigger. Without doubt, buying your own home is one of the best ways you can save money today.

There are a number of reasons why this is true. First of all, when you buy a house, you are entitled to deduct the interest on the loan, or mortgage, on your house. You also get to deduct the local property taxes you pay on your federal tax return. So far, these privileges extend to both married and unmarried couples. A major advantage over being married occurs when, for tax purposes, only one person owns the home and takes the taxes and interest as itemized deductions, while the lower-income member uses the standard deduction. Remember, though, that the deduction for interest and taxes paid goes to the person who owns the house.

Another good reason for owning a home is inflation. If the house you buy now increases at the rate most houses have been going up for the last ten years, you will make more than enough on the house to offset any initial costs. Almost always assuredly, you can at least get back whatever money you invested in the house when you sell it.

Getting a Loan

One thing should be obvious from the start: Two unmarried people are going to have more difficulty obtaining a home loan than a married couple. Some banks (though they are few in number) just won't loan to nonmarrieds at all. Some banks will consider only the higher-salaried person's income, no matter how much the other person makes. Some banks will consider both incomes but will not be inclined to give any breaks (interest, points, prepayment penalties, etc.), making it difficult to "shop around" among a number of banks for the best deal on a home loan. And yes, more than ever before, there are some 20th-century banks which show no favoritism to married over non-marrieds.

How do you find a bank like this? Other than talking to unmarried friends who've bought a house this way, your best bet is just to walk into a bank and start asking questions. Start with the savings and loans in your neighborhood since home mortgages are their specialty. When the economy is healthy and business is booming, these banks will generally have plenty of money to lend. However, in an economic recession, the money supply dwindles and you'll not only have to shop around for a loan, you'll also come under closer scrutiny—financial and otherwise.

Buying a House Jointly

When both of you have equal incomes and both want a slice of the homeowner's tax deductions, then the only solution is to buy a place together. You must be very careful when you do this, though, because an unharmonious split later on could cost you the house, plus a portion of the equity you already have in it.

Take the case of Ginny and Bob. Both make $15,000 per year. Ginny pays rent of $175 per month and Bob pays $250. They have already decided that they want to live together. If they add together their rental checks, they will have $425 per month, which ought to allow them to rent a considerably better place than either of them could afford alone. Instead of renting, let's suppose that Ginny and Bob decide to buy a place together. They feel that their relationship will last a long time and they want to save something out of their paychecks besides worthless rent receipts.

The Down Payment

After some looking, Ginny and Bob find a place that is just perfect for them and costs only $40,000 (below the national average for a home). Now all they need is $4,000 (10 percent) for a down payment. Almost always, it is the down payment that stops singles and single couples from buying a house. Usually it's 10 percent of the total price, but it can rise to 20 percent or 30 percent on more expensive homes.

Appraisal

Once Ginny and Bob have made a deal, the bank will send out an appraiser to see if the property is actually worth $40,000. If the appraiser says that the property is worth $38,000, then Ginny and Bob will have to come up with more down payment because the bank will loan only 90 percent of the appraised value, or $34,200, instead of the $36,000 Ginny and Bob were hoping to get. In their case, however, let's say the bank agrees with them that the house is worth $40,000.

Borrowing the Down Payment

Ginny and Bob should have no trouble raising the $2,000 they each need for the down payment. With their incomes, and good credit ratings, they can borrow this amount from a bank on their signatures (no collateral) alone. However, they've been saving for some time and thus have the $4,000 in cash.

Closing Costs

Home buyers have always complained about closing costs, and rightly so. In some states, the laws were so lax that the seller or lender could charge whatever the traffic would bear. Now there is a federal law that requires the seller or lending institution to tell the buyer in advance how much the closing costs will be. Since this law went into effect, closing costs have dropped sharply.

In Ginny and Bob's case, here are their closing costs:

Tax service fee	$ 16.50
Loan charges (points)	540.00
Fire insurance deposit	44.85
Title insurance[1]	——
Tax escrow	118.51
Miscellaneous fees	9.00
Building inspection	100.00
Total	$828.86

"Points"

The biggest item—loan charges, or "points"—is the fee charged by the lending institution for setting up and making the loan. In our example, it was 1½ percent of the amount borrowed. Since the fee is not set, Ginny and Bob should try to dicker with the bank to see if they can get the rate or amount set aside. If they are a customer of the bank, often the charge will be ignored. If you do have to pay points when you buy the house, one good thing is that you can deduct that payment on your tax return as interest paid.

Escrow

The tax escrow account is paid to the lending institution and will continue to be paid monthly. When the county tax assessor sends a bill (usually twice a year) for the

[1] Title insurance guarantees you (and your lending institution) that you will obtain good title to your property, e.g., free of Indian claims. This insurance varies in cost from state to state; it also varies in who has to pay for it: Sometimes it's the seller, sometimes the buyer. In the example above, the seller paid for the title insurance, which cost $250.

property taxes, the lending institution will pay the taxes from the $118.51 deposited each month. This is also the case for the $44.85 charge for the fire insurance premium. Unlike the "points" situation above, the tax escrow account payment is not deductible when paid to the lending institution. It's deductible only when the lending institution makes the payment to the county tax assessor. Usually the lending institution will send a statement each year showing the total amount paid for taxes, and this is the figure you use when you complete your deductions.

If there is no lending institution involved in the deal—that is, if you pay cash for the house or if the seller himself holds the mortgage or there is no escrow account, you pay the taxes and insurance premiums directly, as they fall due, and keep your own accounts for tax purposes.

Building Inspection

The last item of any significant size is the building inspection. Before you can buy the dream house, the state and/or the lending institution wants to make sure that it meets certain building codes and that the foundation hasn't been eaten away by termites. The inspection won't tell you if the plumbing is no good or the stove won't work, however; you will have to find an experienced friend or a professional house inspector to help you there.

Since Ginny and Bob now know the amount of the closing costs, they arrange to come up with the $4,828.86 total they will need to cover the down payment and the closing costs. Now let's look at how the house has affected them from a purely monetary standpoint. (See page 43)

Note that Bob's savings almost offsets Ginny's additional expense. Still, Ginny and Bob seem to suffer a small net loss. But part of their expenses are paying off mortgage principal, which means that if they later sell the house for the same amount they paid, they will get back some money. As we have already pointed out, the house is apt to increase in value, and

Before:

	Ginny		*Bob*	
	Per month	*Per year*	*Per month*	*Per year*
Salary	$1,250	$15,000	$1,250	$15,000
Withholding, federal	(231)	(2,772)	(231)	(2,772)
Withholding, state	(23)	(276)	(23)	(276)
FICA	(73)	(878)	(73)	(878)
Take-home pay	$ 923	11,074	923	11,074
Previous rent payments	(175)	(2,100)	(250)	(3,000)
Cash left over	$ 748	$ 8,974	$ 673	$ 8,074

After:

	Ginny		*Bob*	
	Per month	*Per year*	*Per month*	*Per year*
Salary	$1,250	$15,000	$1,250	$15,000
Withholding, federal	(213)	(2,550)	(213)	(2,550)
Withholding, state	(20)	(240)	(20)	(240)
FICA	(73)	(878)	(73)	(878)
Take-home pay	944	11,332	944	11,332
House payment (including $50 per month utilities)	(238)	(2,856)	(238)	(2,856)
Cash left over	$ 706	$ 8,476	$ 706	$ 8,476
Cost (savings) of owning over renting	$ 42	$ 498	$ (33)	$ (402)

they will get that increase too. Finally, because interest payments can be deducted from income when figuring income tax, there is a large immediate saving. Let's look at Ginny and Bob's tax deductions as tenants and as homeowners:

	Ginny	*Bob*
Standard deduction allowed when they were renting	$2,200	$2,200
Itemized deductions:		
Interest on the mortgage (first year)	1,500	1,500
Taxes on the house	600	600
State income taxes	276	276
Personal property taxes (auto)	53	53
Charge cards	125	125
Contributions	200	200
Sales taxes	225	225
Medical insurance premiums	150	150
Safety deposit box	10	10
Total:	$3,139	$3,139

For purposes of illustration, Bob and Ginny's expenses are shown the same, but of course they would vary. Since each is able to deduct $939 more than they could before, and since they are both in the 35 percent tax bracket, Ginny and Bob each save $329 in federal and state income taxes by being able to deduct mortgage interest. If either or both already can claim more than the standard deduction, because of interest or state income taxes, or whatever, the saving would be equal to the total interest and property taxes on the house, $1,500 each.

It is obvious that one can't simply look at the down payment and the amount of the monthly payment and make an accurate determination of the cost of renting as opposed to buying.

Drawbacks to Joint Ownership

It's very important to decide *before you buy a house* how it will be disposed of in case you split up in the future. The usual way to handle this is with something called a "buy-sell" agreement. All this means is that in the event of a split, and before the house is put up for sale, either partner has the opportunity to buy out the other one's interest in that house. For example, in Ginny and Bob's case, let's assume that five years after they bought the house, Ginny falls in love with someone else and asks Bob to sell her his half of the house and move out. Bob, hurt and angry, refuses. Since Bob won't move out, Ginny then demands that he buy out her interest in the house so that she can move on. But Bob has no extra money at this time and no prospects of a roommate to share expenses. So he forces the sale of the house. This is the same thing that happens in divorce cases many times, and invariably the house commands less than its actual market value because a forced sale makes it "distressed merchandise": that is, the couple is splitting and must sell it. If both of you sign a buy-sell agreement, simply stating that either person has the first opportunity to buy the other partner's share, then you avoid this costly situation.

The other problem involving joint ownership occurs when the two partners' incomes are very disparate. When one person makes $6,000 a year and the other $60,000, it's tough to find a house where expenses can be split up equitably. Further, the lower-income partner usually has a harder time putting to good use all the tax deductions available with home ownership. They have no value if you use the standard deduction. Therefore, some of the tax savings of joint ownership are lost. In this case, it is a much better idea to have just one person buy the house.

Single Ownership

In this case, the partner with the higher income should deal directly with the bank as if he or she were buying the house alone. Then, depending on the income and the financial ability of the other partner, a housing contract or agreement can be drawn up between the two partners. It can be a standard lease-type arrangement between owning partner and renting partner, a 50/50 joint-ownership agreement, with the nonowning partner contributing a lump sum (perhaps the down payment), or goods or services, or some combination of both. (See the example below.)

What Is the Best Way for an LTR Couple to Buy a House?

In most cases, unless you are absolutely sure that yours is a rock-solid relationship, it's better to have just one person buy the house. Dividing up joint property is always a problem, and having a jointly owned house only complicates things immensely. With only one owner, the housing situation is much less complex for both parties.

When only one partner owns the house, however, it means only he or she gets to take the homeowner's deductions at tax-return time. This works out quite well when incomes are disparate. Then the high-income partner buys the house, takes the deductions, and "rents" half the house to the other partner. If the low-income partner uses the standard deduction (as is usually the case), he or she couldn't take advantage of the homeowner's tax deductions anyway, so it all works out to both partners' advantage.

Here's an example. Jane Roe is an accountant earning $25,000 a year. She and her roommate, John Doe, have found an old Victorian house they wish to purchase together. John, a studio musician who earns only $4,000 to $5,000 per year, does have $12,000 in a savings account on which he earns $720 per year in interest. The Victorian is

$60,000—well within Jane's purchasing power[2]—but she has nothing saved for a down payment. John will lend Jane his $12,000 for her down payment, but to protect himself, John requires that Jane take out a second mortgage on the residence (in favor of John) for $12,000. This means Jane can't sell the house unless he is first paid off. If he wants to participate in any potential increase in the value of the house, he could put a stipulation in the mortgage that he was entitled to half the increase.

Now that we have a typical case, let's look at the economics. Assume that John and Jane had been paying $350 per month rent and that the payments (including mortgage, interest, and taxes) on the house will be $500 (normal on a home this price with a down payment of 20 percent). See the table on following page for the full breakdown.

By owning the house, Jane has decreased her federal tax bill by $1,549 per year. This just about equals the $1,800 more that the house costs over renting. The $720 that John pays her per year in rent should be done by check, and a check should be issued to John by Jane for the interest owed to him. (Because of its size, and the personal nature of their relationship, the rent payment generally would not be considered as taxable income to Jane unless she wants to take the aggressive tax position discussed below.) Another item of importance is that Jane now gets deductions for things she could not deduct previously. This is because the house interest and taxes exceed the "standard deduction" allowed single taxpayers of $2,200.

---

[2] The standard rule used by lending institutions for buying a house is that its price not exceed 2½ times your gross income—in June's instance, not more than $62,500. However, since she has no other long-term debts and no children and is reasonably assured of good salary raises in the future, she should be able to comfortably go to $65,000 or $70,000. Conversely, if Jane had several children to support, car payments on a new Porsche, and a fluctuating income, she would do well to lower her housing expectations by $5,000 to $10,000.

Taxes before buying the house:	*Jane*	*John*
Income	$25,000	$5,000
Interest ($12,000 @ 6%)		720
Taxable income	$25,000	$5,720
Federal income taxes on this much income:	$5,176	$ 402
Taxes after buying the house:		
Income	$25,000	$5,720
Interest and taxes	(6,000)	
Medical insurance premiums	(150)	
Sales taxes	(200)	
Interest on purchasing car	(400)	
Interest payments to John	(720)	
Interest on charge accounts	(180)	
State income taxes	(550)	
CPA fee for preparing tax return	(100)	
Taxable income	$16,700	$5,720
Federal taxes on this income:	$ 3,627	$ 402

SPECIAL "SINGLES ONLY" DEDUCTIONS

Jane, an aggressive taxpayer and not afraid of the IRS, took the position that her home was a duplex, and not only did she get the deduction for mortgage interest and property taxes, she also declared John as a renter of half her house, thereby getting deductions for depreciation of 50 percent of the home and the appliances in it. Assuming that the land is worth $10,000, this leaves $50,000 for depreciation. Since her house was old, she claimed depreciation on a "twenty-year-life," or $2,500 per year, of which $1,250 is deductible. This depreciation deduction saved Jane $166 in income taxes.[3]

[3] Remember, she now has to say that the $720 John paid her is rental income, so it has reduced the benefit somewhat.

Before you rush off to do this, however, you should be aware that the IRS has a whole bag of spears which may punch holes in your tax plan. Talk this over with your accountant (or lawyer, if he's knowledgeable about taxes) before proceeding.

In the case of Jane and John, who have a very stable relationship and have already made the decision on how to handle the sale of the house in the future, buying a house proves to be a good investment. If Jane adds in the savings on state income taxes (not computed above), she should have enough money left over to do the repairs on the house. If housing costs keep rising, and they bought the house at the right price, then Jane and John have indeed made the right financial decision.

SHOULD YOU ALWAYS BUY RATHER THAN RENT?

You may be wondering if the decision to buy a home is always the right one. No, not always, although if people ignored the personal side of their relationships and only considered finances, then probably 90 percent of the renters would be buying homes. However, there are drawbacks. If you move from house to house, the real estate commissions will eat up any profits you might make on the sale. Houses require upkeep, both inside and out (buy a condominimum if you don't like yard work). If you have an ex-spouse who is looking for back alimony, he or she can attach your house. Finally, depending on the house's price, you may find it impossible to scrape together enough money for a 20 percent down payment (unless you can get a second mortgage). This last point is sometimes the most critical stumbling block for most people, so explore it fully before you decide to buy.

6

MISCELLANEOUS MONEY MATTERS

Money, which represents the prose of life, and which is hardly spoken of in parlors without an apology, is, in its effects and laws, as beautiful as roses.

—Ralph Waldo Emerson

Credit Cards

LAST YEAR two friends of ours, Annette Smith and Bob Jones had decided to live together. They moved into a larger apartment which they were able to furnish quite nicely, with the exception of the living room. They went down to their local department store—where Bob had a charge account—and after looking at a number of couches and chairs, settled on $900 worth of furniture, which they charged. The salesman quite naturally assumed they were married.

After this episode, there were several other instances when joint purchases were made—new refrigerator, stereo, etc. Finally Annette started using Bob's card to charge some smaller items which they needed for the apartment. She would sign the credit slips either "Mrs. Bob Jones" or "Annette Jones." She was never questioned and the monthly bills were always paid on time.

Then all hell broke loose and they split.

Before she left, however, Annette used Bob's credit card to charge $1,500 worth of new clothes. When Bob received the bill he threatened to take the department store to court because Annette was not "authorized" to purchase anything with his credit card. While it is true that Bob never requested an extra credit card for her or had her signature "authorized," the department store won the case. Why?

Because Bob and Annette purchased several items together, giving at least the impression of being "Mr. and Mrs." And because Annette had made numerous purchases as "Mrs. Bob Jones," and all of these bills were paid promptly by Mr. Bob Jones.

The moral of this story is so obvious it's not worth stating.

Why any unmarried couple would want to own joint credit cards is unfathomable. Not only are they hard to get, but they can cause enormous amounts of trouble for both parties, especially at the end of a relationship. *It cannot be stated too strongly that you should not open any joint-credit-card accounts.* This goes for stores, gasoline, all-purpose bank cards—any kind of joint accounts. If you don't have enough of a credit rating to buy something on your own, then you shouldn't rely on your partner's credit to make a purchase. Just don't buy it, or wait until you have the cash, or wait until you've established a better credit rating on your own.

This is crucially important for women. For some unknown reason, there is often a strong desire in a partnership to "play married"—to talk about one's "husband" or "wife" and to open "Mr. and Mrs." accounts. Don't do it. Especially if you are a woman who has never established credit before. This could lead to your getting a bad credit rating if your "husband" defaults later on. Go out and establish your own credit in your own name.

Worse yet is the woman (or man) who converts her single accounts to joint ones. This is a lot easier to do than opening a joint account. When the company sends you the first credit card, it usually asks if you would like more cards for authorized signers. You agree, get the signature of the other signer, and that's it. You are risking a good credit rating if your partner defaults, i.e., runs up a lot of bills and then departs. Remember: You are always responsible for all of the debts on the account, no matter who originally charged them. If your partner took your Master Charge card and charged $1,000 worth of sarongs plus an air ticket to Tahiti, you can be certain that the bank won't try to collect from someone in a grass shack six thousand miles away—they'll just come to you.

Another good reason for keeping your credit-card accounts separate is that it makes it much easier to deduct the interest from revolving accounts on your tax return. Of course, you must be itemizing deductions on your tax return to get this benefit, but it certainly is one worth taking if you can. With a joint account, it will be difficult for you to support the purchases on which you paid interest. Thus, you risk losing this deduction if you're audited. Why subject yourself to all this hassle? Keep your credit accounts separate.

Checking Accounts

Joint checking accounts are really no better than joint credit cards. In fact, they're worse because they're so much easier to open. The problems, however, remain the same.

You have no protection if your partner (whose signature the bank will honor) goes and withdraws every penny from the checking account and then clears out. And it's been known to happen—especially after fights. Many banks are also reluctant to open double-signature accounts, the kind which requires *both* signatures to validate a check. They have found that these accounts often cause problems, not only for the couples themselves, but also for the bank's computers. Keep separate checkbooks. Your canceled checks (with proper memos) will support your claim to certain jointly used purchases. If you must do something together with checking accounts, then balance both of them at the end of each month and see who comes closest to the penny.

Tax warning: The taxing authorities take the position that where one person removes sums from a joint account in an amount in excess of what that person contributed to the joint account, such funds may be considered to be gifts. If the amount is over $3,000, the donor will have to pay a gift tax.

Savings Accounts

A joint savings account may seem like a truly safe venture, but it is not. Many times both partners want to save for a vacation or larger purchase, and they set up a joint savings account with the stipulation that while either person may make a deposit, *both* signatures are needed for any withdrawals. This is "too" safe. In the case of a husband or wife who empties the joint account after having split up, the other married partner is protected by the courts, which will determine how the property is to be divided no matter who has it. Since this is not so for unmarried couples, they will try to take extra precautions with their monetary assets. Requiring both signatures seems like a safeguard, but it can very easily turn into a trap.

Two former partners, Bill and Julie, had a savings account like this. After a nasty disagreement they split their possessions and went their separate ways. Unfortunately for Bill, who had five times as much money in the savings account, Julie was in no mood to sign a withdrawal slip. So his money sat in the account, collecting 5 percent interest, when he needed cash to buy furniture for his new apartment. Julie was prepared to let it sit there forever, until Bill kidnaped her beautiful black cat, Inky. The ransom for the return of Inky was, of course, Julie's signature on the withdrawal slip. So, unless you get your jollies from catnapping, stay away from two-signature accounts.

> *Tax note:* Remember, too, that you must pay income taxes on interest earned from savings accounts. Since Form 1099 (used by the bank or savings and loan to report interest earnings of $10 or more to the government) is filed by social security number, one of you must use your social security number for reporting interest. Then you split the taxes on interest in proportion to the amount you put into the account.

Example: Jane and John have $2,000 in their joint savings account. Of this, Jane contributed $1,500 and John, $500. Because the 1099 is reported out only under John's social security number, his tax return would have to reflect interest income of $100. But in reality, he only owes tax on $25 interest. If he should be then audited, he should also have proof (canceled checks, etc.) of the amount he deposited into the savings account. He would also tell the IRS agent that Jane owed taxes on the other $75 of interest income, and the agent could check that out if he wanted. The unfortunate part of the situation is that John's tax return may be audited simply because the interest income shown on his tax return does not equal the amount reported to the IRS on the 1099. Perhaps in the future the banks can remedy this problem, but they cannot, or will not, do it now. No matter how you choose to divide the taxes on the interest, it must be reported correctly on your return. You should try to avoid a situation where one person must report interest income which would knock him or her into a higher tax bracket. (If possible, have the lower-income partner report all the interest out on his or her social security number and then on his or her tax return.)

So, while a joint savings account may appear to be a relatively safe venture (compared to checking or credit-card accounts), it still presents you with a number of problems and drawbacks. Invariably, the simplest way is to keep all of your accounts separate.

LOANS

With the exception of a mortgage (see Chapter 5), there is no really *good* reason for the two of you to get a joint loan. In the case of an automobile purchase, one of you will probably be using the car more than the other. That is the person who should buy the car. Loans are much like credit cards—it's all a matter of borrowing on time—and you should use the same rule of thumb. If the purchase price is so large that only your combined incomes can handle it, then it is too expensive for you right now.

Cosigning for Your Partner

This is very, very risky business. A cosigner is obligated to make the remaining payments of the other person's debt if that person defaults. A cosigner has all of the responsibilities and none of the benefits (supposedly) of the loan. Be very careful in this situation. No matter how much in love you are with your present roommate, and no matter how much your roommate needs that loan, try to avoid being the cosigner of that loan. If your relationship ends bitterly, your partner may default on the loan just to get even with you.

Debts

You are responsible for all your own debts. It's as simple as that. No matter with whom you live or what you share, the debts that you bring to the relationship and the debts you incur afterward belong only to you. The problems start when the other partner is in debt. None of your wages can be garnished and none of your property can be taken away to pay your roommate's bills, provided the creditors do not believe the two of you are married. If things get really drastic and your roommate declares bankruptcy, none of your possessions will be taken as long as you have kept them *separate* and as long as you appear to the creditors as a *single* person, not the spouse of your bankrupted partner.

If your roommate is having money troubles, *do not* open joint checking or credit accounts. And don't buy any large items together, or you may lose your equity in them when the creditors come to call.

Travel

Annoying
Hypocritical
Two-faced
Gutless

These are just some of the epithets for the advice in this chapter on unmarrieds traveling together. But as enraged as you may become while reading the next few pages, just remember that the advice here is always designed to do three things: save you money, save you time, and save you hassles. And many times, the first two aren't worth having if you must put up with the third.

Domestic Travel

When you're making hotel reservations in the United States, it's just a lot simpler to register as "Mr. and Mrs." even though it's against the law in most states. That's right

—false registration at a hotel or motel is a crime. This means not only registering under false names, but also registering as "Mr. and Mrs." when you're not married. Then why risk it? Because (1) the hotels really don't care; (2) local gendarmes have better things to do than hold "marriage license" checks at local hotels; and (3) it's cheaper than getting two rooms.

What happens when you feel a moral obligation to register as an unmarried couple? That depends on where you try it. Most hotels across the country are in business to make money and don't care how you register as long as you can pay the bill. However, there are some areas (like the Deep South) and pockets (like small towns in New England and rural Midwest areas) that *do* take exception to liberated attitudes toward sex and *will* mind if you register as unmarrieds. They may mind so much as to deny you a room together for the night. With local ordinances on this subject varying as they do, you're just a lot better off to make it a standard rule to always register as "Mr. and Mrs." and avoid any hassles.

Getting Anywhere

When you are flying—or riding or sailing—anywhere in the United States or abroad, always register your tickets under your own name. Don't get one ticket covering "Mr. and Mrs." even if you think you can take advantage of those "wives fly for ½ off" gimmicks. The airlines phased them out a long time ago. But there's a more important issue at hand here. When someone else takes responsibility for transporting you somewhere, they can be held liable for damages should something happen to you (planes run into mountains, trains get derailed, etc.) Should some disaster like that befall you, your family or beneficiary may have a difficult time collecting insurance on your untimely demise if your real name was Jane Roe, but all the passenger manifest shows is a Mrs. John Doe. The airline's insurance company could argue that legally they are not responsible for damages since you were not traveling under your *legal* name. And maybe, since you weren't listed, your family can't prove that it was you on the plane, or maybe the plane was lost at sea. Granted, it's a fine point and a rare situation, but why even take the chance?

Foreign Travel

The temptation to fly as marrieds will be greatly reduced once you remember that outside these shores[1] you'll need to show your passport, and in nearly all cases those little booklets issued by the State Department definitely won't jibe with your "Mr. and Mrs." airline tickets. But that's just a minor point. The real issue is that domestic and foreign travel rules are the same. You should never travel (fly, ride, sail) anywhere under anything but your real name. In any case, you'll find the real money to be saved in foreign travel is in sharing a room. Unfortunately, like most good deals, this one has a catch.

Foreign Accommodations

If you have traveled abroad before, you are well aware of the fact that many countries are not so free with visitors as the United States is. Checking into any hotel usually requires leaving (or at least showing) your passport at the desk. Thus, if the two of you have booked one double room—no matter what name it was under—it will quickly become apparent to the desk clerk that he is not dealing with a married couple. In large cosmopolitan cities like London and Paris, this will probably make no difference. There,

---

[1] Exceptions are Canada, Mexico, Puerto Rico, and the Virgin Islands.

they are only concerned with your ability to pay the room rate.

However, be careful in very religious countries and behind the Iron Curtain. In countries where Catholicism or Islam is really practiced, you may find it difficult to share a room together (Ireland and the Middle East, for example). Budget the expense of an extra room when you visit these countries, just to be safe.

Deluxe Accommodations

Also, interestingly enough, very high-class hotels all over the world may take exception to putting two unmarrieds in the same room. Chalk that up to either outrageous greed, or just outdated moral standards. Again, you should budget extra money if your reservations are for nothing but the finest hotels.

Your best bets for double-occupancy accommodations are small to medium-sized hotels, boardinghouses, bed-sitters, hostels, pensions, etc. These informal places are less likely to care about your marital status.

Sex and the Iron Curtain

Getting rooms in Communist countries is another story. There you are likely to run into problems not so much from high moral standards, but because two rooms can mean more hard currency (dollars, francs, pounds, marks) for them than one room. Communist capitalism dictates that two rooms paid for in hard currency are worth five to ten room rents from their soft currency. While you may travel all over Eastern Europe without encountering this problem, it still can happen just on the whim of an ornery desk clerk. One handy explanation to try on them is that you were married after your passports and visas were issued. Honeymooners often have this problem. Don't be surprised, though, if you are requested to take two rooms. It has happened before.

Insurance

Other than covering the necessities (property, health), most insurance is unnecessary for singles.

Life Insurance

Unless you have dependents, or want to assure yourself a nice funeral, you don't need life insurance. As fate would have it, this is the only kind of insurance you can get where you will pay no more than a married person. Or to put it another way, it's one of the few forms of insurance which doesn't penalize you for being single.

But do you really need a life policy? Probably not. Even if you wanted to provide for your longstanding partner, it's doubtful that a life insurance policy would be the best use of your capital. In most cases, the surviving partner can work, even if he or she hasn't done so in a long time. And there are other ways to provide for someone. Check to see if your company provides a group life insurance policy or a pension plan for which your partner can be named the beneficiary.

One alternative you may be thinking of is your social security. That's unfortunate, because Uncle Sam doesn't recognize your relationship unless you have, through the years, checked the marital box on your W-4 form. There must be a marriage certificate (and it must be shown to the social security people) or the government will not pay benefits to your partner, no matter how long you lived together.

So, let us hope that you have not left survival in your old age to the social security system, and that you have provided other assets (home, individual retirement account, annuities, or other savings) for the surviving partner.

Automobile Insurance

There's very little discussion on this subject: Car insurance is mandatory in almost all states and you're foolish to drive without it. Beyond that, you'll find yourself discriminated against (because you're not married) in two areas: cost of coverage and special discounts.

Most insurance companies lower the rates for both men and women if they are married. This quickly becomes apparent to males under thirty, and vividly apparent to males under twenty-five, because of the high premium rate they pay (partly due to age). Even if you are a very mature twenty-four, living with someone else in a marriage-type relationship (perhaps with dependents), it still doesn't matter to the insurance company; being under twenty-five, single, and male is going to cost you in higher premiums.

Another area in which nonmarried couples suffer is special discounts—the multicar discounts for families. Under this plan, a married couple can get a discount on the second (or third) car in the family. Nonmarried partners cannot get this advantage, no matter how long they have been living together. So, in balance, car insurance without a marriage certificate may very well be costing you several hundred dollars more per year. What to do to cut the cost? Well, for starters, it's not a good idea to lie. Don't tell the insurance company you're married when you're not. They'll be more than happy to take your word for it at the start, but should you file a large claim and they start investigating, it won't be long before they discover your real marital status. And since you obtained that policy fraudulently, you may not have any insurance coverage at all (unless you want to go to court and pay for a lot of expensive litigation—and even then you may lose). Remember, when you lie to your insurance agent about your marital status, it's fraud.

One way to get the multicar discount when you are not

married is to give the pink slip (title certificate) to your partner and let him or her put your car under the existing policy as his or her own. Needless to say, you had better be very sure of the stability of your relationship before doing this.

The pink slip is proof of purchase, and if you have signed this over to your partner, it is then legally his or hers. One young man of twenty-four, Doug, did this with his Porsche to save on insurance costs. His roommate, an older woman of twenty-six, put the car on her insurance policy and also kept the pink slip. After they split up, she took the Porsche, and when Doug tried to get the police to stick her with an auto-grand-theft charge, she just waved the pink slip at the authorities and they went away. So did Doug, without his car. (He did get the car back—eventually. But it was expensive.)

Three less drastic steps you can take to counterbalance these insurance inequities are:

1. Raise your deductibles. If you're carrying a $100 deductible, raise it to $200 or $250. This will lower the premium you have to pay.
2. If your car is paid for and not relatively new (at least three years old), consider dropping the collision coverage. This simply means that if someone dents your car in a parking lot and leaves unnoticed, or if an uninsured, penniless driver rams you, you'll have to pay for all the repair work on the car.[1]

---

[1] Think carefully about upping deductibles and dropping collision coverage. We once had a friend who liked to frequent some of the "funkier" neighborhoods in San Francisco. He paid dearly for it. In the space of four months, he was whacked seven times: four "unknown" motorists, two uninsured drivers who were on dope at the time, and one high-risk uninsured driver who lied to his insurance company and tied up the case for eighteen months. Even with collision coverage, our friend ended up forking out $700 in deductibles. The upshot of it was that he *dropped* his diductible to $50 and started taking cabs.

3. If your family lives nearby, see about getting your car insured under their policy, with you listed as principal driver. Your rates will be lower; this is especially helpful for young single males.

Renter's or Homeowner's Insurance

You will pay more for this kind of insurance than a married couple, but less than two single people living separately. Every insurance company has different rates and rules, but basically, as nonmarrieds, you'll pay a little more in premiums than a married couple would because two different last names will be on the policy. For example, the rate might be $50 a year for a single person or a married couple, and $60 a year for unmarried roommates. Unfair? Well, perhaps, but if the two of you were living apart, the cost of insurance would be $100. Look at it that way.

Health Insurance

This is no problem as long as you both work. Each of you will probably be covered by your company's health plan, and that's really all the coverage you need. If the plan also offers dental insurance, all the better for you.

The crunch occurs when one partner is not employed and has no insurance coverage. He or she usually cannot be covered under the other partner's plan because they are not married. What to do? First, decide whether you need any health insurance. If your partner is young and in reasonably good health, you may want to skip it altogether. This is, of course, a gamble. When you don't have much in the way of income, the premium payments on a health insurance policy will seem enormous. However, the medical bills from a prolonged illness can be even more devastating (unless you qualify for Medicaid). So this difficult decision is, in the end, up to you. Failing another insurance policy, see if you can't get your partner listed as your dependent.

Most company health insurance policies cover dependents. But you ought to make sure who they classify as a dependent, and how they go about it.

Or, if you've just quit a job which covered you under a group policy, the insurance company will usually offer you an extension on the coverage until you can take out an individual policy. Check to see if their rates are lower.

Women of childbearing age should check out maternity and abortion coverage. This area of insurance has been liberalized in the past few years, and you're the best judge of whether you'll need this coverage or not.

Check to see if your neighborhood offers an HMO (Health Maintenance Organization). Briefly, this is a collection of doctors, hospitals, and others who combine to offer fee-paying members almost total health care (the exceptions being dental work, psychiatric therapy, and care for rare diseases). Since HMOs are relatively new (they were only authorized by Congress in 1973), there is still a great deal of confusion about what they can and cannot charge. If there is an HMO in your area and you are eligible to join, it may provide health care cheaper than a regular insurance policy. But check out all the details and restrictions before you leap into one of these—and by all means *read the fine print*.

If you have little or no income and you get sick, you can probably qualify for Medicaid. Your county health officials can tell you what you need to do to qualify, but usually the less money you have, the better off you are. And when it comes to Medicaid, you are in a much better position as nonmarrieds living together than as a married couple, as the sad story of Kurt and Karen proves.

Kurt and Karen had been married for six years when she was stricken with multiple sclerosis. Now, ten years later, divorce seems to be the only solution to their huge medical bills. Karen, almost totally paralyzed, lives at a nursing home which provides the round-the-clock care she needs, but her medical bills are now more than twice Kurt's $13,000 yearly salary. Before going into the home, Kurt's employer's insurance paid 80 percent of the bills, but now insurance covers none of the nursing home cost and Kurt cannot pay the bills by himself.

He asked about Medicaid and was told Karen's bills would be paid only if he turned over all of his earnings except for $400 a month. However, that was not enough to pay the mortgage and take care of three teen-age children.

Kurt soon discovered that his only alternative was divorce. Indiana, where Kurt and Karen live, controls how Medicaid funds are disbursed, and its rules are that if Karen is single, all her medical bills—even from the nursing home—will be paid. Reluctantly, Kurt and Karen agreed that divorce was their only answer, and after certain legal problems were solved, their happy sixteen-year-old marriage came to an end.

As You Get Older

The same reason that motivates you to insure comfortable retirement benefits should motivate you to reevaluate health insurance as you get older. The health insurance you didn't need at twenty-five may be crucial at sixty-five. This is when a policy for extended hospital care or nursing-home care may be wise. Don't count on Medicare to pick up the tab. Since it is at the mercy of a fickle Congress, Medicare benefits can (and do) change all the time. Also, if there is no second income (retirement or otherwise) for the single couple, and there are no children, then a policy offering more comprehensive disability insurance should be investigated.

7

INVESTMENTS FOR UNMARRIEDS

For age and want save while you may
No morning sun lasts a whole day.
—Benjamin Franklin

DEFINITELY! You should be thinking along the lines of investments and money management as your income grows. If for no other reason than this: As a single right now you have few cares or worries, almost no financial obligations other than to yourself. The temptation is "to live for today, for tomorrow . . ." But tomorrow will come, and sooner than you think. The shocking truth is that this country's social security system, cannot properly handle its burden, even now. Can you imagine what it's going to be like as we near the year 2000? The social security system will resemble a large, inverted pyramid, with all the retirees on top and a slim work force on the bottom. Singles and single couples must be acutely aware of this problem, because it is more than likely that they will have no dependents to fall back on in old age. If you believe that social security payments will be enough to support you at age sixty-five, you are in for a shock. Fixed-income living is almost impossible in an inflationary economy, and that's the kind of ecomony we'll be facing from now until well into the twenty-first century. So plan now. Budget a fixed expense for retirement just as you do for your car payments or your electricity bill.

Investments in Property

Nothing is more advantageous to you than owning your own home. Besides a place in which to build equity, you also get to deduct all the interest from your mortgage and property taxes—something renters cannot do. And the old adage about the value of real estate always going up is still in force. In fact, it carries more weight now than ever before.

With the cost of building materials skyrocketing, you owe it to yourself to make your first major investment in property: house, condominium, co-op, trailer, houseboat, whatever. Start building that equity and getting those tax deductions now.

In 1975, Congress gave a one-shot tax break of $2,000 to persons who purchased a new residence. In a lot of cases, this, coupled with the tax deductions of ownership, allowed people to buy a home or condominium *with no down payment*. If you are a renter and you did not take advantage of this situation, you missed a great opportunity to make some money. Although this provision applied to new home purchases only in 1975, Congress often benefits taxpayers with these kinds of "loopholes." Keep a sharp eye out for what Congress is doing in the area of taxes.

Retirement Investments

If you are not covered by a qualified pension plan, you can start your own individual retirement plan: either a

Keogh (HR 10) Plan for those who are self-employed or an IRA[1] (Individual Retirement Account) for those companies which do not provide a qualified pension plan.

You get to deduct what you contribute to an individual retirement plan, and the interest earned on the principle is tax-free until you begin to draw on it (usually after retirement, when your tax bracket is much lower). See a bank or talk to an insurance agent about setting up one of these plans. They're definitely a good investment.

Other Investment Opportunities

Besides savings accounts and U. S. Savings Bonds, the Treasury Department has just started issuing bargain-basement T-Bills in $1,000 denominations. Before this, you had to plunk down $10,000 to take advantage of the T-Bill's excellent interest rates. Treasury Bills have maturity dates of three, six, nine, and twelve months. (Interest varies with length, so don't commit your funds to these unless you're positive you can live without them for whatever length of time you choose.)

---

[1] An IRA is an especially good investment for the employee involved in a cohabitation contract. It's just extra security that the employer should provide but doesn't.

8

THE HIGH COST OF STARTING A FAMILY

Familiarity breeds contempt—and children.
—Mark Twain

Should You Have Children Without Being Married?

THIS IS A HIGHLY PERSONAL QUESTION, one that can only be decided by you and your partner. Ideally, it should be done before you decide to move in together, but since it's such a touchy subject, it's usually not mentioned until much later. If you are the partner who wants children, especially if you want them in a relatively short period of time, then the burden of discussion rests with you. Don't be surprised if your partner rejects the idea immediately; many people who live together do so because they fear long-term commitments. There is nothing more long-term than children. You should both be totally committed to the idea of raising a family before you start.

It is not out of line to suggest that those who cannot cope with the emotional and legal ties of marriage are not the best parent material in the world. And, of course, they're not the worst either. But it's an especially serious step without marriage, since you are bringing bastards into the world.

What Price Legitimacy?

As with most of the other formerly "taboo" topics covered in this book, legitimacy, or the lack of it, simply doesn't carry the great stigma it once did. But it's still no picnic to be labeled a bastard, and prospective unmarried parents should give this problem a great deal of thought. These days, it is not uncommon for people living together to start a family if, for personal and/or monetary reasons, marriage is out of the question. The most frequent question in the area is, How do we make our child legitimate?

At times there seem to be fifty different answers to this question, depending on what state you live in. Almost every state has its own special rules regarding the legitimizing of bastard children. Probably the best way to handle it is to contact a lawyer to find out what options your state offers. The following list contains just some of the ways you can legitimize a child in various states:

1. Marriage. This can be an extremely expensive means to an end, especially when both parents work.
2. Drawing up a legitimacy or paternity paper in which the father states that he has fathered the child in question and that he intends to provide support and has given the child his last name and intends it to share in his estate. (As you can probably see from this, only the father can legitimize a child in the eyes of the law.)
3. The father can take his child into his home, provide support, and generally acknowledge that the child is his own.
4. In some states all children are considered legitimate

as long as the identity of their parents is not in question. In those states, there is no need to do anything extra to legitimize a child.

These procedures may not seem important or worthwhile to you at the moment, but they can become crucial later on, especially in the area of inheritance matters and other benefits.

What about the birth certificate? Well, in many states the birth certificate does not deal with the question of legitimacy. It lists the father and the mother's maiden name, so there is no way of telling whether they were married at the time of birth. Hence, it is not a valid way to prove legitimacy.

> *Very important note:* If you are the parent, mother or father, who is going to assume responsibility for raising the child, make sure the paternity document is signed. It assures your continued child support in case of a split in the future.

Medical Costs

More pressing for prospective parents than estate matters is the question of prenatal care and maternity medical costs. If you are pregnant and are working, then your company may well have major medical hospitalization and coverage that will pick up at least part of the tab. You are entitled to them whether you are married or not. Also, it is no longer possible for an employer to fire or lay you off after a certain month in your pregnancy. You have the right to work up until delivery time, if you wish.

If You Are Not Covered

Talk this subject over thoroughly with your partner. Getting covered under his employer's health insurance is unlikely, unless you want to get married (rather drastic). You both should investigate various health insurance plans that cover only maternity and related costs. Also, contact a nearby women's self-help organization, your local health department agency, or a free clinic for advice on where and how to have your baby at a minimal cost (for example, many women now leave the hospital the day after birth to cut down on room costs, which can average over $100 a day). Of course, hospital, surgical, and doctor bills—along with contraception, sterilization, and abortion costs—are all deductible. But to get this deduction, your medical costs must total 3 percent of your adjusted gross income. So if you have $15,000 adjusted gross income, you would have to come up with at least $450 worth of medical bills before you could deduct anything. This is a snap if you have a baby.

You'll also run up a lot of nondeductible costs—layette miscellaneous items, maternity clothes, etc. If you budget $2,500 to $3,000 to cover all the costs of having a baby, you'll be lucky to have anything left over after the baby arrives. Remember, this is for a normal pregnancy. Complications (Caesarean delivery, etc.) will send your total costs skyrocketing because of the high cost of hospitalization and doctor fees.

Abortion

If you don't want to have the baby, arrange for your abortion as soon as possible. After the first three months of pregnancy, most states enter the picture and regulate abortion procedures with respect to the health and safety of the mother. It's also a good idea to contact Planned Parenthood for suggestions on where to have an abortion. Prices *do* vary and you can shop around. The IRS does allow the cost of an abortion to be deducted as a medical expense. However, cost should not always be the determining factor. You can get cheap rates from a local free clinic, but they must perform "assembly line" abortions to keep costs down. Many women have suffered terrible psychological effects from these kinds of abortions, some requiring extensive psychoanalysis later on. Many cheap abortions cost far more than you would at first think. If you have any moral reservations about an abortion, talk it over not only with Planned Parenthood, but also with your gynecologist.

SUPPORT—WHO'S RESPONSIBLE?

If you are the parent—either mother or father—of an illegitimate child, you must provide support for that child. Most states put most of the burden on the father, by allowing the mother to sue him for child support, even though he has no right to custody of the child (support payments, however, open the door to visitation rights). In certain cases, if the father is raising the child, the mother (depending on her earnings) must supply a portion of the child's support.

HEW now has a functioning service known as the Parent-Locator System, where they match missing fathers (who are in arrears on child support) with the counties searching for them. Social security numbers are the vehicles used for tracing. These deadbeats are then incarcerated in the county jail until they come up with the back payment. It's a remarkably effective system: HEW boasts a 70 percent success rate in finding the men, and after a few days in the cooler they seem to "discover" the child-support funds to free themselves. The system was initiated to cut burgeoning welfare payments, and it's working to the tune of over $1 billion a year in savings. If you are raising a child whose father has evaded his child-support duties, contact your county welfare department. They should be able to handle your request and get the necessary information about your ex-husband to the Parent-Locator computer.

Benefits for Illegitimate Children

Social Security

A long time ago the social security system used to routinely discriminate against claims by illegitimate children to their father's retirement benefits. This is unconstitutional and supposedly no longer occurs. An illegitimate child can claim death, disablement, and retirement benefits from both father and mother's social security.

Union Funds, Pension Plans

This is a more difficult, less well-defined area. Pension plans, already unbelievably complicated by the Employees Retirement Act of 1974, will require a careful reading to decide if benefits can be claimed by illegitimate children. If such discrimination does exist in union or private pension plans, it's very likely that it is unlawful and can be overturned in court.

This situation is further clouded if the father dies intestate (without leaving a will). Then it will be necessary to prove that the child was dependent on the father for support *and* that the deceased was actually the father. In some states, even this is not enough to allow the illegitimate child to inherit benefits. When you have a "paternity paper" to prove this, it makes things a lot easier.

Wills and Trust Funds

The way to skip most of these problems is to leave a will. It involves a few simple estate-planning techniques, a lawyer, and maybe an accountant. Leaving a will usually guarantees that the people you want to have your estate will actually get it, and without having to go through a tremendous legal tussle.

Estate Planning Is Important for all LTR Couples

Even if you plan never to have children, leaving a will is an excellent idea. In this way, you can be sure that your LTR partner will inherit from your estate. It will keep other relatives from interfering in probate matters after you're gone. And, especially when you have children, a will is the best way to provide something for all of them.

One item you should be aware of: Wives can inherit a large portion ($240,000) of their husband's estate tax-free. This option is not open to LTR partners. Therefore, a late-in-life marriage is not such a bad idea, especially if your estate (including life insurance) is large. As long as it doesn't cut into your social security benefits too much, this is one time you should seriously consider marriage.

9

LIVING TOGETHER IN RETIREMENT

True happiness is of a retired nature.
—Addison

NO DOUBT you've seen the TV situation comedy built around the Sun City couple who have decided to "live in sin" rather than marry and lose a portion of their social security benefits. Well, there's nothing funny about living on a fixed income these days, and it becomes an outrage when the government steps in and takes away part of your retirement benefits because you changed your marital status. This is just another form of the marriage tax. Any single retired person contemplating a change in marital status should check with the local social security office to see if his or her benefits will change after marriage.

WHO'S AFFECTED?

Primarily, it's a widow receiving survivor benefits. Remarriage could cut into her benefits if her deceased husband earned more money during his lifetime than her prospective bridegroom did. The rule in force here is that a widow is allowed one of two options: either her own retirement or half of her husband's, whichever is greater. If her husband's benefits were greater, and she remarries, she loses them.

An example of this is Ellen, a sixty-six-year-old widow of a corporate executive. Assume that she is receiving $225 per month, half of her late husband's benefits. Ellen is considering marrying Archie, also retired, who receives only $190 in monthly benefits. Clearly, she has a difficult decision to make, because if she remarries, she will be going from $225 per month support for one person to $190 for two people. That's a cut of $35 a month. Ellen would be better off just living with Archie.

Now, does a widower whose wife left him with healthy benefits get to collect half of hers instead of all of his? Yes, he does. But it wasn't always this way. Before a recent Supreme Court decision, a man was not entitled to the same option a woman was in terms of retirement benefits. He could only retire on his own benefits, no matter how much his deceased wife's benefits were. Now he can collect her portion, if it's larger. Even the Social Security Administration has to keep up with the times.

Divorcées Beware

If you are divorced and about to retire, you should know that you are not eligible to share in your ex-husband's benefits unless you were married to him for ten years.[1] This remains the same whether he is living or deceased, still single or remarried. Obviously, if you are in the middle of planning for a divorce and you've been married for nine years,

---

[1] Until 1977, this used to be twenty years. Congress lowered the "time married" regulation partially in response to the increasing divorce rate.

you would be very wise to put off the final decree until your marriage reaches the ten-year mark.

A note for the men: If you were married for more than ten years, then divorced, and are now retired and remarried, your retirement benefits will be reduced, since your ex-wife shares in them. This is not a dollar-for-dollar reduction, so you will have to check with the Social Security Administration to see exactly how your benefits are affected. Naturally, if you're thinking about getting a divorce from your wife of eight or nine years, you would be better to do it before you celebrate your tenth wedding anniversary.

What About Contract Cohabitation?

The only problem with retirement cohabitation contracts is that they can cost you your social security benefits if you're not careful. In the example used during the previous discussion on contract cohabitation, the employee was earning $500 per month. This sum would wipe out most people's social security benefits, since you are only allowed to earn a nominal income while retired without losing your benefits. It's probably a bad idea, then, to enter into contract cohabitation if you are going to be the employee and you are receiving retirement benefits. A better way would be to work out an "understanding," using the checklist in Chapter 13 or devising an agreement of your own.

Tips to Remember

Social security benefits are reduced only if you receive *earned income,* i.e., salary or similar payments. Benefits are not reduced if you receive dividends or interest payments, annuities, or separate pension-plan benefits.

Once you reach age seventy-two you may earn all the income you like without losing a penny in social security benefits.

If you are planning to earn extra income after retirement, try to bunch the payment of that income into one or two months. Social security benefits are paid on a monthly basis, so if you earn $10,000 one year, try to get the payment made during one month. Then you won't lose any benefits for the other eleven months of the year.

10

COMMUNAL LIVING

Morality consists of suspecting other people of not being legally married.
—George Bernard Shaw

NO DOUBT the suggestion of communal living strikes a note of debauchery in the minds of some people—many of whom may be landlords. And, without doubt, the majority of your money problems in communal living will have to do with rental or mortgage payments.

Renting for More Than Two

It's not really necessary to go into detail on why landlords do not like to rent to a group. If one defaults out of a group of six, he still has to go to court for eviction papers. Six people can make that much more noise to disturb the neighbors. They also can do that much more damage to their living quarters. Plus, there's the so-called "morality question."

Frankly, it's a lot easier for one person to rent a place

for the group. But there are drawbacks in that, too. So if you all want to get into the rental act, here are some tips.

Take stock of each person's salary and follow the ¼ rule (see Chapter 5) when determining how much total rent you can afford. If your group is large, say five or over, protect yourselves further by eliminating one person's contribution. In the event that one person should default, then the others can make up the difference without strain. Suppose the six people living together earn between $6,000 and $10,000 per year. This would average out to $125 per person per month ($8,000 less 25 percent for deductions equals $6,000, or $500 per month; ¼ of $500 is $125).

Remember, this is for rent *and* utilities. If you have six people, you'll probably need a house, which also brings with it extra garbage, heat, and water charges. Still, with six people, you can afford $750 in rent quite easily. To protect against a default in the group, limit yourselves to rentals in the $600 to $650 range.

Once you've found a nice place to live, you'll have to convince the landlord that you're all reliable and upstanding citizens. One way is to present a financial statement covering all members of the group. Divided into one section for each person, the statement should list name, age, occupation, salary, other income, bank references, credit cards, any outstanding loans or credit balances. Type it up so that it looks neat and professional. This will go a long way toward convincing a reluctant landlord. You might also consider offering to double the security deposit, or pay both first and last month's rent plus deposit. This will underscore your financial responsibility and show that you mean business. As a group, you should definitely have a set of house rules everyone can follow. Such things as rules on division of chores (cooking, cleaning, shopping) and restrictions (on playing music, having parties, etc.) will ease a landlord's mind. A group rental agreement, signed by everyone, will also help your cause.

Still, even with all these suggestions, you'll find it's easier in the long run to have just one person rent for the group.

Warning: Don't try to fool the landlord into thinking there are only one or two people renting a six-bedroom house, when you are actually a large nonrelated group. Why not? Because:

1. There may be a clause in the lease preventing more than two unrelated people from renting.
2. There may be a local ordinance preventing communal living.
3. The landlord will eventually find out, no matter how discreet you all are.

The reason a landlord prefers to have only one person sign a lease is this: He then has only one person to hold accountable for back rent and damages. Conversely, think carefully before you sign a lease for a large group. You will be held responsible for *all* the rent whether one or all of the other people in the group default. Of course, it's possible to sue those who run out on you, but that takes time and money in itself. Before you sign, you should be *more* than reasonably sure that:

1. Everyone has steady employment or other income to meet the monthly bills.
2. Everyone carries little or no debt. Anyone facing imminent bankruptcy should be viewed with the utmost suspicion.
3. Everyone gets along well. It only takes one person breaking the rules to create a great deal of tension. Weed out the malcontents now.

Buying Your Communal Home

If you think it's difficult to find a bank which will grant a loan to two nonmarrieds, try it with six. It's almost impossible. If you feel that your group is solid and stable enough to commit itself to property ownership, then you should proceed in basically the same manner as outlined in Chapter 5. Since you'll be looking for a larger house with a bigger price tag, the buying member of the group will have to have a fairly sizable income to secure a loan or have lots of money for a big down payment. Alternatively, two people from the group (preferably male and female) should find a "liberal" bank or savings-and-loan institution willing to lend to an unmarried couple. Regardless of how you do it, the tax advantages are still there for your share of the loan.

11

HOW TO GET A "DIVORCE" AFTER LIVING TOGETHER

There are very few people who are not ashamed of having been in love when they no longer love each other.
—La Rochefoucauld

YOU CAN'T IMAGINE it on the day you move in together, but some time in the future you may decide to go your own separate ways. How you approach the separation and how you deal with your partner during the final days can make all the difference between friendliness and bitterness, between a fair sharing of your community property and a battle to see who can rip off the most.

SHOULD YOU SEEK COUNSELING?

You'll know well in advance if the relationship is not working out. The question then arises, Can it be saved? It is not at all unusual for LTR people to seek counseling today. Here are some suggestions to hold down the costs.

Ask a mutual friend to moderate a "bitch session." Perhaps your problems are really not as great as they seem.

It is common in our mobile society to just pick up and move on rather than stay and face the serious counseling married couples regularly experience. The friend you pick should be a mutual one both of you met *after* you started living together. No matter how friendly you are with his old fraternity buddy, don't use him as a moderator. The difference is crucial: the moderator should not be a "his" or "her" friend, but an "our" friend.

Use county-provided family services. These people (usually clinical psychologists) are provided by the county at little or no cost to you, depending on how much you can afford to pay. Use them when you can't find a mutual friend to help, or especially when you've been living together for a long time and you feel your grievances are serious ones.

Private marriage counselors have had a dramatic increase in business from single couples in the last ten years. The American Association of Marriage and Family Counselors is a national organization for accrediting and certifying marriage counselors. It is located at 225 Yale Avenue, Claremont, Ca. 91711. The AAMFC will supply you, at no charge, with the names of accredited marriage counselors in your area. One of the AAMFC's requirements is that its members have at least a master's degree in one of the behavioral sciences, plus two years of clinical experience in marriage counseling.

If counseling fails and you decide it's time to split up, sit down together with your contracts, agreements, and living-together checklist (if you used one) and review the material possessions which must be divided. Do not attempt this in a highly charged emotional state, like right after an argument.

Tips on Splitting Up the Household

Don't start out by "claiming" any of the community property. Items (especially large ones) you purchased alone should be protected by sales receipts or contracts. If you both remain calm and reasonable, there should be no discussion on these things. On smaller community items, be prepared to give up more than you get. Your generosity will go a long way toward making the split an easy one.

Most important, follow your best instincts when it comes time to split up joint household items. If he was the gourmet chef during your relationship, then let him pick first from the kitchen items. Don't insist on taking a crêpe pan that you'll never use just to get his goat.

If you are the one who's insisting on the split, let your partner (who really will be the injured party) divide up all the small household items. It's great therapy—provided he or she doesn't try to take it all—and will go a long way toward rebuilding a shattered ego and making your final parting less traumatic.

> *Important note:* The most serious problems will occur if you've been living together for many years and ownership lines have been blurred, and/or if one partner stayed home to take care of the home and raise children. Then it is very much like a regular divorce, and you should read the third part of this book carefully. In these situations, the stay-at-home partner must take extra precautions to protect himself or herself.

What to Do When You Have Problems

If the split is a hostile one, you are getting a *divorce.* View it this way from the start and things will be much easier for you in the long run.

Use Arbitration

You don't necessarily need a lawyer to referee your "divorce." You can use a mutual friend as arbitrator. The advice here is the same as for counseling. A mutual friend can referee your property settlement sometimes with more effectiveness than a lawyer. Or you can consult the American Arbitration Association. (Based in New York City, this association can guide you to an arbitrator in your area and give you some idea of the various fees for such services.)

Use a Lawyer

As a sort of last resort you can contact a lawyer to handle your split. To save money, you may try to get by with just one lawyer. This can work, provided hostilities have not escalated to the point of all-out war and provided each partner is free of excessive paranoia. But there are certain precautions you should take when using just one lawyer.

One partner must call to set up an appointment. If you are the one to do this, speak to the lawyer very briefly. Set up a time and place for the meeting. *Do not* discuss any of the facts of your relationship. To do so, or to have any prolonged discussion with the lawyer, will make him think of *you* as his client. This negates the lawyer's usefulness to both partners and is patently unfair to the other person. If possible, have a friend arrange your appointment with the lawyer, so that he greets both of you "cold" and can arbitrate the situation with no previous frame of reference.

A lawyer's fee for this kind of consultation can run anywhere from $20 an hour up, but the going rate is now about $50. Forget about Legal Aid—they only take cases for the very poor. If you're so destitute that you qualify for legal aid, you probably have nothing to wrangle over in the first place.

However, if the stakes are very high, you won't want to put the arbitration and final settlement in the hands of one lawyer. When this happens, you're getting a divorce and should read Part Three to get some idea of what awaits you.

What Happens When It Goes to Court

Yes, you can take your "divorce" to court. Times have changed tremendously in the judiciary.

The courts first began to remove judicial stigma from couples living together when they refused to prosecute "Cohabitors," even though every state in the union had some sort of law on its books outlawing fornication, cohabitation, or other "lewd" sexual practices. Now those laws are either gone, rewritten to protect only minors from sexual offenses (the so-called "consenting adults" laws), or never enforced. For example, until 1976, California's Penal Code made "adulterous cohabitation" a crime. Any person living with another person who was still married was committing a crime. Had this section of the Penal Code been enforced, California authorities would have had to use every football stadium in the state for detention centers.

From this relaxation sprang the liberalization of alimony and child custody: The courts have been reducing or eliminating alimony payments when the ex-spouse was found to be living with another person and that person was providing partial or total support. Conversely, it's getting harder to prove that a divorced parent with custody of the child is "unfit" or "immoral" just because he or she is living with another person of the opposite sex.

Can you see a trend here? The courts are moving closer and closer to viewing all partnerships (married or not) on the same grounds. So when an LTR divorce goes to court, the partner who ran the household and/or took care of the kids may be granted alimony in addition to the obligatory child support. That's what happened to Lee Marvin.

KID SHELEEN AND THE SHOWDOWN AT ALIMONY COURT

As mentioned earlier, in one of the more celebrated California cases of this kind, Lee Marvin was sued for a portion of his property by the woman he lived with for six years. In her suit, Michelle Triola Marvin (she changed her last name legally) questioned whether or not property acquired during an LTR should be divided equally just as community property is divided at the end of marriage.

The attorney for Ms. Marvin stated that she and the actor had an oral agreement to share their earnings and any property accumulated during their patnership; to present themselves as husband and wife; and that she would give up her own career aspirations to serve as companion and housekeeper.

Ms. Marvin's attorney asked the Los Angeles Superior Court to move away from traditional concepts and apply the principles of marriage and divorce to lasting nonmarried relationships. During the course of a pretrial proceeding, however, the court ruled that property rights applied only to valid marriages and threw out the case.

Undaunted, Ms. Marvin's lawyer appealed to the California Supreme Court. It agreed to hear the case and in its ruling said that "agreements between nonmarried partners fail only to the extent that they rest upon consideration of meretricious sexual relationships." Translation: People who live together for only one reason—to have sex, or sex in exchange for money—do not fall under this ruling. *But* if a couple lives together to share companionship, housekeeping, etc., and there is an agreement (oral or written) between them to do this, then that agreement must be honored. The court said in effect that property rights of unmarried couples stem from general principles of contract and equity laws, not from community-property laws.

Because of the Supreme Court's ruling, the case was returned to Los Angeles for trial in order to divide the property. Gay activists were quick to point out that although the decision involved a heterosexual couple, the ruling should apply equally to gay couples. It seems obvious that all California's LTRs—regardless of sexual preference—will be affected by the Marvin decision.

12

WARNING: WHEN NOT TO LIVE TOGETHER

This is the place for tears.
—Vitellio Scarpia

THE LAW WORKS in many mysterious ways, especially when two people are living together. For most couples, however, day-to-day cohabitation should cause no major traumas—legal or otherwise. The courts and lawbooks are not exactly filled with cases of unmarried couples slugging it out over community property, custody of the kids, support, and visitation rights. Beware, though, of those few instances when living with another person can be disastrous . . . for both of you.

Divorce Pending

Do not live with a new person if either of you are getting a divorce—especially when there are children and/or visitation rights involved.

Usually, bitterly contested divorces take a long time to reach the final decree. Because of the long time involved, one of the parties of the divorce may decide to live with another person of the opposite sex. It could be that this third person provided the original impetus for the divorce, although this has no bearing on the case subsequently. Sometimes, divorces take so long that two people who might otherwise marry end up living together because they think the divorce will never come through.

Take the case of Brad. He was involved in a long divorce action, the primary stumbling block being the question of visitation rights. When his wife moved out of state, Brad became very lonely. After his divorce action was initiated, he met Helen, a single career woman, and after a year of dating, they decided to live together. Had Brad been divorced, they would have gotten married. Their idea was that they would start housekeeping immediately and then marry as soon as his divorce came through.

Brad knew his soon-to-be-ex-wife was dating, and he believed she would have no objections to his new relationship. Unfortunately for Brad, one of their mutual "friends" promptly told his wife. Her immediate reaction was to stop all visitation rights. Brad fought back and went to court to enforce the court's original order on visitation. The court refused to force Brad's wife to let him see his children, citing his adulterous relationship with Helen. No matter what preliminary legal steps he had been through or how long they had been separated, Brad was *married* until that divorce decree was final. The court, not being totally heartless, made the following changes in his visitation rights:

1. He could see the children only in their home state during daylight hours.
2. He could not bring Helen or talk about her when he visited the children.
3. His visitation rights were limited to once a month.

Brad thought the issue was all over, but when tax-return time rolled around, his wife refused to sign the joint return.

Brad noted that in his tax bracket, this increased his federal income taxes by $3,000. Since they didn't get divorced by the end of the year, the money Brad had been paying her as support would not qualify as alimony. She finally signed the return, after Brad paid her $2,500. Even then it was not over, since there still was some community property to split.

Not surprisingly, Brad became very bitter and frustrated, and he began to take his feelings out on Helen. Finally she moved out. When this became known, his divorce action speeded up considerably. However, it was too late to save his relationship with Helen.

What it boiled down to was that Brad's wife was angry because he was able to find someone special quicker than she could. She had utterly no reason to end the divorce until it suited her. She had the kids and was receiving financial support. If she had been divorced, she would have had to pay taxes on the support payments because they would then be called alimony. Actually, it would cost her money to get divorced.

What's Good for the Goose . . .

It works in reverse. If you are the mother of two children and their father is dragging his feet on a divorce, you may be tempted to live with another man for companionship, because you can't get that divorce, or to establish a stable home environment for your children. No matter how many good intentions you have for doing this, the father can petition the court for custody of the children on the old "fallen woman" grounds.

With more and more men being granted custody of their children from previous marriages, it is important for mothers to be careful in the new life styles they choose. This is not to say that all divorced women with children should deny themselves the opportunity of living with someone.

Just be sure, if this is your situation, to talk things over with a lawyer, to find out how your state courts have ruled on those cases in the past, and to talk things over with your husband. Don't, however, pop an opener like this on him: "Frank, if I shack up with Sam Smith, will you sue for custody of the kids?" For one thing, you'll probably put an idea in his head that he may not have thought of before. And you'll certainly incense him. Many ex-husbands find that this is the fastest way to prove that their former wives are emotionally unstable and the courts often agree with them—especially if a husband can show that "sexual indiscretion" is a part of the wife's instability. It's better to sound him out discreetly—talk about your individual plans for after the divorce, etc. Obviously, all this rests on the assumption that the two of you are still speaking. If this is not the case, then proceed with the utmost caution.

Alimony and Child Support

Do not live with someone else if you are divorced and solely dependent on alimony and child support, and if your new partner cannot or will not support you and your children.

Again, this pertains to the parent who has custody of the children and/or is receiving spousal support. While it can be either man or woman, in 90 percent of the divorces occurring today, it is the *woman* who is in this situation. So, this advice is geared to her.

It is probably a very bad idea to live with a man who cannot support himself, much less you and your family. There are a number of reasons for this. If your ex-husband perceives this man as a "bum," he may resent his children being exposed to an "unsavory" character. He may also resent even more the idea of supporting this person. Never mind that the bum in question is a writer who will win the Nobel Prize for literature next year—right now your ex-husband believes your roommate is a bum and that's all that counts. What does it mean to you? Well, if your ex-husband really gets mad, he could take it to court and possibly get the support reduced or eliminated. In extreme cases, you might lose the custody of your children.

A totally unworkable piece of advice for situations like this is to stick to accountants or lawyers for roommates. Even the most unsavory of this bunch has a patina of respectability, plus you can get free tax and legal advice.

Seriously, even if you are living with a pillar of the community, you still face losing your alimony and, in rare cases, your child support. The reason for this is the increasingly liberal attitude of the courts. Where once a man was tied to the spousal support of the divorce decree—no matter *what* his ex-wife did—now he can petition the courts for a change in circumstance, i.e., your live-in lover. The courts are looking at these situations *very closely*. If they are convinced that the former wife is self-sufficient (working, for example) or if she has another form of support (roommate), they may well decrease or discontinue her ex-husband's alimony payments. Child support, however, is much harder to change. In both cases, you should check the rulings of your state's courts to get some idea of your chances for a decrease.

Again, your ex-husband's attitude toward you and the divorce will play an important role in these circumstances. If things have mellowed between the two of you and your children are happy, chances are good he won't spend the time and money to go back to court to lower his payments. On the other hand, if hostilities have not abated, if he feels bitter about the settlement, if you make it difficult for him to visit the children, he may end up trying to get back at you through the courts.

Should any of these situations fit your circumstances and you are living with someone, you'll have to choose some course of action. One is not to tell your ex-husband about your new roommate. This requires discretion on your part, especially around old mutual friends. It might be wise to move away to lessen the chance of discovery. These are sound suggestions, provided there are no children involved.

Problems for Single Mothers in LTRs

Obviously, things change drastically with children in the picture. For starters, it's a bad idea to move far away from your former husband, especially out of state. It adds hundreds or thousands of dollars more per year to the cost of his visits and gives him more firepower when petitioning the courts for reduction of child support, since you have caused the increase in his child-related expenditures.

Even worse, you've taken you and your children out of the jurisdiction of the court which originally granted the divorce and which will hear all future petitions for change in support or custody. If your ex-husband goes back to court, you will have to appear before the court to defend your position. Sometimes it is also necessary to bring your local lawyer and pay all of his travel expenses, as well as your own. This, on top of a possible support reduction, can really end up costing you money.

Can You "Hide" a Roommate?

Whether you're in state or out of state, it's going to be hard to hide the existence of your new roommate from your ex-husband, considering a child's natural tendency to "blab" during visitation periods. Even if you have exceptionally reticent children, they will certainly undergo a form of interrogation, albeit subtle, from the visiting parent. It won't be long before they're talking about their "Uncle" John, and your cover is blown.

In light of this, it's best to be up front with your ex-husband about any new relationships. You should already have some idea about how he will react, and you can go from there. Be subtle (and tactful) about it, and try to show that the children are better off having the influence of an opposite-sex partner around them. If your ex-spouse is a reasonable, rational person, there should be no trouble.

Different Race or Same Sex

Be very careful about living with a person of another race, or of the same sex.

It's extremely sad, and distasteful, to have to write about this subject and give advice along these lines. But in trying to deal realistically with these situations, you should be aware that many courts do not view racially mixed couples with the same equanimity as other couples. If a non-custodial parent objects to his or her children being raised in a racially mixed household, that parent can petition the court for custody. Again, each court, each judge will vary. This is such an emotional issue that when the court does award custody to the other person, it may go to great lengths to explain it was not on the grounds of racial prejudice.

Recently a Pennsylvania Superior Court let stand a ruling that gave the custody of two young girls to their father in light of the mother's "immoral conduct." The mother and her children had lived with another man, a black, while her husband was stationed in Korea. The lower court went to great lengths to state that while the husband's custody suit "had been heightened by the fact that the wife's paramour is a member of the Negro race," its decision was not affected by that fact. Well, perhaps not, but you can't help wondering. Perhaps this woman's divorce was not amicable, or her ex-husband was just a bigot. Whatever the reason, she lost her two daughters because she misjudged her husband's reaction to her cohabitation with a black man.

The same advice holds true for couples of the same sex. If you are in this situation you should be aware of judicial prejudice against your life style.

It is not difficult for an ex-spouse to prove to the court that you are an "unfit" parent when you are living with a same-sex lover. Prejudice against gay parents stems from the so-called immoral or unsavory sexual aspects to which children are exposed in these relationships. Although gay parents have recently started winning a few of these cases, the majority of these couples are still faced with a hard choice: their children or their life style.

13

CHECKLIST FOR LIVING TOGETHER

Living together is the best revenge.

SOMETIMES IT HELPS to have a broad overview of important situations. That's why there are so many marriage manuals on the market these days. People want to know what they're getting into (or have already gotten into) with the holy state of matrimony. It is no less important for unmarried couples. There are certain preliminaries to be discussed, certain agreements to be reached, and certain problem areas of which you should be aware.

Always try to approach any item of this checklist in a good humor; after all, you're not signing the Magna Carta, you're just agreeing to a few basic rules.

In some instances, items need only be read and mentally checked off. In others you will need to complete a "laundry list" agreement. And in a few cases, there will be an agreement that needs to be signed by both of you.

When You're Discussing the Possibility of Living Together

1. Have you considered the economic impact of living together? Is your estimate of costs in line with what you expect to save by living together?
2. Are you really ready to settle down? If question 1 represents a cash savings to you, then it's important to weigh this item carefully. Often people see only dollar signs and limitless sex when they discuss the advantages of cohabitation. After the newness wears off (and it will), your partnership will be in serious trouble if one, or both, of you contracts a case of "wandering eye." As much as possible, make sure there is a solid base for your partnership.
3. Check to see if you are living in a common-law-marriage state (see appendix). If so, and you see no advantage to filing a joint return with your partner, be sure you do not hold yourselves out to the community as a married couple. Don't use "Mr. and Mrs." appellations. Don't start joint bank accounts or make time purchases together. To avoid possible legal problems, keep your financial affairs as separate as possible.
4. How are household expenses to be paid? Are both of you going to work? Make sure both partners understand the division of income for rent, food, utilities, etc. Decide now if you're going to use a petty-cash system, or a weekly or monthly accounting system.
5. How are household chores going to be divided up? Ignoring this rather mundane point could cause trouble later on if there are differences of opinion over who's supposed to do what. Don't box yourselves in: "You do the dishes every Monday, Wednesday, and Friday. I'll dust on odd-numbered days if you wash windows on the full moon." No one can keep to that

strict a schedule. Of course, you should have some idea about who's going to do the shopping and laundry, but lend a hand when your partner occasionally can't meet his or her end of the bargain.

6. Now's the time to bring up the subject of children. If you both believe that it should wait until marriage, fine. End of discussion. But if you are both unalterably opposed to marriage at any time, or if one of you is just dying to start a family, hash this problem out *now,* before you go any further.
7. If your prospective partner has been married before, check the status of that marriage. No final decree? It's best to wait until all things are settled before living together. Encourage your would-be partner to discuss this new relationship with his or her ex-spouse. There can be problems, especially relating to alimony payments. It's always wise to get an ex-spouse's grievances out in the open before starting an LTR.

Before You Move In Together

8. Property. How will it be used? Completely separated or all mixed in together? It will be extremely hard to keep all your possessions separate, especially when there is only one of a kind (dining-room set, dishes, stereo, etc.). It may not be a good idea to catalogue everything you own, but definitely make a list of all the big-ticket items you're adding to the partnership and those small valuable or irreplaceable items that could easily get mixed up or "misplaced."

Expensive items	*Small valuables*
Large appliances	Old records
Furniture	Rare books
TVs, stereos	Antiques
Paintings	Crystal and/or silver
Ten-speed bikes	Anything that you could not replace

9. What are you going to do if you decide to purchase things together after moving in? Small items like wine glasses or linens don't pose much of a problem because they can easily be split up. However, what about that bedroom set you both crave? Going to purchase it together? Be careful, even if only one of you actually pays for it. Keep all receipts and at least agree as to who gets possession of the item in case of a split.
10. When looking for a place to live, agree, beforehand, on how much rent you both can afford, the neighborhood in which you want to live, the necessities your apartment or house must have (fireplace, dishwasher, etc.). Try to look for the place together. If one of you already has a big enough apartment, make sure that you, the present tenant, get clearance from the landlord before your new roommate moves in.
11. Make sure both partners understand financial arrangements. If you are strongly opposed to joint bank or credit accounts (and you should be), your partner should understand and agree to this. Also, discuss any insurance you may need and who will pay for what when you're entertaining at home, on dates, or while traveling together.
12. All long-term investments, stocks and bonds, retirement plans, and income property should always be kept separate.
13. Birth control and the end result of not using it: Decide early on who's going to take responsibility for family planning. Don't expect her to stay on the Pill indefinitely; don't try to rush him to the doctor's for a vasectomy. If you plan to have children, make sure you legitimize them in some manner (marriage, paternity paper, whatever). If the mother is not working, she may have no insurance; try to get her

covered under some sort of medical insurance as soon as possible.

When Things Go Wrong

14. Suggest some form of counseling for you and your partner. Don't give up on your partnership just because of a few arguments or misunderstandings.
15. If all attempts at reconciliation fail, do everything you can to make the split an easy one. If there are any children involved, support payments and visitation will have to worked out. Don't be afraid to see a lawyer on this point, especially if you are the partner who will end up with custody of the children. They must be supported by both parents, absence of marriage license notwithstanding.

PART TWO

FOR MARRIED COUPLES: TWO CANNOT LIVE AS CHEAPLY AS ONE

14

SOME PREMARITAL MONEY SUGGESTIONS

Keep your eyes wide open before marriage,
half shut afterwards.
—Poor Richard's Almanac

THE DECISION to marry is a major event in your life. You have no doubt weighed many factors before deciding on such a step. Besides all the mental and physical adjustments you will have to make, there will be assorted money matters to iron out: joint versus separate bank accounts, who's going to pay for what, the extra burden of the marriage tax. There is also a certain amount of "advance planning" you should do before marching down the aisle.

A Personal Inventory of All Your Belongings

Here's another one of those calculating, cold-blooded suggestions that people "in love" really hate. But here it is anyway. If you've objectively considered marriage in this day and age, you are undoubtedly aware of the staggering divorce rate. Like the road to hell, the path to divorce court is paved with good intentions. Don't get caught looking. The items you bring into a marriage are your personal property, and in the event of a divorce, they should never be considered along with the community property. This is crucial in those marriages of short duration where little community property is accumulated.

To protect yourself, make a list of everything you own before the wedding. Include full descriptions of all items, or better yet, take snapshots of them. If you have a portable tape recorder, you can walk from room to room and record descriptions of your personal property. However you do it, make sure you have another person witness your list or have some way to prove that the inventory took place before you were married.

What About Wedding Gifts?

In general, the personal gifts you receive before the wedding (from relatives and friends) are yours. Community-property gifts are those you *both* receive as wedding gifts. For example, if your parents help you complete a twelve-place silver flatware set before your wedding, that's considered your personal property. But the color TV Aunt Sophie gave you and your new spouse on the big day will be lumped in with the rest of the community property you accumulate during your marriage.

Prenuptial Agreements

Although they seem to be all the rage these days, marriage contracts, or prenuptial agreements, have actually been around for a long time. The classic use of the marriage contract was as a hedge against alimony-seeking golddiggers and gigolos. It's still around today, but with several refinements. Before getting married, some people enter into an agreement which contains clauses stipulating how property will be split in the event of a divorce, how much and how long spousal support will be, and which property remains separate and which becomes community. Sometimes these agreements are entered into even after the marriage has taken place. The general rule is that if both parties have bargained in good faith (and knew what they were bargaining away), then the agreement will be upheld by the state courts.

Prenuptial agreements have been particularly useful in the state of New York, where, until recently, the only grounds for divorce was adultery. Because of this, one of the parties would have to testify that he or she committed adultery, whereupon the judge would then give all the property to the other spouse. In these cases, prenuptial agreements alleviated these problems.

However, it is important to remember that if one spouse can prove that he or she signed the agreement without fully understanding what was being bargained away, the courts will usually try to rectify the situation. As a general rule, though, you can feel reasonably confident that a prenuptial agreement will be upheld as written in most courts.

Especially for Women: Money Tips Before You Marry

Now that credit cards are so widely used, you ought to know how to handle them, especially before you get married. First of all, always protect your credit rating. Today, more than ever before, many women getting married for the first time have been out on their own, working for a number of months or years. During their single years, they have collected a number of credit cards from oil companies, department stories, banks—almost any firm that does business these days has a method of providing credit to its customers.

So, here you are, Sally Smith, with a fistful of credit

cards, about to say "I do." What do you do with those cards? Change them all over to your new married name, "Mrs. John Jones"? (No.) Ask the credit department to have your new name, "Sally S. Jones," and your husband's name appended to your charge account? (No.) Keep on using them under your old name and let your husband use them occasionally by signing John Smith? (No.) Close all your accounts and destroy the cards immediately? (No.)

Here's what to do with those cards: Take all of them out of your wallet, file them in a separate envelope, and put them away in a safe place (a safety deposit box, home safe, or some place well hidden from burglars).

Why? There are a number of reasons for this, starting with your (presumably) good credit rating. Don't jeopardize it. A good credit rating is invaluable in today's society. If your husband turns out to be fiscally irresponsible, he could get you in debt faster than you think. And nothing's worse than finishing off a bad marriage with a bad credit rating. If you ever get divorced, you will need credit and probably a good deal of it to hold you over while you look for a new job or furnish a new apartment. Even in the best of marriages, it's comforting to know that you can always fall back on the "ready cash" system that credit provides should you find yourself suddenly single again.

It doesn't always take a divorce to bring this about. Take the case of Bob and Lisa. Bob was a high-flying entrepreneur, always into one "scheme" or another. He might have realized his ambition to become a millionaire if he had not been killed in an untimely accident. What he left Lisa with was an incredibly chaotic financial mess, no will or estate plan, and almost all of their property mortgaged to the hilt. With children at home to feed and take care of, she had no way to raise money or go back to work. Things looked pretty bleak until she remembered all those old credit cards she hadn't used for several years. First, she reactivated them all by making small purchases and paying them off immediately. Then she went back to her old bank, where she had established an excellent credit rating (a car loan paid off early, a credit-card account paid in full each month) and arranged for a $5,000 short-term loan to see her and her children through the probate of Bob's estate. It would have been really rough for Lisa if she had not kept her old credit in perfect shape.

Start Joint Accounts

So put those credit cards away and get your husband to add your name to his accounts. In many cases, he will have the larger income and the larger limits. Avoid the situation where you use your Master Charge card exclusively, and he uses his the same way. Why send two checks to the same company each month? It's a waste of time, checks, and postage. Besides, it's a lot harder to keep track of expenses, especially deductible ones (gasoline and sales taxes, for example).

What About the Uniform Credit Act?

Passed in 1975, the Uniform Credit Act is designed to protect women against discrimination in the granting of credit. The only criterion they must meet is financial responsibility—the same standard men must.

Is it a success? That depends on what kind of credit is being discussed. Credit-card accounts and small loans seem to be no problem, but success with the big ticket items (home mortgages, for example) is far from 100 percent. It is, however, a tremendous improvement over what went on before the Act was passed. For example, before the Act was passed, if you wanted to attach a new last name to your department-store credit card, the store would automatically close your old account and send you a new application for *your husband* to fill out. Once they got the financial dope on him, they would open a new account for you as "Mrs. John Jones," with a new account number and new limits if his income was different from yours. Not only that, but your past credit record, good or bad, long or short, was gone with the wind. It meant nothing to them; only your husband's income was important. It was the same story at banks when a working husband and wife went to apply for a home loan. The wife's income was never considered in issuing the loan or deciding on points and prepayment penalties. When banks had their arms twisted on this injustice, they started considering *part* of the wife's income, many times making her sign demeaning statements that she was using birth-control devices regularly and that she swore not to get pregnant for a certain number of years. Happily these war stories are now a thing of the past.

Today, the name game with credit cards has changed, too. Now you can add any last name that you want to your card, whether you are married or not, and the company should not ask you for additional financial information. Even though this is a fairly painless procedure, don't do it. You're much safer using your husband's credit or starting new joint accounts for both of you.

What If I'm the Only One with Credit?

What if, for example, you are working and have credit and your husband does not? Perhaps he's going to school, or is unemployed, or just never bothered to open any accounts. Well, if he's working even part time you can still establish joint accounts, even if he's never bothered to open any of his own. At this point, he seems to have income, but no credit rating. Not true! Unless he was a complete hermit before marrying you, he does have some sort of credit rating, because anything from buying a car on time to paying an electric bill puts your name on file with the credit bureau. Remember, you don't have to have a great deal of income to start a joint account, as long as the income you earn is steady.

But He's Unemployed

Then you must assess exactly how unemployable he is. If it's a momentary thing (he's between jobs or just out of school), then this situation will not last long. As soon as he lands a new job, get your joint accounts. Under no circumstances should you let him use your credit cards for more than two or three months. Such habits are hard to break after that.

If he is chronically unemployed, you might want to reevaluate your plans for marriage altogether. That's what Louise should have done before she married Julian, but her parents' strong objections to him ("He's just a hippie bum, dear") actually propelled her into this very bad union. Louise, having worked for several years before marrying Julian, had established a respectable, if modest, credit rating. After the wedding, she wrote to all of the credit-card companies and had them send her new "Mr. and Mrs." cards so that Julian could use them too. What a mistake! Julian, an unpublished writer, found the all-purpose bank cards a boon when treating old friends to lunch, dinner, and nights out on the town. He also refurbished his worn wardrobe and got a new typewriter. About the time the monthly bills were beginning to exceed Louise's credit limits, she was laid off from her job. Faced with the prospect of no income, Louise suggested to Julian that he get a job. He declined and shortly after that left her for good. Louise eventually had to declare bankruptcy to get out of the financial mess Julian had put her in, and her previously unblemished credit rating was gone forever.

So, if there's a Julian in your future, resign yourself to paying cash at all times. You can always fall back on your cards for little emergencies; just make sure you're the only one using them. Remember: You worked hard to establish your good credit rating. Protect it and it may someday help you out of a tight spot.

15

FINANCIAL ADVANTAGES OF BEING MARRIED

Wives are young men's mistresses, companions for middle age, and old men's nurses.
—Francis Bacon

AS WELL AS BEING MISTRESSES, companions, and nurses at different times, wives are tax deductions all along the way, provided they never earn any significant income on their own.

For those breadwinners lucky enough to be in the top 40 percent of all wage earners (those able to support a family of four on one salary), there is a tax deduction for supporting a nonworking spouse. Depending on how high your income is, your spouse can earn close to $5,000 before the marriage tax begins to take its toll (see graph in Chapter 17).

COLLEGE STUDENTS TAKE NOTE

This is especially important for those people who are putting their husbands or wives through college. Your spouse may want to take a part-time job to help defray the cost of that education, but caution him or her against working too much. Two significant incomes will only be eaten away by the marriage tax, and the time spent working could probably be put to better use by studying.

Estate Tax Advantages

Under the current tax laws, a man or woman may bequeath $240,000 tax-free to his surviving spouse. This is an advantage only legally married people have. In order to calculate the advantage of this benefit, assume that a man dies leaving his entire estate of $100,000 to an LTR partner instead of to a wife. The tentative tax on this amount is almost $24,000. It's obvious from this example that a marriage would have saved an enormous sum of money.

Your Estate Is Larger Than You Think

You may think that the numbers mentioned above are quite large, but they include such things as life insurance benefits. So, while you may not be able to count your net worth in terms of $240,000 at first, you may find that you actually have more than that when you include your insurance death benefits. When you're drafting a will, it's crucially important that you take maximum advantage of all the estate and gift-tax provisions Congress allows so you can save every tax dollar possible. When you're ready to draft a will, consult an attorney and, if your estate is large, a CPA who specializes in estate taxes to assist you in getting all the benefits the law allows.

Marital Status

Remember that your marital status for tax purposes is determined on December 31, or on the date of your death. For tax purposes, then, if you were to marry on your death-bed, you would be dispensing all of your property to your spouse and he or she would be entitled to the aforementioned $240,000 exemption from estate taxes.

Yearly Benefits

In addition to survivor benefits, you're entitled to give away $3,000 a year tax-free to anyone you choose. If you and your spouse both agree, you then can give away $3,000 to each recipient without paying any gift taxes. If you want to make outright gifts to your spouse, you may give your spouse $100,000 free of gift taxes. Any subsequent gift over and above this amount will subject you to a gift tax.

Tax Planning for Gays

In most circumstances, gay couples are already receiving the maximum benefit from our tax laws because both are working, and their single status avoids the "marriage tax" levied on married persons where both spouses work. However, for those gay partnerships in which one person does not work, or for those gay couples who want to be aggessive in their tax planning and are not afraid to pioneer new fields, here are some pointers.

First of all, you must decide whether or not you can be married in the state in which you live. Some states, like California, used to regularly issue marriage licenses to homosexuals until there was a public flap about it, and the legislature banned the procedure. Prevailing attitudes in most states now seem to be against issuing same-sex marriage licenses, but this thinking may change.

However, for those states which do grant these licenses, the question now is, Are these marriages legal for tax purposes? The IRS has always been restricted in its determination of the marital status of a given couple by the applicable state law where the couple resides. This means that if a gay couple has gone through the procedures necessary to be legally married within their state, the IRS must recognize that marriage as being valid for federal tax purposes. Indeed, their marriage will be legal for tax purposes until the state declares it invalid, and this can only come about if one of the members brings an action to have the state rule on its validity.

For example, this is what would happen if the IRS examined a couple's tax return and decided to fight them on the issue of their marriage. The IRS would disallow the use of joint-return rates and assert a deficiency (that is, taxes owed them), stipulating in the examination that the couple was not legally married. The gay couple then would have to refute this allegation by proving to the tax court that they were married.

OK, let's assume that this couple resided in Texas, a common-law-marriage state, and that they had already done everything necessary to be married under the Texas law. (Note: Many gay couples in the common-law-marriage state may be married now and not even realize it. If they live as "husband and wife" and tell the community they are married, they probably are.)

Since the Texas courts have not categorically ruled that gay couples cannot qualify under the state's common-law-marriage act, the IRS has no way to prove that the gay couple's marriage is illegal. And because of legal limitations on who can bring a court action, the IRS cannot ask the state of Texas to declare the marriage invalid; only the couple themselves can do that. The Tax Court would have no choice but to rule against the IRS. There are some two hundred court cases that have found that if the couple is legally married under the laws of their state, they are legally married for tax purposes until a state court declares their marriage invalid.

Once the couple is legally married, they can obtain the benefits of filing a joint tax return. This means that if one partner doesn't work, the couple will obtain approximately a 20 percent reduction in their federal and state tax bills.

Aren't There Any More Deductions for Married Couples?

No, basically, there aren't any more. Strictly in terms of tax savings for married couples, you get a break in estate taxes and you get an extra tax deduction as long as there is only one breadwinner in the family, and that's all. Those are the only major advantages you have over two people just living together. Remember, though, that this is only in the narrow sense of tax savings. Obviously, there are many advantages to being married. A couple just can't depend on Uncle Sam for them.

16

THE MARRIAGE TAX

O curse of marriage!
—Shakespeare

THE SEEMINGLY UNSHAKABLE MYTH in American financial and marital circles is that two people are always better off on their tax return if they are married. In other words, they will pay less in taxes if they are married by the end of the tax year (December 31). OK, let's put this myth to rest: Unless one of you has no income, you will almost always pay more for the privilege of being married—anywhere from $6.00 to $6,000 more.

Why?

Well, there are two basic reasons for this. First of all, Congress has always wanted to encourage the formation and continued strength of the traditional American family, consisting of father-breadwinner, mother-homemaker, and children. Congress, however, has never allowed for two incomes, such as when the mother gets a part-time or full-time job.

Congress has not yet faced squarely the quality of life in the last quarter of this century. Double-digit inflation, the decline of the dollar, and unfavorable balance of trade in the end means only one thing: Everything costs more, from disposable diapers right on through to college degrees—food, heat, light, fuel, clothes, housing—everything. It's not just the luxuries which are out of reach now, it's the basic staples of everyday life. It is currently estimated that only 40 percent of single breadwinners earn enough to support a family. That translates into 60 percent of all families needing two breadwinners in the home. This statistic, like all the others, is bound to climb in future years.

Second, for those couples fortunate enough to be able to get by on one income, there is the impact of women's liberation. The movement is probably responsible for getting more women out of the house and into jobs than anything else except possible foreclosure. The women who twenty years ago were content to stay at home and cook, clean, and raise the children now want the challenge and stimulation of a job in addition to all those other duties. Even if it's only four figures, that salary they're bringing in is having a tremendous financial impact in terms of taxes.

The Marriage Tax Chart

Want to know exactly what the marriage tax costs you? The following chart[1] shows how much extra you pay each year. Just locate you and your spouse's income and read across to the applicable box.

That's right, two people who are both earning $25,000 pay Uncle Sam over $2,500 a year just for the privilege of

---

[1] Based on 1978 percentages. While changes in the rates are likely, the progressions will remain close to this chart, with the usual variance of $10–$50. This chart assumes the standard deduction in all cases. Figures in parentheses denote a gain for married couples.

Your Spouse's Income	Your Income								
	5,000	7,500	10,000	12,500	15,000	17,500	20,000	22,500	25,000
–0–	(274)	(366)	(459)	(609)	(756)	(919)	(1,100)	(1,491)	(1,722)
5,000	173	200	211	209	168	110	15	(254)	(345)
7,500	198	281	348	398	410	326	379	161	119
10,000	211	348	467	570	615	679	724	555	581
12,500	219	398	570	706	840	955	1,049	948	1,005
15,000	168	410	615	840	1,025	1,189	1,351	1,281	1,389
17,500	110	385	679	955	1,189	1,226	1,614	1,595	2,127
20,000	15	379	724	1,049	1,351	1,614	1,858	2,083	2,275
22,500	(254)	161	555	948	1,281	1,595	2,083	2,148	2,376
25,000	(345)	119	581	1,005	1,389	2,127	2,275	2,376	2,690

being married. And it gets worse. If you're both earning $50,000 a year, you pay more than $5,500 in federal taxes for that marriage certificate.

In all but a few cases, you are going to have to either find some way to circumvent the marriage tax or resign yourself to paying the extra tax to the federal government. Or you could just shelve the problem and worry about it tomorrow, hoping in the meantime that Congress will change its mind and give all you old married folks a new tax break. Don't count on it. For one thing, Congress has a way of taking even the simplest tax change and complicating it beyond belief. Also, if they try to give marrieds an extra break that singles and single couples don't have, there'll be a tremendous uproar. The last one in part brought about the Tax Reform Act of 1969, when singles were so incensed over having to pay more in taxes than married couples that they practically beat down their Congressmen's doors until they received some tax relief.

The obvious answer is to make all people in this country pay tax according to the same rates. For example, if everyone owed taxes according to Schedule Y (the married-filing-jointly rate), then each person earning $20,000 per year would pay the same amount in tax each year no matter whether he or she was married, single, divorced, widowed, head of household, left-handed, purple, or tangerine.

Needless to say, this kind of solution is so simple that it is light-years away from Congressional enactment, if ever.

Other Forms of the Marriage Tax

The marriage tax affects you in more ways than just on a 1040 tax-return form. It can reduce a retired couple's income from social security. It can have disastrous effects when a long illness depletes a married couple's funds and exhausts their insurance. This usually occurs in terminal cases, or when the disability is less serious but drags on for years. It can happen to any couple, at any age, and usually the only relief is to seek aid from the welfare system. Unfortunately, the first thing the welfare people do is to inquire whether you're married and, if so, how much support your spouse is providing. Then they usually ask the working spouse to turn over almost all of his paycheck before they will part with any welfare money to help pay the medical bills. If there are children in the family as well, this is clearly an unacceptable alternative, because the working spouse has no money left over to support them.

However, if the couple is divorced, then the ill spouse can get welfare aid because he or she qualifies as a *single* hardship case with no income. But there must be a divorce first.

Under any circumstances, this is a senseless and tragic end to a marriage. But when you consider that it is the elderly who suffer most from this form of the marriage tax (in many cases ending happy marriages which have lasted for over half a century), it becomes cruel and inhuman treatment.

What to Do?

OK, let's assume you've decided on a more positive course of action than just saying to hell with it. You have just two choices: Pay the tax or get divorced. Sorry, those are your only options, and if you are morally opposed to paying extra taxes, then you're really down to only one.

Take heart. This kind of divorce is not as repugnant as you may at first think. For starters, it is relatively painless and can actually be enjoyable if you combine it with a vacation. But to find out exactly how to pull this off, you'll have to read the next chapter.

17

HOW TO BEAT THE MARRIAGE TAX

MARRIAGE, n., a community consisting of a master, a mistress and two slaves, making in all, two.
—Ambrose Bierce

MR. BIERCE, one of America's best-known misogynists, composed the above definition long before the Sixteenth Amendment to the Constitution introduced the federal income tax system. Had he been around later to see the havoc it created, he no doubt would have enlarged the community in his definition to include Uncle Sam.

Redefining Your Marriage

Yes, that's precisely what married couples must do today—rework their definition of marriage to the point of using two marriage definitions: one for themselves and one for the IRS. It certainly can be argued that people who live together are redefining the entire concept of marriage, and successfully so from a monetary standpoint, since they legally escape the marriage tax. But many "traditionalists" still like the idea and the commitment to marriage, even in light of ever-increasing divorce statistics. For those hardy individualists, there is no substitute for wedding bells. Unfortunately, there appears at first glance to be no getting around the marriage tax either. In fact, this is *not* true, but you do have to know *how* to get around it. And not surprisingly, this entire sleight-of-hand trick rests on a few definitions.

Exactly What Constitutes a Marriage?

Marriage, as defined by the law texts, is the "voluntary union for life of one man and one woman, to the exclusion of all others; a civil contract made in due form, by which a man and woman agree to take each other for husband and wife, during their joint lives, and to discharge towards each other the duties imposed by law upon such relation."

Whew.

This union, replete with license, flowers, and flying rice, is acknowledged by you, your new spouse, your friends, and the state in which you live. It is not recognized by the IRS until you tell them so by checking the appropriate box on your 1040-tax-return form or your employee W-4 form. In other words, the definition of marriage for tax purposes is when you tell the IRS, "Hey, I'm married."

So what happens if you don't tell them at all? Well, for starters, you sign the tax return under penalty of perjury. That means you can go to jail if they catch you lying to them. How can they catch you? By that tried-and-true method: *the audit,* where you, the auditee, are caught with an unaccounted-for spouse. It's possible to get away with a few questionable deductions during an audit, but hardly an unreported husband or wife. If you are legally married, always file as marrieds. The trick is to become legally unmarried in a way that the IRS acknowledges.

Beating the Marriage Tax: The First Method

The whole idea behind beating the marriage tax is to be able to prove to the IRS that you're not married. One way to do that is to get married in the Bahamas, Mexico, or some other foreign location. Then there is no local, county, or state record of your marriage anywhere. If the IRS comes to call, just tell them you're living together. Of course, this requires different last names; you'd be Mr. and Mrs. to your family and friends only. Joint bank accounts, if you have them, will require different last names. Don't lull yourself into thinking you can "hide" a joint account with your married names on it. Like customs agents, IRS auditors have an uncanny ability to sniff out things like that. How? Well, let's say you used your covert account to pay all the small community bills: phone, utilities, garbage disposal, etc. Don't you think an agent going through your entire year's bills might become suspicious if he never found a single check made out to the phone company? Besides that, you may need to support a deduction sometime that was paid for from that joint account. Even if none of these situations ever happens to you, an IRS agent who suspected you were married could check with all the local banks to see if you had any joint accounts.

So, in case you decide on a foreign marriage, don't advertise it at all. Don't plan any joint accounts (checking, savings, or credit) with your new married name.

What are the Drawbacks to a Foreign Marriage?

Well, there are some, of course, but probably not the ones that would first pop into your mind. For example, in the case of a divorce action by one partner, the other is protected in court via the "putative spouse" law. A foreign marriage is legal as long as one spouse does not protest or question the legality of the marriage. Take the case of Steve and Alice, a working couple who have decided on a foreign marriage to circumvent the extra tax. During their eight-year marriage, they both continue to work, although Steve earns five times as much as Alice does. Steve has bought all the big-ticket items in their marriage—house, cars, boats, furniture, etc.—while Alice uses her salary for the consumables.

One day Steve comes home and announces that he wants a "divorce." Not only that, but since he's paid for "everything," he's keeping it all and Alice had better be packed and out by sundown. She protests. Steve counters with the fact that since there was no legal U.S. marriage, Alice has no right to division of property or spousal support. Well, not only is Steve an insensitive clod, he is also wrong. Alice takes their foreign marriage license to court, along with all the particulars of their eight-year union, and is promptly awarded an equitable property settlement, plus alimony. Alice is called the "putative spouse" because she really believed that they were married, even though Steve "protested" in court that they were not.

Therefore, either spouse is protected by the courts in the case of a divorce. The same thing holds true for death. Your spouse's estate will go to you, provided there are no previous unresolved marriages. In the above case, let's assume that instead of running out, Steve dies without leaving a will. Alice naturally believes that she is the beneficiary of Steve's estate, until Steve's first wife shows up to claim her share of the estate. Seems that Steve never bothered to dissolve that first union, which makes him a dead bigamist and consequently leaves Alice out in the cold. In all cases of two marriages, it is the first one that is considered legal and in force. Even with a proper divorce, it is always a good idea to have a will, so that you can specifically spell out who does *not* share in your estate (an ex-spouse, children from previous marriages, etc.). In this way, your will minimizes any questions about, or challenges to, your estate.

Beating the Marriage Tax: The Second Method

If you are now the owners of a U.S. marriage license, then your next option is the foreign divorce.

This can be achieved in one of two ways: You can get divorced once and remain divorced after you return to the United States, or you can turn your divorce into a yearly vacation in the Bahamas, getting divorced every December and then remarried in January.

There are many reasons why the second option is more popular than the first. Most people who get married like to stay married, thus the idea of only a temporary divorce appeals to them. They find it disagreeable to be permanently nonmarried, even if it is only for tax purposes. Or they fear the reaction of family and friends. Another reason couples like to remarry is that they are afraid that once a tax divorce is achieved, a real legal one will not be far behind. And, of course, it is not all that much more difficult to get remarried before coming back from your vacation.

Why Not Do It?

Despite all those seemingly great reasons for getting remarried every year, there is one reason even more powerful for staying tax-divorced: the IRS.

Recently, after one couple's much-publicized year-end divorce and remarriage, the IRS—smarting from their impudence—issued a regulation which said that these divorces were "shams" and that the couple could not file under the more advantageous single rates. Well, there's been a lot of discussion about this ruling, with some tax-court experts stating that the IRS cannot "moralize" when it's in direct conflict with the tax law—a sort of "taxation of the bedroom," if you will. On the other hand, some experts feel this particular IRS ruling will stand up in Tax Court because the important issue here is the *intent* of the law, which is like saying, "Well, what did this couple really want to do?" Well, what they really wanted to do was to stay married, except for a couple of days at the end of the year, which would in turn save them $4,000 every year. But, says the IRS, since it was the couple's actual intent to be married for the year, they must figure their taxes from the married rate tables.

One thing's for sure: This is a point in the tax law that is going to be argued about endlessly until our tax laws are changed to stop such discrimination. It won't be soon, either. Prior to 1969, single people were taxed very unfairly, too, and it took years and years before their screams of protest were heard in Congress. Now, nearly a decade later, there's still nothing to lead us to believe that things have changed much up on Capitol Hill. So, if you are married and are paying extra taxes, you can't afford to wait for Congress to straighten out this injustice. The only answer is to get some sort of tax divorce, and then stay "divorced."

It's Not As Bad As It Sounds

Indeed not. In fact, this is the most painless divorce you can get. First of all, it's practiced in a sunny climate (usually the Bahamas; Mexico recently stiffened its residency requirements). It takes only a few minutes at the local magistrate plus the fee for your counsel. Your biggest expense will be the actual cost of the vacation (which, by the way, is not deductible).

What Happens When We Get Home?

Nothing unusual, until you file your tax return, which will be under the cheaper single rates. You need never tell anyone else about it; in fact, you might be better off by just telling friends and family that you went to the Bahamas for a vacation. This tax divorce is just between you and the IRS.

Will It Stand Up in Court?

It depends on which court you mean. Tax Court? Yes, because you were and still are divorced. State court? No, not if one of you contests it. Let's say that one of our previous fun couples, Steve and Alice, get a tax divorce. Two years later, Alice decides she's had it with Steve and takes her tax divorce into court to get it recognized by the state. Steve contests her action. In this case the court will rule that the divorce is invalid because it occurred *outside* the state, and one party now objects to it. So, once contested, you are no longer "divorced" in the eyes of the state (and the IRS), and you must go through regular legal channels to get a state-recognized divorce.

Beating the Marriage Tax: The Third Method

OK, let's assume that you don't like the Bahamas, or can't afford that kind of a vacation. Does that mean you can't get a tax divorce? No. There's yet another way.

You can get what amounts to a tax divorce by filing for a Decree of Separate Maintenance. You are not legally divorced with this decree (a final dissolution must still be filed), but the IRS regards you as divorced for tax purposes.

The drawbacks of a separate maintenance decree are huge or insignificant, depending on the state in which you live. Some states still make it a crime to cohabit with another person of the opposite sex. Under these statutes, your Decree of Separate Maintenance might be declared invalid. Also, watch out in common-law-marriage states, where "representing yourselves as husband and wife" could void the decree.

Consult a Lawyer

No matter what state you live in, you should talk to a lawyer before proceeding with a Decree of Separate Maintenance. He will provide the best advice on any peculiarities that might be contained in your own state's laws. He can also help you file the decree if it proves to be to your financial advantage. The cost of all this shouldn't run you over $100, and you could end up saving several thousand dollars every April 15.

18

MISCELLANEOUS MONEY MATTERS FOR MARRIED PEOPLE

The sum which two married people owe to one another defies calculation. It is an infinite debt, which can only be discharged through all eternity.
—Goethe

Credit Cards

THE DEBT mentioned above should not, however, be run up on your credit card. Of course, we're not bad-mouthing credit. Credit cards, when used properly, are indeed a boon to a family's financial planning. The term "used properly" means paying the bill in full when it comes due. The interest charged on most credit card accounts is equal to 18% simple interest per year. Don't borrow money from credit cards; go to the bank and borrow the money directly. Almost any bank will be happy to loan you money at 12% to 15% interest rates if you will just make the effort to make an application.

Juggling Interest

The major benefit of credit cards is that they enable a couple to indefinitely earn an amount equal to one month's upper limit. For example, if a couple charges $500 worth of goods on their credit cards that they would normally purchase in cash, the couple has in fact earned the first $500 tax and interest free! It's as if Uncle Sam had advanced them $500 that they could keep forever provided they pay all of each month's charges on time.

Here's how it works: All during the month that they are buying and charging $500 worth of goods, they have the use of that $500 (in cash) that they would have otherwise spent on the charged items. To make maximum use of their $500, this couple should have it invested in a savings account earning interest. Then, when the credit card company bills them *at least a month later,* the couple pays the credit card bill of $500 out of their second month's earnings.

As an example, Tom and Carol get paid on the first of June. They estimate that they will need $500 worth of chargeable items that month (food, clothing, etc.). They purchase these goods with their cards, and put $500 of their earnings in a savings account drawing 5% interest. Next month, the charge account bill comes due. Tom and Carol pay this *in full* from July's paycheck. In the meantime, they've earned interest on their original, still untouched, $500.

> *Very important note:* Pay the bill in full when it comes. Otherwise you lose more in interest to the charge card company than you save in the bank's savings account.

Also note that there have been some rumblings on the part of certain bank card companies to charge for their previously "free" cards. If this comes about, you will have to evaluate bank charge cards against the interest being earned on the original $500 which you have invested in the savings account.

Bank Accounts

Probably the best of all worlds is to have a single joint bank account. Most couples have trouble each month balancing the family checkbook, and multiple bank accounts merely compound the problem. However, there are certain advantages to having separate bank accounts in different banks. The reasons are somewhat complicated.

Sometimes, when money is "easy" (not in a recession or depression), banks institute procedures to encourage new depositors to their savings and checking accounts by offering certain free services. Often these free services can be used to your advantage. Free checking, no minimum balances, and free safety deposit boxes are all extras that most people can use.

Other times, once you have had a checking account in a bank for a given amount of time, it alone amounts to a kind of good credit rating and will encourage the bank to loan you needed cash in an emergency.

Separate checking accounts also have an additional benefit because usually joint accounts are closed upon the death of a spouse. After that, it often takes the actions of a lawyer to get at the funds in the joint account. When you maintain your own separate account, your funds are available for necessities.

Separate savings accounts have benefits, too. When couples have sufficient money to split their accounts, they get the maximum amount in interest plus having their accounts under the maximum amount guaranteed by the federal government. Another advantage to splitting accounts is that if the money is separately owned, a small savings in state income taxes may follow because some of the interest earned can be reported by the spouse with the lower income. For the benefits to you in your particular state, check with your tax adviser.

Debts

Various state laws range between total responsibility in all cases for your spouse's debts to no responsibility except for the necessities. The major problem here is in determining what particular items of previously incurred debt are paid out of community funds in each jurisdiction. The general rule is that debts incurred before marriage continue to be separate debts, and only the separate property of the spouse incurring the debt may be used to pay off those debts. However, when certain separate debts are incurred, based upon the promise of forthcoming marriage, then community property and/or the property of the other spouse can be levied to satisfy those debts.

Probably the best premarital planning device is to agree in writing as to what debts exist and what property will be used to satisfy such debts. It is probably difficult for a couple in love to sit down and enter into mundane contracts relating to potential liabilities, but it could possibly save the marriage later on and also possibly save both partners some money.

Debt and Divorce

Many times you see an ad in a newspaper stating that Mr. X will not be responsible for any debts other than his own after the date of the ad. The effect of this ad is to give the required publication notice to creditors so that they cannot look to Mr. X for payment of his wife's subsequent debts. But are these ads really effective? It depends. When the wife, for example, has joint charge accounts and credit cards and successfully uses them, some state laws require the couple's community funds to be used to satisfy those debts. This is true, *even though* the store may have been notified that that particular card and charge account was no longer valid. The store's defense is that as long as Mrs. X has a valid card, and they honor that card, they are not required to make good for her debt. However, if you're in this situation, contact your attorney for legal advice. Once properly notified, no store should grant credit on any card or charge account.

Most states are now taking the position that both debt and income earned after separation become the separate liabilities and incomes of each particular spouse. In general, the term "separation" means the separation from bed and board, but in many states (California, for example) it does not have to be a legal separation. Technically, even moving into the other bedroom would constitute separation of bed and board and would render subsequent earnings and liabilities separate property.

Insurance

Insurance is probably one of the largest bugaboos for any family. It is particularly difficult and trying for families with young children to determine what kind and how much insurance they need. Unfortunately, a friendly insurance salesman is probably the worst possible person to analyze a young couple's financial situation and problems. Many times the salesman himself has the same financial problems as the couple to whom he's trying to sell some life insurance.

In the usual situation, the young couple has a relatively modest income, high monthly payments for furniture, house, and the car, and the greatest need for insurance coverage they will ever have in their life. This, coupled with the fact that a death has only a small chance of happening, they do indeed have a tough decision.

Why Buy Insurance at All?

Probably most people don't even analyze whether their families would be better off if the principal wage earner was not covered. Suppose we have a father who earns $15,000 a year, and his wife stays at home to care for the two small children. In all probability, they are staying just above water and just ahead of their creditors. Then let's assume the father is killed in an automobile accident. Several things may happen. First, the wife may be able to collect insurance from the other driver, or her husband's employer may have him covered under a company plan. His company plan may even double if he was on company business. On the other hand, she may get sued by the other driver because her husband was at fault. If their automobile insurance wasn't enough to pay for the claims, she may be forced to shell over any money she did receive if her husband had been covered by life insurance.

One thing is certain, though: If her husband was insured, a few days after being notified of her husband's death, she would have received a check for the amount of his insurance coverage. This check will be a tremendous psychological boost to her morale, because it will give her breathing time after her husband's death to decide what to do and how to do it.

But How Much and What Kind of Insurance?

First it's necessary to look at some definitions.

Term insurance means that you get what you pay for, life insurance. You aren't buying any of the frills such as forced savings or borrowing power for the kid's college needs. Term insurance is the cheapest of all kinds of life insurance. It can be written with lots of options. For example, you can write it with the guaranteed right to change it in the future, adding more coverage or extending the life of the contract.

Whole-life insurance generally means the type of life policy that you write for your entire life. Unlike term insurance, which is for a given period, such as twenty years, whole-life policies are written for your life. Unlike some term policies, which can be canceled at the end of their term, whole-life policies cannot be canceled except for nonpayment of premiums.

Cash-surrender value means that your whole-life policy is building up a value over its life that you can borrow if you need the money.

What the insurance company has done in the latter two cases is to say that if you will pay a higher premium in the beginning than you would pay on term insurance, the company will give you your money back after twenty years with interest at 5 percent, and your insurance coverage will cost you nothing. Of course, the insurance company is betting that you will live and that they will earn more than the 5 percent they have to give you back.

Sounds like a crapshoot, doesn't it? If you have a $10,000 policy and you die, your spouse will get $10,000 regardless of whether you have a term or a whole-life policy. The extra cost of the whole-life policy isn't worth it if you die, but it is if you live.

Term Insurance Is the Answer

For those of you who have decided that you are interested in life insurance coverage and in a gamble, term insurance is the way to go. As a rule of thumb, you can figure that for the same amount of money, you can get six times the coverage under term insurance that you can get under whole life. However, since life insurance companies are forever changing rates options of their policies, ask your agent to give you both costs.

How Much?

The amount of insurance you buy depends on several factors. Maybe you want your wife and kids to live better after your death than they did before. The usual situation is that you buy as much insurance as you can afford, and that always seems to be less than you need. Suppose that you are a father who earns $12,000 a year (after taxes), and you die leaving an insurance policy of $100,000. Your wife can invest that in high-grade U.S. bonds and earn $8,000 per year. Remember too that she will receive social security benefits until the children reach eighteen (twenty-two if they go to college) of about $300 per month. This means that she is now getting about the same income she got when you were alive, and she doesn't have to touch the $100,000 (or put up with you).

Maybe that is too much insurance coverage. Probably a better case would be to have just enough insurance coverage so that when your youngest child is eighteen, the insurance money would be all gone. Of course your wife will have to go to work at that time, but that is your decision.

One final word of advice about insurance: Find a good agent who knows what he's talking about and is more interested in serving you than making a commission, and stick with him and listen to his advice.

Retirement Planning for the Very Married

Unfortunately, most financial and tax-planning devices available go only to those couples who have the ability to save from their current income or have inherited some wealth from other sources. The old saw "You have to have money to make money" may be trite, but it is also true. Do not despair, though, if you are not independently wealthy. There are many ways our capitalistic society forces us to save. Sometimes, after a period of many years, we find ourselves with quite a large nest egg; one of these automatic nest eggs is the equity you build up in your home. With current inflation, the equity in a home over a married couple's lifetime can be surprisingly large.

Equity, to a homeowner, is that magical difference he gets when he sells his house and pays off the mortgage. It's not uncommon for the equity in a home over a thirty-year period to build to $30,000, or even $50,000, in today's dollars as the value of the house keeps rising. The interest on this alone, coupled with social security, can enable a couple to retire without straining their resources. Some couples may wish to sell their homes and move into lower-priced rental apartments, but they should be forewarned that homeowners have tax deductions and inflation benefits that are not available to renters. After thirty years, even the monthly rental may be higher. But you do have a good deal more freedom when you rent, along with less upkeep on your residence.

Selling a home also provides one other benefit: A decreasing annuity may be purchased by the couple with the equity that they had in their home. For example, the equity in a home (fully paid for) at today's average prices would be about $50,000. If a couple were to convert this equity into a lifetime annuity, they would never have to worry about income again. The annuity would pay them the same amount, month after month, for the rest of their lives, no matter how long they lived. You should check with an insurance agent to see how much monthly income you could get with the amount of equity you have. Annuities can be developed in many ways; for example, they can provide that if the couple does not live to a certain age, the insurance company granting the annuity will make a payment to the couple's beneficiaries. By using these "liquidating" annuities, along with social security, a couple will have a monthly paycheck for as long as they live with never a worry about future income. They will also generate more income than they would have by simply living on the interest from $50,000 put in a savings account. However, the "liquidating" annuities will not leave anything for heirs.

Tax Effects of Social Security

The social security laws are as complex in their application as are the tax laws. This is particularly unfortunate because it so often traps the unwary and the uninformed and causes their social security payments to be less than they ought to be.

The general rule of eligibility for social security is that you must earn taxable wages at least one month per quarter, for ten quarters. This means that to receive coverage, you must have worked for a period of two and one half years. In order to qualify, you must have earned *at least* $50 per quarter. If you are a self-employed person and have net earnings of $400 or more in a year, this will also count as four quarters in coverage for that year. In order to be fully covered—that is, to get the maximum social security benefits payable—you must have forty quarters of coverage. This means that you must have worked, earning at least $50 per quarter or, if self-employed, $400 per year for at least ten years.

To show how social security can trap the unwary, take the case of John and Frieda. Frieda was six years older than John and they had been married for thirty years. During all of those years, John was self-employed as a farmer, and Frieda worked by his side every day, in addition to caring for the house. When John and Frieda filed their tax returns, only John paid social security taxes; Frieda did not. When they retired, Frieda turned sixty-two first and wanted to draw social security benefits. However, since she had not worked at least ten quarters (or forty quarters to be fully covered), she could not draw any social security until John reached at least age sixty-two. Had Frieda listed herself as being self-employed along with John, their only tax cost would have been the social security payments he would have paid into the system and eventually it would have been returned to her many times over in social security benefits for the six years prior to John's reaching age sixty-two. This is indeed a small price to pay. A word of planning, then, for those couples who are self-employed: Based upon the ever-increasing social security payouts, it is well worthwhile to the wife who does work alongside her husband, in any business, to file her tax return, listing herself as self-employed along with her husband. In addition, she will obtain valuable benefits because she can put a fair portion of her earnings into a Keogh Plan which would not be taxed to her or her husband until they retired.

If a married woman is fully covered because of her own employment, her social security payments when she retires will be *the greater* of one half of her husband's benefits, or her own benefits.

In only a few cases can persons who are living together earn more social security benefits if they were to marry. In most circumstances, the woman is drawing benefits equivalent to her deceased spouse, and she would take a substantial reduction in social security benefits if she were to marry her retired lover. Unfortunately, we are once again faced with another form of the "marriage tax." The social security laws generally discourage marriage by reducing a couple's benefits.

Divorce Planning for the Very Married

Even when everything and everyone is friendly, more than one third of all the marriages in this country end in divorce. That's a fact of life. During your married life, and especially when things start to sour, always keep in mind certain procedures and financial measures that would enable you to weather the economically devastating effects of divorce.

There are certain steps that anyone, husband or wife, can take, which entail such things as socking away a few pennies here and there and keeping track of community funds to know where the assets are going. It is always important to take title to property jointly, so that none of the property can be sold without both of you approving. This is particularly applicable to such things as accounts with stockbrokerage firms. Often one spouse will have this under his or her own name, and can generaly move funds in and out of them at will without having to ask the other spouse's permission. This is not so with real estate, since most state laws require consent of both spouses in writing before real estate can be purchased or sold.

If you are unsure of your family's financial affairs, refer to Chapter 19 for assistance. That chapter may alert you to steps being taken by your spouse preparatory to suing you for a divorce. If you are forewarned, perhaps you can head him or her off at the pass or take steps yourself to make the divorce easier for you.

Tax-Sheltered Annuities

Another popular type of investment is the tax-sheltered, or investment, annuity. Essentially what it amounts to is that a certain amount of money (at least $10,000) may be set aside, and then the income earned currently on this annuity will not be taxed to the owner until the interest is withdrawn from the account. In effect, you're allowed to have your full interest accumulating in accounts guaranteed by the U. S. Government and, at the same time, you don't have to pay taxes on the interest. Obviously this allows a person to accumulate considerably greater funds over a period of time. One of the major benefits of a tax-sheltered annuity is that funds can be withdrawn in amount equal to the principal initially invested without paying a current tax.

Series E Savings Bonds

Don't overlook the value of Series E Savings Bonds. Many people scoff at Series E bonds because of the low rate of interest they pay. However, Series E bonds are currently paying a fraction over 6 percent if held to maturity. (For more information on Series E bonds, read the chapter in the third section.)

A word of caution: A complete rundown of various types of investments are beyond the scope of this book. These suggestions are merely intended to point out certain areas that have often been neglected by couples looking at their financial status. Perhaps these hidden hints will provide some additional means and motivation to investigate alternative means of financial security.

19

HOW TO FIND OUT WHAT YOUR TAX RETURN REVEALS... OR CONCEALS

The power to tax involves the power to destroy.
—John Marshall

AN INCOME-TAX RETURN is a sort of diary of economic events which have occurred during a taxable year. *Any* tax return of *any* size has a wealth of information if you know how to read it and what to look for. The following ex-

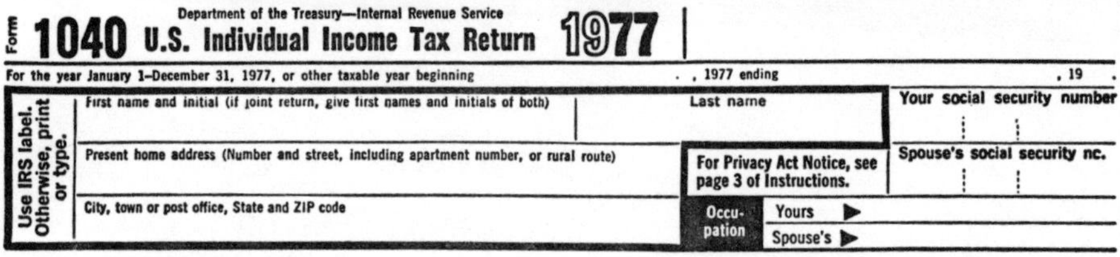

Form 1040 Department of the Treasury—Internal Revenue Service U.S. Individual Income Tax Return 1977

For the year January 1–December 31, 1977, or other taxable year beginning , 1977 ending , 19 .

Use IRS label. Otherwise, print or type.

First name and initial (if joint return, give first names and initials of both)	Last name	Your social security number
Present home address (Number and street, including apartment number, or rural route)	For Privacy Act Notice, see page 3 of Instructions.	Spouse's social security no.
City, town or post office, State and ZIP code	Occupation: Yours ▶ Spouse's ▶	

planations will help you to discover what is actually in your return and is intended to be a useful guide for both men and women. It is particularly valuable for the spouse who has had little exposure to the family's financial affairs, or when a divorce is anticipated.

The explanations may seem a bit complex at times, but this is because the tax laws are complex. Throughout this entire chapter are comments relating to tax planning and hints of what to watch for if you are trying to determine the existence, size, or location of assets. Alternatively, the hints work as well to make the search for assets more difficult by suggesting how certain items can be removed from the reporting required in the tax return, or how reporting can be delayed to subsequent years when they are not so important.

What to Do If You Don't Have a Return to Study

If you do not have a copy of your tax return, you can obtain one simply by writing to your regional IRS office. They will need to know the names and social security numbers the return was filed under and the year you want. The IRS currently charges $1.00 per page for the copy.

If you are the woman involved in a divorce, you have every legal right to copies of all tax returns filed. You will need these returns to help you or your lawyer ascertain the existence of all assets and to determine the amount and source of income. If your husband balks at giving you copies, either get nasty or send away for the returns yourself.

Don't do what one enterprising ex-wife did, however. She suspected that her ex-husband's income had increased substantially since the divorce, but she couldn't prove it. (Apparently he continued to live in his normal life style and did not purchase any boats or expensive cars.) She wrote to the IRS, giving them his social security number and the address he used when he filed his tax return, and they promptly sent her his last tax return. Of course, she broke several laws, but she hasn't been charged with anything—yet. Thereafter, she petitioned the court to increase her spousal support. Apparently no one suspected how she came to know so much about her ex-husband's financial affairs.

The Structure of a Tax Return

The tax-return format itself is built upon the principle of moving from the easy to the hard. Following this format, this chapter goes from the easy to the hard. For income and deduction items beyond salary and a small amount of dividends and interest, the IRS provides separate forms, which are summarized on the front of Form 1040. The forms are constructed to reflect the application of the tax law to a particular item of income or deduction.

Unfortunately, because of the complexity of the tax laws, it is not possible to cover all areas in this chapter. For those fortunate enough to afford it (or need it), a good CPA or lawyer specializing in income taxes should be hired to help explain your return.

This chapter is divided into two sections. The first is for those who have primarily salary income and use the standard deduction or itemize. The second section deals with the more complex returns, such as those involving self-employed persons or those with high salaries. In addition, the discussion goes into considerable detail about how to find (and hide) income and assets. Don't be misled, however; in no way does this discussion contain any recommendations which are illegal. All are perfectly proper and conform with the tax laws. The commentary relating to how to read your return is relatively brief and is intended to explain to you the application of the tax law in language you can understand. The tax law is fraught with enough complexities and exceptions as it is. Judge Learned Hand once remarked that tax laws change at the pace of a second hand compared to the hour hand for other laws. The explanations and the discussion are intended to give you a clue as to tax or financial considerations and should be read in that light. If you want to investigate one of the areas further, and are not sure of the way to proceed, ask your lawyer or CPA. If you're like most taxpayers, however, the majority of tax situations you'll need to know about will be covered here, and you'll have no trouble understanding the issues.

EASY RETURNS

How to Start

Beginning on page 1 of Form 1040, following the names and address section, is the section noting filing status and exemptions.

Filing Status			
Check Only One Box	1	☐	Single
	2	☐	Married filing joint return (even if only one had income)
	3	☐	Married filing separately. If spouse is also filing, give spouse's social security number in the space above and enter full name here ▶
	4	☐	Unmarried Head of Household. Enter qualifying name ▶ See page 7 of Instructions.
	5	☐	Qualifying widow(er) with dependent child (Year spouse died ▶ 19). See page 7 of Instructions.

Box 1: Single

Since everyone begins life in the single status, it takes a deliberate action (although some people claim it happens inadvertently) to become subject to the other filing-status classifications. After such action, most everyone fits in box 2. This is true even for those in the process of getting a divorce. As one attorney said, "If you aren't divorced, you're married." This means that any situation other than a final divorce decree or a Decree of Separate Maintenance requires you to check either box 2 or 3.

A Decree of Separate Maintenance (which is called a legal separation in most states) will allow a couple to use the single rates, as the tax law treats the marriage as if it were terminated. However, the couple will still be married under state law, even though earnings and assets and liabilities remain separate. To qualify for this status, however, the couple must actually obtain the legal decree.

It's reassuring to note that the IRS doesn't have a box to check for those persons who are divorced, or just living together. But who can tell? If people start getting divorced in December to save the marriage tax, look out for a question on future tax returns for the date the divorce was granted.

Marital status is determined at the end of your taxable year, usually December 31. So, if you are married on that day, the IRS considers you married for the entire year. Conversely, if you are divorced on that day, you are considered divorced for the entire year.

If you can't find your erstwhile spouse, the tax law gives you a break from the killing married-filing-separately rates and allows you to file as a single person if you meet certain tests:

1. The missing spouse is not supposed to live with you at any time during the year (it is not necessary for you to be ignorant of his or her whereabouts).
2. You must maintain a home for your children or stepchildren and be entitled to count them as dependents, and they must live with you for at least six months of the year.
3. You must furnish over one half the cost of maintaining the home.

Once all those tests are met, you can use the head-of-household rates, which are almost as favorable as the joint-return rates. Unless your missing spouse also has a child, he or she will not meet the test and must use the married-filing-separately rates.

Box 2: Married Filing Joint Return

The tax law does not specifically define the state of being "married" but instead defines all other potential states of existence. So, if you examine these and you do not fit, you must be married.

Whether a marriage between persons of the same sex is legal for the purpose of filing a joint tax return has not been tested in court. Some states, however, are issuing marriage licenses to persons of the same sex. If they go through whatever formality is required, presumably they would be married under state law. This would in turn make them married for federal tax purposes and give them the ability to file a joint income-tax return.

> *Important note:* A major item that should not be forgotten in filing a joint return is that *both* spouses must sign the return. However, the courts have ruled that if the nonsigning spouse had knowledge of the joint return, then it would be allowed. Apparently, the joint-return election will be voided only if the nonsigning spouse brings a legal action to have it set aside. This signing requirement is a potent legal weapon in divorce negotiations, particularly where one spouse has income considerably greater than the other.

Box 3: Married Filing Separately

The married-filing-separately status results in a tax savings only in extremely rare instances. It usually results in a horrible penalty to the primary-income-earning spouse in a divorce situation where the other spouse refuses to sign the joint tax return. When you check box 3, the tax on $12,000 of income is $2,064 versus $1,679 using the single rates. That's 23 percent more. The percentage differential between single and married filing separately increases from zero at lower-income levels to appoximately 25 percent when taxable income is $20,000. The differential then begins to decrease so that when taxable income is $100,000 or more, the rate penalty is only about 1 percent. Obviously this penalty hits hardest at the level affecting most people.

Box 3 is a sort of punishment factor and applies primarily to the errant spouse who leaves the home. The spouse who stays at home usually has custody of the children, and the tax law specifically provides that those persons are not subject to the penalty.

Box 4: Unmarried Head of Household

Unmarried-head-of-household status is reserved for those single individuals who maintain a home where one or more certain dependents live. The rates for this status generally fall midway between those for singles and marrieds. It is also available under certain circumstances to those singles who provide support for their parents.

Box 5: Qualifying Widow(er) with Dependent Children

Persons whose spouse died during the year are entitled to use the joint-return rates in their last return. If they also maintain a home for their children, they can use the joint-return rates for the two taxable years immediately following the date of death. After that, they have to use the head-of-household rates.

Exemptions

Lines 6a and b are relatively straightforward and allow a deduction of $750 for each dependent. The general rules to qualify as a dependent are that you must have provided

Exemptions

Always check the "Yourself" box. Check other boxes if they apply.

6a ☐ Yourself ☐ 65 or over ☐ Blind

b ☐ Spouse ☐ 65 or over ☐ Blind

Enter number of boxes checked on 6a and b ▶ ☐

c First names of your dependent children who lived with you ▶ ....

Enter number of children listed ▶ ☐

d Other dependents: (1) Name	(2) Relationship	(3) Number of months lived in your home.	(4) Did dependent have income of $750 or more?	(5) Did you provide more than one-half of dependent's support?

Enter number of other dependents ▶ ☐

7 Total number of exemptions claimed . . . .

Add numbers entered in boxes above ▶ ☐

more than 50 percent of the person's support. There are special rules for parents, college students, and other persons who are not part of your family, and these should be consulted if you think you might be entitled to claim any of these persons as a dependent.

For fathers paying child support: Notice that line c, listing the names of dependent children, is only for those children that live with the father. Even though the fathers can legally claim their children as dependents, they are required to list them under line d. This is strictly for the benefit of the IRS. Their computers are programmed to check every listing on line d, but do not bother with line c.

This section may tell you whether or not your spouse is claiming exemptions for children from a prior marriage, a mother, or a mistress or lover. Don't laugh. Under certain conditions, mistresses and lovers qualify for dependent exemptions.

Taxable Income

The next section of the tax return includes the various items of taxable income:

Income				
8	Wages, salaries, tips, and other employee compensation. (Attach Forms W-2. If unavailable, see page 5 of Instructions.)	8		
9	Interest income. (If over $400, attach Schedule B.)	9		
10a	Dividends (If over $400, attach Schedule B) .... , 10b less exclusion .... , Balance ▶ (See pages 9 and 17 of Instructions)	10c		
	(If you have no other income, **skip** *lines 11 through 20 and go to line 21.)*			
11	State and local income tax refunds (does not apply if refund is for year you took standard deduction)	11		
•12	Alimony received	12		
13	Business income or (loss) (attach Schedule C)	13		
14	Capital gain or (loss) (attach Schedule D)	14		
15	50% of capital gain distributions not reported on Schedule D	15		
16	Net gain or (loss) from Supplemental Schedule of Gains and Losses (attach Form 4797)	16		
17	Fully taxable pensions and annuities not reported on Schedule E	17		
18	Pensions, annuities, rents, royalties, partnerships, estates or trusts, etc. (attach Schedule E)	18		
19	Farm income or (loss) (attach Schedule F)	19		
20	Other (state nature and source—see page 9 of Instructions) ▶	20		
21	**Total income.** Add lines 8, 9, and 10c through 20 ▶	21		

Wages and Salaries

Line 8 shows wages and salaries from W-2 forms. In

general, the wages and salaries will be gross; that is, no deductions will have been taken from them.

For those persons interested (for whatever reason) in keeping their income as low as possible, here are a few suggestions which might be helpful. First, suppose you are offered a transfer at a substantial increase in salary and your spouse refuses to go. If you go and a divorce results, you will be faced with higher support payments. In light of this, it may be possible to negotiate with the company for a larger bonus or deferred compensation in lieu of a raise currently. If you have an opportunity you might forgo a raise for other perquisites, such as more paid vacation days.

A case recently decided in Idaho stipulated that a bonus which was paid every year, and equal to a year's salary, was not to be counted in determining support because the bonus was at the discretion of the employer and depended upon net profits. A word of caution, however: One New Jersey fellow got stuck when his income before the divorce was $40,000 per year and immediately went to $80,000 afterward. When his ex-wife found out, she sued for increased support. Even though he quit his job when she sued, the court set the support level based on the $80,000 income. The court reasoned that because the husband had the ability to earn that much, quitting his job was capricious and the fact he no longer had any income was not important.

Interest Income

Interest income is entered on line 9, and if the amount is over $400, the payer must be listed on page 2, part I, Schedule B. The most important thing to remember is that there are certain kinds of interest income which will not be recorded here. The major one is interest income from municipal bonds. This interest is not subject to federal taxes (indeed, it doesn't even have to be reported) and is exempt from most state taxes, as well. One of the greatest tax-planning devices of all times was the case of the woman who converted all the property she inherited from her deceased husband into "tax-free" municipal bonds. She enjoyed an income of $1 million per year and didn't even have to file a tax return.

Dividends

Dividend income is reported on line 10. Each person is allowed to exclude the first $100 of dividends from taxable income. Where one spouse owns all the stock, the limitation is $100 unless the couple lives in a community-property state which specifies that this kind of income is community property (Texas, for example, but not California). Both spouses, if they have dividend income, should own enough stock individually to take advantage of the $100 tax-free income. If the divided income is over $400 the individual amounts must be listed on page 2, part II, Schedule B. For additional information for those who are interested, read the detailed discussion on that section.

The second major area of interest income which may escape current taxation is the interest accruing on Series E U. S. Savings Bonds. These bonds are bought at a discount, and if the taxpayer so elects (by not reporting the appreciation), the interest will not be reported as taxable income until the bonds are cashed in.

The third major area of nonreported interest income applies to the tax-sheltered annuity plan. But you had better investigate before investing because these plans are currently under IRS security. Generally, these plans provide that if you put up $10,000 or more for a minimum time of ten years, the interest earned on the principal is not reported by you as income until such time as you request the interest to be paid to you. This vehicle is becoming very popular with the money set. One of its major benefits seems to be the ability to withdraw a portion or all of the principal for emergency use without withdrawing any of the interest, which would then be taxable.[1]

For Those Receiving Alimony

This year, for the first time, the IRS has provided a special line to report the receipt of alimony. Apparently the agency was afraid that too many persons were not reporting their alimony receipts as taxable income; the IRS wants to help them remember that they must pay taxes on this income.

Other Items

Lines 13 through 20 don't affect most people, so they are discussed in depth later in the chapter.

Adjustments to Income

Lines 22 through 27, and line 30, adjustments to income and the sick-pay exclusion, are those deductions allowed even though the standard deduction is taken.

This includes such things as picking up the tab for a business dinner for which the company did not provide reimbursement, or the use of a personal automobile on company business. Moving expenses, alimony, and certain other deductions are subtracted here, which gives a total known as adjusted gross income (AGI). It is from your AGI that deductions for personal exemptions, medical expenses, contributions, and interest and taxes can be taken. This final figure (AGI minus deductions) is your taxable income, i.e., the portion of your income upon which your tax is computed.

Line 22 reports the deduction for moving costs from one

---

[1] For additional information and planning hints, see the detailed discussion later in the chapter on interest and dividend income (Schedule B).

Adjustments to Income	(*If none,* **skip** *lines 22 through 27 and enter zero on line 28.*)			
22	Moving expense (attach Form 3903)	22		
23	Employee business expenses (attach Form 2106)	23		
24	Payments to an individual retirement arrangement (from attached Form 5329, Part III)	24		
25	Payments to a Keogh (H.R. 10) retirement plan	25		
26	Forfeited interest penalty for premature withdrawal	26		
27	Alimony paid (see page 11 of Instructions)	27		
28	**Total adjustments.** Add lines 22 through 27 . . . . ▶		28	
29	Subtract line 28 from line 21		29	
30	Disability income exclusion (sick pay) (attach Form 2440)		30	
31	**Adjusted gross income.** Subtract line 30 from line 29. Enter here and on line 32. If you want IRS to figure your tax for you, see page 4 of the Instructions . . . . ▶		31	

city to another. Supposedly, the original idea behind allowing such deductions was that if people moved to get better jobs which paid more money, they would owe *more taxes.* More probably, the moving industry did a little lobbying in Congress to get this deduction. The upshot was that everyone started moving south, with part of the cost being absorbed by Uncle Sam. So, to qualify for this deduction (limit $3,000) in the year you pay the expenses, you must be gainfully employed for a year after you get to the new location. Otherwise, you lose the deduction and must give back the tax savings.

Employee business expenses are those expenses incurred by you on behalf of your employer for which you are not reimbursed. An example of this is when you use your car to visit a client's office. No doubt you have heard of lavish parties and such allowed on expense accounts. Line 23 is where these are reported. Basically, the rule for expense accounts is that you must have a receipt for any expenditure over $25. Any meal, which may include wives, must be in a surrounding which is conducive to discussing your business. If your employer reimburses you for the expenses, the reporting requirements are somewhat lessened. Note, however, if your employer reimburses you for more than you would be entitled to deduct, the excess may be *income* to you. An example of this would be where you send a dozen roses to your lover and you pad the expense account to cover the amount (and you are caught). Unfortunately, most wives do not have access to their husband's expense-account reports and are therefore unable to verify whether he was having dinner on such and such a night with such and such a client as he said he was.

Lines 24 and 25 are the lines to report your deduction for a contribution to your retirement plan. Individual retirement accounts are for those salaried persons who are not covered by their employer's pension plan. The maximum deduction is 15 percent of your salary or up to $1,500. This amount can be increased to $1,750 if your spouse doesn't work and you want to give her half of your retirement benefits. The Keogh deduction is equal to the lesser of 15 percent of self-employed (earned) income or $7,500. Although it's never been tested, a person receiving alimony might consider reporting the alimony as "earned income" so as to qualify for the deduction.

The general rule for both of these plans is that once you put money into them, you can't get it out until you retire (no earlier than age fifty–nine and a half).

Computing the Tax Owed or Refund Due

Once the taxable income has been determined, the amount is entered on line 32, on the back of Form 1040. The next step is to determine if your itemized deductions exceed the standard deduction allowed.

The itemized-deductions provision allowed by Congress is rich with political favors and is discussed in more detail under Schedule A.

Tax Computation

Lines 33 through 36 contain the directions for computing the taxes due. If your return includes more than just the basics, good luck if you try to do it yourself. Even the IRS cautions you on line 33. Some people feel that if they check that box, the IRS will automatically examine their return to make sure they computed their taxes properly. The form called for on line 33, 4563, is not included in the tax package sent to taxpayers, and it is not explained in the instructions. If you must know, it is a form to report income excluded from U. S. possessions. Lastly, on line 33, a dual-status-alien question does not ask for sexual preferences, but applies to those persons who are both resident and nonresident aliens.

Line 36 requires you to compute your taxes on special forms if you have certain things happen to you during the year. Note, too, they don't send you these forms either. In order, the forms are as follows: 4970, tax on accumulation distribution of trusts; 4972, special ten-year averaging method (for lump-sum distributions from pension plans); 5544, multiple recipient special ten-year averaging method; 5405, recapture of credit for purchase or construction of new principal residence; and the Section 72(m) (5) penalty tax on premature or excess distributions from a retirement plan. (For this one, they don't have their own form, so you are allowed to make your own up.)

If you have trouble computing your taxes, don't despair —ask the IRS to help you. National studies indicate they pass out the wrong answer only once in ten questions. (The

Tax Computation

32 Amount from line 31 . . . . | 32

33 If you itemize deductions, enter excess itemized deductions from Schedule A, line 41 . . . .
If you do NOT itemize deductions, enter zero . . . . | 33

Caution: *If you have unearned income and can be claimed as a dependent on your parent's return, check here* ▶ ☐ *and see page 11 of the Instructions. Also see page 11 of the Instructions if:*

- You are married filing a separate return and your spouse itemizes deductions, OR
- You file Form 4563, OR
- You are a dual-status alien.

34 Tax Table Income. Subtract line 33 from line 32 . . . . | 34

Note: See Instructions for line 35 on page 11. Then find your tax on the amount on line 34 in the Tax Tables. Enter the tax on line 35. However, if line 34 is more than $20,000 ($40,000 if you checked box 2 or 5) or you have more exemptions than those covered in the Tax Tables for your filing status, use Part I of Schedule TC (Form 1040) to figure your tax. You must also use Schedule TC if you file Schedule G (Form 1040), Income Averaging.

35 Tax. Check if from ☐ Tax Tables or ☐ Schedule TC . . . . | 35

36 Additional taxes. (See page 12 of Instructions.) Check if from ☐ Form 4970, ☐ Form 4972, ☐ Form 5544, ☐ Form 5405, or ☐ Section 72(m)(5) penalty tax . . . . | 36

37 **Total.** Add lines 35 and 36 . . . . ▶ | 37 national studies conducted, however, did not indicate how hard the questions were that were posed to the IRS agents.)

It is obvious that this is an easy section to complete. All you have to do is spend about six years studying to be a CPA. Observe the different computations required on lines 33, 34, and 35, depending upon your marital status. If the government would quit fooling around taxing people differently because of their marital status, two-thirds of the above computations would be eliminated.

The first item on line 33 refers to those wealthy kids who have unearned income such as interest and dividends of over $750 and who are counted as dependents by their parents. If so, they can't take the standard deduction but must itemize.

As you can see, if your return is complicated enough, you would have to use twelve different forms just to compute your gross taxes, and there are seven different forms to report credits against those taxes. If you earn that much money, you can hire someone to help you find your correct tax.

Tax Credits

With the exception of the credit for the elderly and the foreign tax credit, all of the other credits are new. The child and dependent care credit was formerly a deduction. This will probably be the case for exemptions if Congress decides to allow a credit of $250 per exemption instead of a deduction of $750. This is a benefit only for those persons earning under $15,000 per year.

The investment tax credit is for those individuals who invest in certain depreciable business property. Foreign income taxes are allowed as credits against U.S. taxes. The next two credits are for those persons employing others in certain circumstances. The "new jobs credit" is new for

1977 and will presumably be the "old jobs credit" after 1977.

Line 45 was for some solar credits that were never approved by Congress.

Credits			
38 Credit for contributions to candidates for public office	38		
39 Credit for the elderly (attach Schedules R&RP)	39		
40 Credit for child and dependent care expenses (attach Form 2441) .	40		
41 Investment credit (attach Form 3468)	41		
42 Foreign tax credit (attach Form 1116)	42		
43 Work Incentive (WIN) Credit (attach Form 4874)	43		
44 New jobs credit (attach Form 5884)	44		
45 See page 12 of Instructions	45		
46 Total credits. Add lines 38 through 45			46
47 Balance. Subtract line 46 from line 37 and enter difference (but not less than zero) . . . . ▶			47

The other tax schedule serves primarily to collect social security taxes from self-employed persons. If such persons took credit for taxes on line 41 above, and have failed to meet all the criteria, the credit must be repaid on line 50 in this part.

Other Taxes		
48 Self-employment tax (attach Schedule SE)	48	
49 Minimum tax. Check here ▶ ☐ and attach Form 4625	49	
50 Tax from recomputing prior-year investment credit (attach Form 4255)	50	
51 Social security tax on tip income not reported to employer (attach Form 4137)	51	
52 Uncollected employee social security tax on tips (from Form W–2)	52	
53 Tax on an individual retirement arrangement (attach Form 5329)	53	
54 Total tax. Add lines 47 through 53 . . . . ▶	54	

The minimum tax noted on line 49 does not mean that everyone has to pay some taxes, but it was originally aimed at those wealthy individuals who could shelter their unearned income with various (legitimate) tax schemes. However, since it didn't raise very much money, Congress changed the rates in 1976 so that if, for example, you sell your house for a $15,000 profit, you will owe $750 minimum tax on the deal, even if you have no other income. The tax rate is 15 percent of your gain after an exemption of $10,000 or one-half your regular tax, whichever is greater.

Payments and Tax Due

Included in this section are the credits against the tax due after the credits for the other taxes due in the preceding section. Here you list your withholding, estimated tax payments, excess FICA payments, etc., and if they exceed the taxes due, you get a refund. Otherwise you owe the government money.

Payments	55 Total Federal income tax withheld (attach Forms W–2, W–2G, and W–2P to front)	55	
	56 1977 estimated tax payments (include amount allowed as credit from 1976 return)	56	
	57 Earned income credit. If line 31 is under $8,000, see page 2 of Instructions. If eligible, enter child's name ▶	57	
	58 Amount paid with Form 4868	58	
	59 Excess FICA and RRTA tax withheld (two or more employers) . . .	59	
	60 Credit for Federal tax on special fuels, etc. (attach Form 4136) . .	60	
	61 Credit from a Regulated Investment Company (attach Form 2439)	61	
	61a See page 13 of Instructions	61a	
	62 Total. Add lines 55 through 61a . . . . ▶		62
Refund or Due	63 If line 62 is larger than line 54, enter amount **OVERPAID** . . . . ▶		63
	64 Amount of line 63 to be **REFUNDED TO YOU** . . . . ▶		64
	65 Amount of line 63 to be credited on 1978 estimated tax . . . . ▶	65	
	66 If line 54 is larger than line 62, enter **BALANCE DUE.** Attach check or money order for full amount payable to "Internal Revenue Service." Write social security number on check or money order . . . ▶ (Check ▶ ☐ if Form 2210 (2210F) is attached. See page 14 of Instructions.)		66

Note the credit allowed on line 60. This is for those persons who purchased gasoline or oil for use in a nonhighway vehicle such as a boat or an airplane. The credit is for taxes for the improvement of highways, which is added to the cost of the gasoline and oil. The theory is that you don't have to pay the tax if you don't use the gas or oil on the highway.

Signing the Form

The last area on page 1 of Form 1040 is the signature section. There are two major considerations here: The first is that the return must be signed under the penalties of perjury, and the second is that if a joint return is being filed, both spouses must sign the return.

Please Sign Here

Under penalties of perjury, I declare that I have examined this return, including accompanying schedules and statements, and to the best of my knowledge and belief, it is true, correct, and complete. Declaration of preparer (other than taxpayer) is based on all information of which preparer has any knowledge.

Your signature — Date

Spouse's signature (if filing jointly, BOTH must sign even if only one had income)

Paid preparer's signature and identifying number (see instructions)

Paid preparer's address (or employer's name, address, and identifying number)

☆ U.S. GOVERNMENT PRINTING OFFICE : 1977—O-235-057 #95-238446

Note the place for the paid preparer's signature and social security number. Under recently enacted legislation, this person has come under some fairly rigorous rules relating to what he or she can do in preparing the return. Basically it means they will accompany you to jail if they are found guilty of helping you commit tax fraud.

Before proceeding to the rest of Form 1040, you should understand a few things about withholding tax and about refunds.

Withholding Too Much and Other Devious Tricks

For those persons who are getting divorced, it is important to remember that monthly support payments are generally based on "after tax" income. Because of this, many primary-income-earning spouses lower their take-home pay by additional withholding of federal and state income taxes. This is accomplished with special forms (called W-4s) that the income-earning spouses prepare and sumbit to their employers which will increase the amount of withholding and thereby decrease the after-tax income. Obviously, this is patently unfair to the other spouse, who is depending upon a fair split. Although this is used by about everyone, it is relatively easy to check. If you know the gross amount of salary, call the IRS and they will tell you how much federal income tax, including social security, must be withheld. You will also have to call your state tax office to get the state amount. They will ask for the filing status—married or single, etc.—and the number of personal exemptions.

Two things to watch for are the effect of itemized deductions and the filing status. Currently, the IRS allows a lower withholding rate if your itemized deductions exceed the standard deduction. The way you get your withholding reduced is to count additional exemptions on your W-4 form. This is an "option" granted you and carries severe penalties if misused. Obviously, if you want your take-home pay lower, thereby possibly decreasing your support payments and increasing your tax refund, you won't want to risk those penalties. Some persons, in determining their filing status, don't make the rash assumption that their spouse will sign the joint return. Using the married-filing-separately rate will significantly increase their withholding. If their spouse does sign the return, or they are single by year's end, they will have a nice refund. Otherwise they have covered themselves and should they have to pay higher income taxes their spouse will share part of the cost through lower support payments.

You now know both how to increase your withholding legally, and how to determine if and how it is being done. A word of caution: If the opposing attorney has any idea that this trick is being used or understands it, he will be quick to point this out to the court, which, in turn, may be inclined to adjust your after-tax earnings and not believe you when you claim you need a certain income level to live on.

Refunds

If a tax return is filed during the time the divorce proceedings are in progress, and there is a refund indicated on the tax return, each spouse will be entitled to one-half the refund in most circumstances. Make sure you get your half!

Also, do not overlook the fact that there may also be a refund due on any state income-tax return filed as well. Note that refund checks on all joint returns are made out to both spouses, and both must endorse the checks before they can be cashed or deposited.

Itemized Deductions

Itemized deductions constitute the biggest loophole in that they are used by more people than any other tax shelter. The two biggest items are the deductions for home-mortgage interest and state income taxes. It is primarily through the itemized-deduction section that the average salaried person can affect his taxable income. Although you may ask your employer to defer your bonus or not ask you to work overtime, you run a certain risk that he may think you don't need the money and will adjust your future raises accordingly. However, he will never see what you do on your tax return.

Schedule A, which reports your itemized deductions, is shown on page 166.

The first part of Schedule A allows a deduction for certain large medical expenses. Other than the first $150 of medical insurance premiums, your medical expenses have to be more than 3 percent of your adjusted gross income. For example, if your taxable income is $12,000, your medical expenses would have to be over $360 before any of them would be deductible over the minimum of $150 allowed.

Some persons quite effectively manage their taxable income in this area by properly timing their medical payments. They schedule their dentist and medical appointments late in the year and insist on paying before year end. Then they wait until after the first of the year to turn in their expenses to the insurance company for reimbursement. Therefore, their medical expenses have not been compen-

Schedules A&B—Itemized Deductions AND Interest and Dividend Income

(Form 1040)

Department of the Treasury
Internal Revenue Service

▶ Attach to Form 1040. ▶ See Instructions for Schedules A and B (Form 1040).

1977

Name(s) as shown on Form 1040 | Your social security number

Schedule A Itemized Deductions (Schedule B is on back)

Medical and Dental Expenses (not compensated by insurance or otherwise) (See page 14 of Instructions.)

1 One-half (but not more than $150) of insurance premiums for medical care. (Be sure to include in line 10 below)
2 Medicine and drugs
3 Enter 1% of line 31, Form 1040
4 Subtract line 3 from line 2. Enter difference (if less than zero, enter zero)
5 Enter balance of insurance premiums for medical care not entered on line 1
6 Enter other medical and dental expenses:
a Doctors, dentists, nurses, etc.
b Hospitals
c Other (itemize—include hearing aids, dentures, eyeglasses, transportation, etc.) ▶
7 Total (add lines 4 through 6c)
8 Enter 3% of line 31, Form 1040
9 Subtract line 8 from line 7 (if less than zero, enter zero)
10 Total (add lines 1 and 9). Enter here and on line 33 ▶

Taxes (See page 14 of Instructions.)

11 State and local income
12 Real estate
13 State and local gasoline (see gas tax tables)
14 General sales (see sales tax tables)
15 Personal property
16 Other (itemize) ▶
17 Total (add lines 11 through 16). Enter here and on line 34 ▶

Interest Expense (See page 16 of Instructions.)

18 Home mortgage
19 Other (itemize) ▶
20 Total (add lines 18 and 19). Enter here and on line 35 ▶

Contributions (See page 16 of Instructions for examples.)

21 a Cash contributions for which you have receipts, cancelled checks or other written evidence
b Other cash contributions. List donees and amounts. ▶
22 Other than cash (see page 16 of instructions for required statement)
23 Carryover from prior years
24 Total contributions (add lines 21a through 23). Enter here and on line 36 ▶

Casualty or Theft Loss(es) (See page 16 of Instructions.)

25 Loss before insurance reimbursement
26 Insurance reimbursement
27 Subtract line 26 from line 25. Enter difference (if less than zero, enter zero)
28 Enter $100 or amount on line 27, whichever is smaller
29 Casualty or theft loss (subtract line 28 from line 27). Enter here and on line 37 ▶

Miscellaneous Deductions (See page 16 of Instructions.)

30 Union dues
31 Other (itemize) ▶
32 Total (add lines 30 and 31). Enter here and on line 38 ▶

Summary of Itemized Deductions (See page 17 of Instructions.) **A**

33 Total medical and dental—line 10
34 Total taxes—line 17
35 Total interest—line 20
36 Total contributions—line 24
37 Casualty or theft loss(es)—line 29
38 Total miscellaneous—line 32
39 Total deductions (add lines 33 through 38). ▶
40 If you checked Form 1040, box:
2 or 5, enter $3,200
1 or 4, enter $2,200
3, enter $1,600
41 Excess itemized deductions (subtract line 40 from line 39). Enter here and on Form 1040, line 33. (If line 40 is more than line 39 see "Who MUST Itemize Deductions" on page 11 of the Instructions.) ▶

sated for *in that year*.

The second part of schedule A is for your allowable deductions for taxes paid. If you wish to lower your taxable income for a given year, you may prepay next year's real estate taxes and deduct them this year. You can prepay state income taxes as well, but the amount you prepay is supposed to be about the amount you will owe on the return. If you are in a divorce proceeding, it probably does not help much to prepay taxes to lower your income. Although your taxable income will be smaller by the amount prepaid, conversely your taxes due will be smaller as well. However, if you can arrange to borrow the funds to make the prepayment, you might luck out. The borrowing would count as a community debt and would be satisfied out of family liabilities. You, of course, will get the benefit of the prepayment cost by getting a tax refund, or having next year's property taxes already paid on your house. However, the other side of the coin is that you may lose by not getting all the state tax refund, or the prepaid real estate taxes if you lose the house in the settlement.

Real Estate Taxes

Pay attention to the real estate tax deduction; it may provide a clue to hidden assets. If your spouse has purchased or inherited some real estate you don't know about, the real estate taxes paid on the property will show up here (nobody is going to pass up a tax deduction). Call the local tax assessor and ask for the amount of the property taxes levied on your house. If your deduction is more than the amount, become suspicious and ask about the difference.

Interest Expenses

Lines 18 through 20 contain the interest-expense deduction in Schedule A. Although the deduction for prepaid interest has all but been eliminated, it is still possible to borrow funds and pay interest which will be allowed as a deduction. If borrowed before your date of separation, the liability will be a community debt, i.e., your spouse must pay half. What you do with the funds is your own business. On the other hand, note that the interest-expense deductions have to be itemized. If there are some interest deductions and you don't know what the funds were borrowed for, or where they are, ask.

Charitable Contributions

The charitable-contributions section is next on Schedule A. Although the rules have been tightened considerably, you can still get a deduction for contributing property to the right organization. Note, however, there is no deduction for that fifty cents you donate to that needy person on the street. To qualify as a deduction, the gift must be to a charitable organization registered with the IRS. If you happen to be involved in divorce proceedings, and have already replaced your wardrobe with new duds as recommended, don't give that old stuff away until you are able to file your own separate tax return. Otherwise, you will have to share the tax benefits of the donation with your soon-to-be ex.

Casualty and Theft Losses

The next section deals with casualty and theft losses. For one reason or another, Congress allows a deduction for these. Apparently they figure that if they can't stop the muggings, they will at least give you part of your money back through tax deductions. However, you only get to deduct the part of the loss that's over $100. Does that give you any ideas? In general, the definition of a casualty loss requires the loss to have occurred because of a fire, storm, or shipwreck. Therefore, if you chopped one of your toes off with a lawnmower, you might think you had a casualty loss, but you probably wouldn't because you couldn't prove what your toe was worth. You don't get a deduction if you merely lose or misplace your property. However, where a husband slammed a car door on his wife's hand and the door broke two fingers, and the diamond on the wife's ring was lost, the loss (of the diamond) was deductible as a casualty loss. One word of advice: If you want your deduction of a theft loss to stand up, you should report the theft to the police and have a police report to back you up.

Miscellaneous Deductions

This miscellaneous section of Schedule A is primarily for such things as union dues, the cost of safety deposit boxes, tax-return-preparation fees, and the cost of this book. (Yes, it's deductible!)

Should You Itemize?

If you have calculated all your itemized deductions and the amount comes to more than $3,200 if you are married, or $2,200 if you are single, you will want to itemize on your tax return. As a general rule of thumb, you can assume that for every dollar over those amounts you will save thirty cents. This makes the effort worthwhile.

Every so often, Congress increases the amount of the maximum standard deduction allowed to encourage people not to itemize and to simplify their tax return. As a comparison, the maximum standard deduction in 1967 was $1,000 for everyone. Unfortunately, interest expenses and state income taxes have increased so rapidly that the larger maximums have very little effect today. In 1967, $10,000 of taxable income would have allowed a person the maximum standard deduction. This has been changed to a flat $3,200 for married persons and $2,200 for a single person. Still, this means that as your income increases, the benefits of itemizing become more and more important.

Dividend and Interest Income

The next major area to examine is Schedule B, which is shown on page 171.

How to Find Out About Other Investments

The first half of Schedule B indicates interest income. In this column, all interest earned in savings accounts and bonds and other loans, with the major exception of Series E U.S. Savings Bonds and municipal bonds, is listed. In general, people do not report the interest earned on Series E bonds until the bonds are cashed in. Under the current regulations, it is possible to buy Series E bonds and continue to hold them indefinitely, with the interest accruing and not being reported on federal or state tax returns until the bonds are cashed in. Congress has obliged by providing that those bonds issued in 1940 and after still earn current rates of interest and still do not have to be redeemed. This means that the interest from these bonds does not show up on Schedule B, and so it is not possible to tell of their existence by means of the tax return. Some persons have used the savings bonds as collateral for loans, although technically banks are not supposed to accept them. The bank loans show up as family liabilities in divorce settlements, and the interest expense as a deduction which tends to lower the money left for support payments, and "family" assets are used to pay off the loan. One enterprising husband, who was getting a divorce, may have avoided the problems of perjury in listing his assets by having the bonds issued in the names of his children with himself as the "or" owner (the other person besides the original owner who can cash the bonds). The "or" ownership listing provides the greatest flexibility, in that he can cash the bonds in himself, for such things as college expenses, which otherwise might have to come out of other income.

In the case of both dividend and interest income, per-

Schedules A&B (Form 1040) 1977 **Schedule B—Interest and Dividend Income** Page 2

Name(s) as shown on Form 1040 (Do not enter name and social security number if shown on other side) | Your social security number

Part I **Interest Income**

1 *If you received more than $400 in interest, complete Part I.* **Interest** includes earnings from savings and loan associations, mutual savings banks, cooperative banks, and credit unions as well as interest on bank deposits, bonds, tax refunds, etc. **Interest** also includes original issue discount on bonds and other evidences of indebtedness (see page 17 of Instructions). **(List payers and amounts.)**

2 Total interest income. Enter here and on Form 1040, line 9 . . . .

Part II **Dividend Income**

3 *If you received more than $400 in* **gross dividends** *(including capital gain distributions) and other distributions on stock, complete Part II (see Note below and page 17 of instructions).* **(List payers and amounts**—write (H), (W), (J), **for stock held** by husband, wife, or jointly.)

4 Total of line 3 . . . .

5 Capital gain distributions (see page 18 of Instructions. Enter here and on Schedule D, line 7). See Note below . . . . .

6 Nontaxable distributions (see page 18 of instructions) . . .

7 Total (add lines 5 and 6) . . . . . .

8 Dividends before exclusion (subtract line 7 from line 4). Enter here and on Form 1040, line 10a . . . .

Note: *If you received capital gain distributions and do not need Schedule D to report any other gains or losses or to compute the alternative tax, do not file that schedule. Instead, enter 50 percent of capital gain distributions on Form 1040, line 15.*

B

Part III **Foreign Accounts and Foreign Trusts**

If you are required to list interest in Part I or dividends in Part II, **OR** *if you had a foreign account or were a grantor of, or a transferor to a foreign trust, you must answer both questions in Part III. (See page 18 of Instructions.)*

1 Did you, at any time during the taxable year, have any interest in or signature or other authority over a bank, securities, or other financial account in a foreign country (except in a U.S. military banking facility operated by a U.S. financial institution)? . . . . ☐ Yes ☐ No

If "Yes," see page 3 of instructions.

2 Were you the grantor of, or transferor to, a foreign trust during any taxable year, which foreign trust was in being during the current taxable year, whether or not you have any beneficial interest in such trust? . . . ☐ Yes ☐ No

If "Yes," you may be required to file Forms 3520, 3520–A, or 926.

☆ U.S. GOVERNMENT PRINTING OFFICE : 1977-0-235-067 94-2249262

haps the best way of telling whether or not these items exist is through the discovery procedure that may be used by your attorney.

How to Find Out How Much Stock Is Owned

The second part of Schedule B reports dividend income. If dividend (or interest income) is over $400, the payors and amounts must be separately listed. It is possible to determine the number of shares owned and their value from this listing. Look in the financial section of any major newspaper. The first number immediately following the name of the stock is the dividend paid per share over the last twelve months. If you divide this number into the dividend income shown, you will have the number of shares. Multiplying the number of shares by the price shown in the paper will give you the value. However, remember that the shares may have been pledged as collateral for bank loans or a margin account (a loan from the stock brokerage firm). If this is so, the value should be reduced accordingly. A good way to tell if this is the case is to look in the interest-deduction section of Schedule A to see if there are any interest deductions for amounts paid to banks or stock brokerage firms.

There are many stocks that do not pay dividends. It is not possible to determine the existence of such assets from the tax return. The best way to trace these investments is to determine the possible source of the funds used to buy the stocks. For example, if your spouse received a gift or sold other stock (it would be reported on this or a previous return), inquire as to the whereabouts of the money.

On Simplifying the Tax Laws

The issue of tax simplification is extremely difficult. The usual demand from taxpayers and consumer advocates is to have a straight across-the-board tax rate and no deductions. This would allow everyone to do his or her own tax returns without all the conniving and scheming that goes on with tax shelters and loopholes. In addition, it would put a large number of lawyers and accountants out of work, perhaps into more productive jobs.

Unfortunately, the situation is more complex than that. The tax laws are made by elected representatives in Congress who have to pay attention to their constituents. For example, if Congress should do away with the deduction for home interest, one or more of the following could happen:

1. Houses would go down in value because without the benefit of the tax deduction, there would be less demand for them, since they would cost more to own. Conversely, apartment buildings would go up in value, and their rents would rise, too.
2. With less demand for homes, the housing industry would be forced into a major retraction of employment, thereby causing thousands of people to be out of work with the attendant possibility of starting a mini-depression.
3. With home interest no longer deductible, state income taxes would rise, because most states follow the federal tax base.
4. If the value of houses was to plummet, it stands to reason that property taxes should also go down. But they probably wouldn't, since most jurisdictions automatically raise the valuation by 1 percent per month.
5. Without the demand for home mortgages, savings-and-loan institutions would lose a big chunk of their business. To balance things out, they would have to lower interest rates they pay on savings accounts and look for other, riskier sources of loans which could easily default, leaving many such institutions in perilous situations.
6. With the demand for rental property going up, the

urge for rent controls would grow stronger. This could subject large parts of the nation to the same problems of dislocation that New York City has.

7. Thousands who planned to retire on the equity in their homes would be affected.
8. For a majority of people, the American dream of a little white house with a picket fence would come to an end.
9. Many new faces would be seen in Congress after the next election.

As you can see from the above nine points, the major problem with tax simplification is the unknown repercussions of a given action. And this is only one small area of the tax laws! The U. S. Government, through several administrations, has endeavored to fine-tune the economy through tax rebates. A major change in the tax laws could throw this delicate system out of balance. Of course, there are some items, such as the deduction for gasoline taxes, which can be eliminated without any serious repercussions, and with the right amount of pressure, Congress will begin to make progress on the things it *can* change.

COMPLICATED RETURNS

The second section of this chapter is for those persons who have income from other than salaries and wages. As in the first section, the explanations and discussions are intended primarily for those who want to know more about the family finances or who are planning a divorce.

Let's return to line 13, page 1, of Form 1040, the summary of various types of income and deductions:

13	Business income or (loss) (attach Schedule C)	13	
14	Capital gain or (loss) (attach Schedule D)	14	
15	50% of capital gain distributions not reported on Schedule D	15	
16	Net gain or (loss) from Supplemental Schedule of Gains and Losses (attach Form 4797)	16	
17	Fully taxable pensions and annuities not reported on Schedule E	17	
18	Pensions, annuities, rents, royalties, partnerships, estates or trusts, etc. (attach Schedule E)	18	
19	Farm income or (loss) (attach Schedule F)	19	
20	Other (state nature and source—see page 9 of Instructions) ▶	20	
21	**Total income.** Add lines 8, 9, and 10c through 20 ▶	21	

Each line concerns a different type of income and poses different problems, whether you are trying to find out a spouse's income, conceal your income from a spouse, or simply minimize the taxes you must pay.

Self-Employed Business Income

Schedule C, mentioned on line 13, is used to report the income for self-employed persons. (If the self-employed earnings come from a partnership, another tax form, 1065, must be used to report the earnings.) Schedule C is shown on page 176.

Income from a Business

Lines 1 through 5 report the gross receipts and the cost of sales. There are primarily two ways of reporting receipts as income, the accrual method and the cash method. The accrual method records as taxable income those items which have not yet been reduced to cash, whereas the cash method records as taxable income only the cash or fair market of any goods actually received. An example of the cash method is a doctor's receivables from his patients on December 31. Even though he has sent out statements to his patients, until he actually receives their checks or the cash, he does not have taxable income.

The phrase "returns and allowances" on line 1 means the cost of exchanging or refunding the purchase price for items returned. If a person purchased a pair of shoes and later returned the shoes for a refund, the refund paid would be

SCHEDULE C (Form 1040)
Department of the Treasury
Internal Revenue Service

Profit or (Loss) From Business or Profession

(Sole Proprietorship)
Partnerships, Joint Ventures, etc., Must File Form 1065.
▶ Attach to Form 1040. ▶ See Instructions for Schedule C (Form 1040).

1977

Name of proprietor | Social security number

A Principal business activity (see Schedule C Instructions) ▶ ....; product ▶ ....
B Business name ▶ ....
C Employer identification number ▶ ....
D Business address (number and street) ▶ ....
City, State and ZIP code ▶ ....

C

E Indicate method of accounting: (1) ☐ Cash (2) ☐ Accrual (3) ☐ Other ▶ ....

	Yes	No
F Was an Employer's Quarterly Federal Tax Return, Form 941, filed for this business for any quarter in 1977?		
G Did you own the business at the end of 1977?		
H How many months in 1977 did you own this business? ▶		
I Check valuation method(s) used for total closing inventory: ☐ cost, ☐ lower of cost or market, ☐ other (if "other," attach explanation).		
Was there any substantial change in determining quantities, costs, or valuations between opening and closing inventory? If "Yes," attach explanation.		

Income

1 Gross receipts or sales $........ Less: returns and allowances $........ Balance ▶	1	
2 Less: Cost of goods sold and/or operations (Schedule C–1, line 8)	2	
3 Gross profit	3	
4 Other income (attach schedule)	4	
5 Total income (add lines 3 and 4)	5	

Deductions

6 Depreciation (explain in Schedule C–2)	6	
7 Taxes on business and business property	7	
8 Rent on business property	8	
9 Repairs	9	
10 Salaries and wages not included on line 3, Schedule C–1 (exclude any paid to yourself)	10	
11 Insurance	11	
12 Legal and professional fees	12	
13 Commissions	13	
14 Amortization (attach statement)	14	
15 a Pension and profit-sharing plans (see Schedule C Instructions)	15a	
b Employee benefit programs (see Schedule C Instructions)	b	
16 Interest on business indebtedness	16	
17 Bad debts arising from sales or services	17	
18 Depletion	18	
19 Other business expenses (specify):		
a		
b		
c		
d		
e		
f		
g		
h		
i		
j		
k		
l		
m		
n		
o		
p Total other business expenses (add lines 19a through 19o)	19p	
20 Total deductions (add lines 6 through 19p)	20	
21 Net profit or (loss) (subtract line 20 from line 5). Enter here and on Form 1040, line 13. ALSO enter on Schedule SE, line 5a ▶	21	

Did you claim a deduction for expenses of an office in your home? ☐ Yes ☐ No deducted from the gross receipts on this line.

Deductions for a Business

Lines 6 through 20 report the items of allowable business deductions for self-employed persons.

The depreciation deduction applies to those items purchased in a business which have a useful life of more than one year. Depreciation may be illustrated by the following example.

Suppose a typewriter with a useful life of ten years is purchased for $500. The depreciation deduction would be $50 for each year or portion of a year the typewriter is owned. The back of Schedule C (not shown) lists the dates of purchase, method of depreciation, cost, etc., for each depreciable item.

The only remaining item of expense which needs clarification is amortization. Amortization is a rarity for personal returns, but it may be defined as similar to depreciation in that the item has a useful life of more than one year.

The cost of goods sold, section C-1, applies to merchandise purchased for resale. It also includes other items such as freight on the purchased goods.

Special Planning Techniques for Self-employed Persons

The following comments are primarily for those looking for ideas on how to determine the value of a self-employed business, or how to lower income for divorce purposes. The list is by no means complete, but it does contain the most popular procedures.

Income

Except for self-employed persons in retail or manufacturing businesses, most people use the cash method for reporting income. If this is the case, the easiest way to lower the income shown on the tax return is to delay sending bills to customers, clients, or patients until after the end of the year. There is a certain risk in this, of course, as the bills may lose some collectibility, and it is useful only toward the end of the year.

A good way to test whether deferred billing is being used is to look at the gross receipts reported on line 1 on tax returns for the last couple of years. If the amount reported has not increased in the year under question in line with the previous years, ask some pointed questions. There is, of course, nothing to prevent a self-employed person from simply not working so hard the last year before the divorce.

Expenses

There are three major ways in which expenses can be used to lower taxable income. The first is depreciation. The tax laws provide for several different methods of computing depreciation. In using the typewriter illustration above, the most favorable method of depreciation yields a deduction of $180 versus $50 as used in the example. This is known as accelerated depreciation. For a person contemplating divorce (or embroiled in any divorce-type action), the purchase of equipment needed in the business yields two favorable results. The first is that the purchase gives all sorts of depreciation deductions and tax credits, and the second is that the liability for purchasing the equipment will be a liability of the family (this means your ex picks up half the cost). Although the value of the equipment (which may include a new car used in the business) will be counted as a family asset, the value may be less than the liability since the equipment (car) is now used. The only real defense against a practice of this sort is to recompute the depreciation deduction using nonaccelerated methods, so that the court can be fully aware of the "real" income as reported on Schedule C.

Pensions

The second area of importance is the pension-plan deduction. Currently, self-employed persons may deduct 15 percent of their net income, as shown on line 21 of Schedule C, with a maximum of $7,500, for contributions to their personal retirement plans. The deduction noted on line 15, however, is for the self-employed person's employees. His own deduction is reported in Part II on the back of Form 1040. The tax laws levy a very heavy penalty for distributions from these plans before retirement. For this reason, most courts are reluctant to require a current division of the assets of the plan, but will provide for a division for the other spouse upon retirement. Some courts, apparently because the judges do not fully understand the complex provisions of pension plans, simply ignore the plan and sometimes even allow the pension-plan deduction in determining spousal support. Because of the overall favorable treatment given to these plans by the courts, self-employed persons should avail themselves of their advantages. The plans are relatively easy to start and almost any savings-and-loan association can handle the paperwork.

Prepaying Expenses

The last major area for consideration is prepaid expenses. For certain taxpayers, a deduction is allowed currently for payment of expenses that have not been incurred. The IRS and the Tax Reform Act of 1976 have narrowed this ability somewhat, but a competent CPA still should be consulted for the potential to lower taxable income by prepaying expenses. Although difficult to detect for those spouses in doubt, a comparison of expenses with prior years' tax returns should indicate if this prepayment procedure is being used.

Phony Deductions

Finally, sometimes certain aggressive taxpayers report deductions in Schedule C, knowing full well that upon examination by the IRS the deductions will probably be disallowed. If you suspect this to be the case, retain a good tax CPA to examine the returns.

Valuation

There are no hard-and-fast rules for valuing a business. However, the IRS has published a procedure which specifies what to look for and how to compute it. For a self-employed person such as a doctor or lawyer, the value of the business will be because of the professional's personal skills. The general rule of thumb in this case is a value equal to one year's gross receipts (line 1, Schedule C) plus the net value of the business assets, including any unbilled receivables not yet reported on line 1. The value tends to be more if the practice is located in a growing, highly desirable location and, conversely, less if located in an undesirable location.

Where the skills of the self-employed person are not a major factor in the income of the business, such as a retail business, the IRS uses a concept known as book value. Book value is determined by adding together the value of all the assets and subtracting all the business liabilities. Caution: This procedure will probably not reflect the fact that the fair market value of the assets may be considerably greater than the cost shown on the business's books. Look up a good tax CPA for assistance in valuing this type of business.

CAPITAL GAINS AND LOSSES

Line 14 on Form 1040 is used to report the gain or loss on the sale of capital assets via Schedule D, shown on page 181. In general, the term "capital assets" applies to any

SCHEDULE D (Form 1040) Department of the Treasury Internal Revenue Service

Capital Gains and Losses

(Examples of property to be reported on this Schedule are gains and losses on stocks, bonds, and similar investments, and gains (but not losses) on personal assets such as a home or jewelry.)

► Attach to Form 1040. ► See Instructions for Schedule D (Form 1040).

1977

Name(s) as shown on Form 1040 | Social security number

Part I Short-term Capital Gains and Losses—Assets Held Not More Than 9 Months **D**

	a. Kind of property and description (Example, 100 shares of "Z" Co.)	b. Date acquired (Mo., day, yr.)	c. Date sold (Mo., day, yr.)	d. Gross sales price	e. Cost or other basis, as adjusted (see Instruction F) and expense of sale	f. Gain or (loss) (d less e)
1						

2	Enter your share of net short-term gain or (loss) from partnerships and fiduciaries	2	
3	Enter net gain or (loss), combine lines 1 and 2	3	
4	Short-term capital loss carryover attributable to years beginning after 1969 (see Instruction I)	4	( )
5	Net short-term gain or (loss), combine lines 3 and 4	5	

Part II Long-term Capital Gains and Losses—Assets Held More Than 9 Months

	a.	b.	c.	d.	e.	f.
6						

7	Capital gain distributions	7	
8	Enter gain, if applicable, from Form 4797, line 4(a)(1) (see Instruction A)	8	
9	Enter your share of net long-term gain or (loss) from partnerships and fiduciaries	9	
10	Enter your share of net long-term gain from small business corporations (Subchapter S)	10	
11	Net gain or (loss), combine lines 6 through 10	11	
12	Long-term capital loss carryover attributable to years beginning after 1969 (see Instruction I)	12	( )
13	Net long-term gain or (loss), combine lines 11 and 12	13	

Part III Summary of Parts I and II *(If You Have Capital Loss Carryovers From Years Beginning Before 1970, Do Not Complete This Part. See Form 4798 Instead.)*

14 Combine lines 5 and 13, and enter the net gain or (loss) here . . . **14**

15 If line 14 shows a gain—

a Enter 50% of line 13 or 50% of line 14, whichever is smaller (see Part IV for computation of alternative tax). Enter zero if there is a loss or no entry on line 13 . . . **15a**

Note: *If the amount you enter on line 15a is other than zero, you may be liable for minimum tax. See Form 4625 and instructions.*

b Subtract line 15a from line 14. Enter here and on Form 1040, line 14 . . . **15b**

16 If line 14 shows a loss—

a Enter one of the following amounts:

(i) If line 5 is zero or a net gain, enter 50% of line 14;

(ii) If line 13 is zero or a net gain, enter line 14; or,

(iii) If line 5 and line 13 are net losses, enter amount on line 5 added to 50% of amount on line 13 . . . **16a**

b Enter here and enter as a (loss) on Form 1040, line 14, the smallest of:

(i) The amount on line 16a;

(ii) $2,000 ($1,000 if married and filing a separate return); or,

(iii) Taxable income, as adjusted (see Instruction J) . . . **16b** ( )

Note: *If the amount on line 16a is larger than the loss shown on line 16b, complete Part V to determine Post-1969 Capital Loss Carryovers from 1977 to 1978.*

property, but, with certain minor exceptions, these are not important for our discussion. If you sell your car, your kitchen table, or your stocks for more than you paid for them, you must report the gain on Schedule D.

Any amount entered on line 7 (capital gains distributions) indicates that mutual fund shares are owned. Unlike dividends, the names of the mutual fund shares owned are not listed. If you don't have a list of the shares owned, and you want to determine the value, a rough rule-of-thumb measurement is to divide the capital gains distribution by .025. The best method is to obtain a listing with the number of shares and determine the value from the financial section of the newspaper.

Special Planning Techniques for Capital Gains

For those persons interested in lowering their net worth, a sale of securities at a loss to report lower earnings will not give the desired result. This is because the loss is generally limited in deductibility to capital gains. The best bet is to sell those separately owned securities which have appreciated in value over cost. Since the sale will be at a gain, income taxes will have to be paid on the gain, and the taxes will be a liability of the family and shared equally as a reduction of net worth. Had the securities not been sold, their full value, without reduction for the tax liability in the event of sale, would have been included in any financial declaration. It is important to keep in mind that in a non-community-property state, the division of joint property in certain ways can trigger a tax event, even though you are the person who winds up with the security. Perhaps the best planning techniques in this complex area is to include the tax implications on the financial declaration of the sale of any securities owned, whether at a gain or loss.

Mutual Fund Gains and Sale of Business Property

The next line, 15, of Form 1040 reports the distributions from mutual funds not included in line 7 of Schedule D. This is just an alternative location. If you see an entry here, read the above discussion relating to mutual funds.

Line 16 of Form 1040 is to report the net gain or loss from the sale of equipment or real property used in their business by self-employed persons. The gains and losses are ordinary, i.e., includable in taxable income in full or deductible in full. Read the section on Schedule D for tax-planning hints and suggestions.

Income from Pensions, Annuities, Rents, etc.

Line 17 of Form 1040 is used to report supplemental income from pensions, rents and royalties, partnerships, estates, etc., via Schedule E, shown on page 184.

Pensions and Annuities

Part I of Schedule E reports pension and annuity income. This section is for taxable pensions only. Since social security is tax-free, it is not reported anywhere in the tax return.

Generally, for persons already receiving pensions, no problems exist in the event of divorce because the pension proceeds will merely be divided as received.

Annuities are similar to pensions but with certain variations. For example, if you give $10,000 to an insurance company, they will agree to pay you a certain amount of money for life, regardless of how long you live. You can purchase one now and have the annuity start paying you when you retire. The amount they pay you over the amount you put in is taxable to you.

Rents and Royalties

Part II of Schedule E deals with rental and royalty in-

SCHEDULE E (Form 1040)
Department of the Treasury
Internal Revenue Service

Supplemental Income Schedule

(From pensions and annuities, rents and royalties, partnerships, estates and trusts, etc.)
▶ Attach to Form 1040. ▶ See Instructions for Schedule E (Form 1040).

1977

Name(s) as shown on Form 1040 | Your social security number

Part I **Pension and Annuity Income.** If fully taxable, do not complete this part. Enter amount on Form 1040, line 17. For one pension or annuity not fully taxable, complete this part. If you have more than one pension or annuity that is not fully taxable, attach a separate sheet listing each one with the appropriate data and enter combined total of taxable portions on line 5.

1 Name of payer..........
2 Did your employer contribute part of the cost? . . . ☐ Yes ☐ No
If "Yes," is your contribution recoverable within 3 years of the annuity starting date? . . . ☐ Yes ☐ No
If "Yes," show: Your contribution $.........., Contribution recovered in prior years . . . | 2 |
3 Amount received this year . . . | 3 |
4 Amount excludable this year . . . | 4 |
5 Taxable portion (subtract line 4 from line 3) . . . | 5 |

Part II **Rent and Royalty Income.** If you need more space, use Form 4831.
Have you claimed expenses connected with your vacation home rented to others? ☐ Yes ☐ No

(a) Kind and location of property If residential, also write "R"	(b) Total amount of rents	(c) Total amount of royalties	(d) Depreciation (explain below) or depletion (attach computation)	(e) Other expenses (Repairs, etc.—explain below)
6 Totals . . .				

7 Net income or (loss) from rents and royalties (column (b) plus column (c) less columns (d) and (e)) . | 7 |
8 Net rental income or (loss) (from Form 4831) . . . | 8 |
9 Net farm rental profit or (loss) (from Form 4835) . . . | 9 |
10 Total rent and royalty income (add lines 7, 8, and 9) . . . | 10 |

Part III **Income or Losses from Partnerships, Estates or Trusts, Small Business Corporations.**

Enter in column (b): P for Partnership, E for Estate or Trust, or S for Small Business Corp.

(a) Name	(b)	(c) Employer identification number	(d) Your share of gross farming or fishing income	(e) Income or (loss)	(f) Additional 1st year depreciation (applicable only to partnerships)
11 Totals . . .					

12 Income or (loss). Total of column (e) less total of column (f) . . . | 12 |

13 **TOTAL** (add lines 5, 10, and 12). Enter here and on Form 1040, line 18 . . . ▶ | 13 |

Explanation of Column (e), Part II

Item	Amount	Item	Amount	Item	Amount

Schedule for Depreciation Claimed in Part II above. If you need more space use Form 4562.

(a) Description of property	(b) Date acquired	(c) Cost or other basis	(d) Depreciation allowed or allowable in prior years	(e) Method of computing depreciation	(f) Life or rate	(g) Depreciation for this year
1 Total additional first-year depreciation (do not include in items below) →						
2 Totals . . .						

E

☆U.S. GOVERNMENT PRINTING OFFICE 1977—0-235-062—87-032-1919

come, including income and expense from rental and oil property.

Most rental-property situations are rather mundane and are not known as glamour investments. The royalty situation is another story. If you have royalty-income items, you need to consult an expert to determine tax-planning opportunities.

One thing to watch for: Most real estate deals generate taxable losses in the earlier years, which need to be adjusted in determining taxable income for spousal-support purposes. Also note that the description schedule (bottom of Schedule E), which includes various information about each piece of property, lists the property at cost and not fair market value. In many cases, the cost of the land is not included in the cost of the property because land is not subject to depreciation. When you are determining the value of any real property, this is a point worth careful study.

Partnerships, Estates, and Small Businesses

Part III of Schedule E is the most complicated. It reports gains and losses from partnerships, estates and trusts, and small business corporations.

You are entitled to copies of any partnership return or corporation tax return where you own at least 1 percent of the common stock. If you want to obtain any returns, consult a qualified CPA specializing in taxes. He will have the necessary information to enable you to obtain copies of such returns and to answer your questions.

A partnership is a legal entity whose income is taxed to its owners. The items of income, expenses, etc., incurred by the partnership are reported on a separate form specifically for partnerships. As a general rule, a partnership is entitled to the same tax-planning techniques as are sole proprietorships outlined earlier in the discussion of Schedule C.

If a person has a very understanding partner, it might be

possible to act in cohort to defer income items or prepay expenses, although this is probably very difficult to achieve in practice.

Estates and trusts are items which are derived from inheritances or gifts. If you have any of these, consult a good CPA for guidance if they are very complex. One of the problems with trusts is that a person may set up a lifetime trust with his own assets (which may be partly yours), which cannot be touched in a normal divorce proceeding. While this ability varies from state to state, you should check with your attorney if you suspect this problem.

Distribution from estates and certain estate trusts indicates that your spouse may have inherited property, or acquired property by a gift. Certain states have provisions for equally dividing property acquired by gift or inheritance and others do not. You may be entitled to part of the assets, which may be used to pay spousal and child support. Consult your attorney for guidance.

Small business corporations are corporations in every sense of the word except they have a special tax election to be taxed as a partnership. As with partnerships and trusts and estates, small business corporations are beyond the scope of this analysis and require detailed study for maximum benefits.

Many small, privately owned corporations do not pay dividends, and are not taxed as partnerships, but may pay a salary or a consulting fee to your spouse. The tax-planning techniques available to the owner in this case to lower income or at least defer income are numerous and complex. If your spouse is involved with a family-owned corporation, get a CPA specializing in taxes to give you advice. He will be able to assist in determining the tax-planning techniques most valuable and the general IRS view of the value of your spouse's interest in the business. He will also be able to assist your lawyer by preparing various computations for the court and to determine if any income items are being deferred.

Especially for Farmers

Line 19, of Form 1040, deals with Schedule F, the reporting of income from farming operations. Although not many people are directly engaged in farming any more, the schedule is used to report any operations from farming or ranching. This schedule should be read in conjunction with Schedule C, as most of the tax-planning techniques apply to both types of business.

One of the major advantages in farm operations is that significant amounts of crop income may be carried over to following years without being sold. Perhaps the best way to discover if this is the case is to check with the particular grain elevators, cotton gins, or other storage facilities normally used, to determine if your spouse has any items which have not been sold and are being stored.

In the case of ranchers, significant increases in the value of raised cattle may escape detection. If the breeding cattle or herd was purchased and has been held a long time, it is probable that depreciation deductions have reduced the cost of the cattle to a very small tax basis. In addition, calves born during the period and added to the breeding herd will not be reflected in the depreciation schedule, and it will be difficult to determine the value of the herd based upon the income figures shown on Schedule F. The best procedure is to get an appraisal of the value of the herd. It should be kept in mind that accelerated depreciation of the herd may significantly lower taxable income during the years immediately preceding the divorce proceedings and should be adjusted, accordingly, to reflect the proper income from the ranch activities. In determining a value for the herd, you will want to subtract income taxes that will be due upon any sale or disposition of the herd.

What About the State Tax Return?

Although most states generally use the federal income-tax return as a basis for computing state taxes, there are certain major differences. Probably the primary difference is that state income taxes are generally not allowed as a deduction on the state tax return. This in turn increases the taxable income subject to state income taxes. One of the major benefits to come from examining the state income-tax return is that most states do not exempt municipal-bond interest received from other states from taxation as the federal return does. The inclusion of the otherwise tax-exempt interest in the state return provides a valuable tool in hunting assets. Where a state income tax is levied in your state, obtain copies of the returns to examine. You might just find all sorts of goodies that do not show up on the federal return.

There are many other specialized forms that go with even a relatively simple personal income-tax return. However, the major categories have been covered here and should provide the reader with the ability to examine most tax returns with relative ease.

20

TAX CHECKLIST FOR MARRIAGE

UNLIKE THE TAX CHECKLIST for divorce, where detailed planning is an absolute must, this checklist is limited mainly to money matters and is based on the idea that your marriage is continuing. There are some potent reasons for taking advantage of the items listed here: As your income rises, you'll have more opportunities for tax planning with real estate investments, municipal bonds, investment annuities, and the like. Remember, though, that it's not possible to list all such opportunities. Indeed, that subject alone can fill several books.

1. Series E U. S. Savings Bonds

Don't dismiss Series E bonds as a serious investment vehicle. They are probably the safest investments around, and they pay almost as much interest as a savings-and-loan institution. They're particularly attractive because you can elect to have the interest on the bonds deferred until you're ready to cash them in; for example, after retirement when your income has been substantially reduced. If you have children and want to provide for their higher education, Series E bonds are a good value, since you can make your children the owners of the bonds and avoid paying taxes on the interest. For more information, read Chapter 38.

2. Keogh Plans

Keogh Plans allow you to put up to 15 percent (limit $7,500) of your self-employed earnings in a retirement plan, thereby providing you with a deduction for investing in your own retirement plan. This money goes into a savings-and-loan account, but the interest earned on it is not taxable to you until you withdraw the funds. Note: If your annual income is less than $15,000, you can put 100 percent (limit $750) of that self-employment income into the plan. Ask any savings-and-loan institution for further details.

3. Individual Retirement Accounts

Investigate whether or not your employer covers you in a qualified pension plan. The company is required by law to make such coverage and literature available to you upon your request. If you're not covered by a plan, by all means invest in an IRA. You can put as much as 15 percent (limit $1,500) per year into an IRA and get a tax deduction for it. As in the case of the Keogh Plan, the interest earned on the account is not taxed to you until you withdraw the funds upon retirement. Again, check with any bank or insurance company for further details.

4. Investment Annuities

An investment annuity is for those people who can scrape together at least $10,000. This annuity is written by a savings-and-loan institution in conjunction with a life insurance company, and again, current earnings are not taxable until withdrawn. They do have one unique feature; in case of an emergency, the principal can be withdrawn before the interest. Technically, then, you can withdraw all your principal without having to pay any income taxes on the interest.

5. Social Security Taxes

If you are a self-employed person and your husband or wife helps in the business, make sure you pay social security taxes on him or her. This is a worthwhile investment, particularly in the last ten-year period before retirement. If your spouse works at least ten years before age sixty-two, he or she will be fully covered, and your retirement benefits will increase significantly.

6. Year-end Tax Planning

Don't overlook the opportunities for year-end tax savings. They're there, even for those people who don't itemize deductions. The trick, at least for these people, is to take certain steps to get above the maximum limit set for the standard deduction. One way you can do this is to increase your payment for state income taxes in the same year that you buy an automobile. People who itemize get to deduct the sales tax paid on an auto, while those who take the standard deduction do not. Keep this in mind when you buy an auto. Of course, the hefty state income-tax payment means that you'll want to file your tax return as early as possible in order to get a refund on the state taxes if you overpaid. Also remember that if you do not itemize your deductions on the following year's return, the refund of state income tax will not be considered as taxable income to you.

7. Tax Planning for Those Who Itemize

Although the 1976 Tax Reform Act somewhat restricted

the ability to deduct prepayment of interest and other items, the prepayment of taxes on your home and state income taxes (within limits)[1] has not been curtailed. View any deferral of tax payments as a permanent deferral. For example, if you prepay $500 of real estate taxes this year and every year for the next seven years, and assuming you save $200 in income taxes doing that, your $200 could be invested in a savings account which will return interest income to you. In other words, by simply writing a check each December for $500 to your county tax authority, you have made $200. Is this a fair return on your time? You bet it is!

8. Buying a Home

Buy a home if you don't already own one. There is no better investment for a family than the purchase of a home. Not only do you get the benefit of any appreciation in value, but you get a whole new group of itemized expenses to take on your tax return. Items such as medical expenses, interest on charge accounts, etc., are now available to you as deductions because with a house, you'll be well over the standard deduction limit (mortgage interest and property taxes, both deductible, will put you there).

9. The Importance of a Good CPA

As soon as you think you need help with your taxes, invest in a CPA. Although he'll charge more than most tax services, he should be able to return his fee many times over in tax savings to you.

---

[1] The prepayment of state income taxes is generally limited to the tax you expect to owe on the return. The IRS frowns on your taking a deduction for prepaying five times your estimated state tax due. However this restriction is based on your "reasonable" estimate, rather than the amount ultimately due.

10. LEASING AUTOMOBILES

Don't do it. The temptation to lease is strong simply because most auto leases require little or nothing down. But make no mistake about it, you're paying considerably higher interest charges on the purchase because of this low down payment. In addition, when the lease runs out, you may end up having to take a significant loss on the contract. It's either that, or coming up with a substantial amount of cash to pay off the final, or balloon, payment in order to keep the car. One consolation: The interest on the lease is deductible.

11. WILLS

Keep your family wills up to date. People who die without wills, or who leave wills that are hopelessly out of date, provide the legal profession with one of its greatest sources of revenue. Unless you want a large portion of your estate to go for lawyer's fees, spend the money *now* and bring your will up to date.

12. JOINT OWNERSHIP OF PROPERTY

Joint ownership is really the only way to go in community-property states. This means that in the event of your death, your spouse will succeed to the property without undue estate taxes or legal problems. In non-community-property states, joint ownership allows you to transfer any separate property to your spouse so that you can get the best possible estate-tax benefits. If you want some of your property to go to someone other than your spouse, then it should be kept under your separate name.

13. INSURANCE POLICIES

Have your spouse own your insurance policies. This way, any insurance proceeds paid as a result of your death will not be included in your estate and will not be subject to estate taxes. In order to qualify for this, however, your spouse must have sufficient separate income either through salary or dividends and interest to make the premium payments. This is a very basic and important tax-planning device; don't overlook it. Consult your insurance agent or company personnel director for more details.

PART THREE

DIVORCE: HOW TO KEEP IT FROM COSTING YOU AN ARM AND A LEG

21

AN OVERVIEW OF DIVORCE

It is fatal to enter any war without the will to win it.
—Douglas MacArthur

THE FOLLOWING PAGES were written especially to help *you* in your divorce. You will learn things that a lawyer or CPA may not ordinarily tell you, or may not even know himself. This part of the book is designed to lead you from the first moment you make the decision to get a divorce until the final dissolution decree is filed. The suggestions and hints you'll find here are designed to save *you* money, *not* your spouse. Make no bones about it, once you start the divorce proceedings, that person you've been living with for so long may become your mortal enemy. The steps recommended here will often be tough and uncompromising, but consider them in this light: If you follow the procedures closely, you will definitely have an edge in the proceedings and you'll be able to be a little more generous in the negotiations. This in turn can provide the "grease" necessary to get a stalled divorce over with so that you can go on with the business of living.

Divorce is one of the biggest, most traumatic steps you will take during your lifetime. Most people have little idea of how shattering even the friendliest of divorces can be. Everyone has trouble dealing with the loneliness and the abject sense of failure which color their every thought and deed.

Occasionally, there are a few divorces made in heaven. If you and your spouse both want the divorce *and* if you are in complete agreement as to the settlement, then you will have little or no trouble. Depending on the size of your assets and liabilities, you may even be able to get by with just one lawyer to draw up the papers.

But more likely, you will find that when you begin your divorce, you will have difficulty even getting to talk to your spouse, much less getting any decisions made.

Men, who don't have the emotional or psychological stamina of women, fare very hard indeed, and the cost in lost job hours is high. It is a sad fact that divorced or separated men have a much higher mortality rate than do married men. Perhaps one of the reasons men seem to fare much worse in a divorce is that they are usually the ones who give up the children and leave home.

Take the case of Henry, a stockbroker. He had been married to Eliza for ten years when she suddenly announced that she wanted a divorce because she was in love with another man. Henry, stunned by this news, agreed to move out of their house and into an apartment. Shortly after that, Henry's slow burn suddenly ignited, and he angrily insisted that Eliza move out of the house so they could sell it. Threatening words and ugly scenes followed. Not taking any chances, Eliza got her lawyer to put Henry under a peace bond so he wouldn't bother her or the kids. (The fact that she had committed adultery was of no consequence.) Henry liked to do woodworking and had transformed his basement into an extensive workshop. He used this hobby to forget the tensions of his job. Unfortunately, there was no room in his apartment for all of his tools, and he had no access to his old basement. These frustrations were compounded by the fact that Henry also missed seeing his children every day; their weekend visits seemed strained and formal. As the months passed, Henry's drinking increased sharply and eventually he lost his job.

Lest you think that only middle-income or long-married people suffer like this, take the case of the famous professional ballplayer who earned almost a quarter of a million dollars each year. When his short marriage ended in divorce, he suffered through the worst season of a fabled career, with all his statistics slumping badly. When his contract with the club ran out, he took a hefty cut in salary before signing again.

Can You Take It?

So the question remains, Is divorce the answer? To try to answer that for yourself, see if you could withstand the following onslaught which usually accompanies a divorce action:

1. Your financial affairs will become public record. Copies of all tax returns will be given to each attorney, who will probably ask someone else to review them. You will be asked for a listing of all your assets and liablities.
2. If you are the primary-income-earning spouse, you will probably be asked to pay all court and legal fees. A contested divorce will be quite expensive.
3. Be prepared never to see your children again. Although this seems drastic, it is a distinct possibility which can be accomplished by the custodial spouse simply by moving from state to state.
4. Your children may be adopted by their new parent.

This particular issue went to one state's Supreme Court. The court ruled that the father had no particular rights in this issue (other than visitation) and granted the adoption. The court said it was more "convenient" for the children to be known by the same last name as their mother.

5. Your divorce never ends! Be prepared for hurts and slights when your children are grown. You may not be asked to their graduation or wedding because it would be "embarrassing." In addition, as long as support is being paid, a *suit for modification* can be brought. What this means is that either of you can go back to court and ask to have the visitation rights or amount of support altered. To do this, however, you usually have to prove that your financial or personal circumstances have changed before the court will order a modification. Note that some divorced spouses regularly haul their ex-spouses back to court to sue for custody of the children, for a variety of real and imagined causes.
6. Figure the divorce will take forever. A good rule of thumb is three times longer than you expect. Be prepared for months to go by without anything happening. Your frantic calls to your attorney will be futile and will merely add to your legal fees.
7. Be prepared to have the county sheriff enter your office with a subpoena for your boss. He can be called to testify about your income and any deferred-compensation agreements.
8. Get ready for long periods of time when your spouse won't even talk to you about a settlement. This is the norm, rather than the exception. Whatever you may think about your spouse's intelligence, business acumen, and ability to compromise, forget it! It all goes out the window in a divorce.

9. This could be the most stressful period of your life. Don't be surprised at the weird physical manifestations: a loss of hair or complete change in color (to gray); sky-high blood pressure, ulcers, heart problems, etc. Watch your drinking, too. It could easily escalate and get out of hand before you know it.
10. In figuring the cost, add together all of the legal and other fees you think you'll incur to arrive at an estimate. Then double it. Also, deduct 50 percent from the value of any assets you may have to sell.
11. Be prepared for a stiff tax bill. If you have any property to be divided up, it must be done properly to avoid a big tax bill. Budget for the fees of a good CPA especially trained in taxes.
12. Allow for many sleepless nights and long hours of frustration. You will have a feeling of sheer helplessness in your inability to regulate your own life.

The Cost of Marriage Counseling

If you suspect that the price of divorce may be too high for you, then definitely explore every avenue of marriage counseling *before* you start having an affair and *before* you see a lawyer for some "friendly" advice.

First of all, talk it over with your spouse. His or her reaction may give you a good idea of how everything will work out in the end. If your partner agrees to such a move, things aren't so hopeless after all. In many instances, the other person has been thinking along the same lines but has lacked the courage or sense of urgency to breach the subject first. If you encounter a less than enthusiastic response, it may be from shyness or an innate sense of failure. Some husbands and wives automatically link the need for counseling with failure, which is not necessarily a valid connection.

Family Service Agency

The third reaction you may get from your partner is one of outright rejection and hostility. He or she will oppose all efforts toward counseling, sometimes countering with the suggestion that any breakdown in the marriage is all your fault—"There's nothing wrong with me or this marriage." (A good offense is the best defense.)

If this is the case, there is probably little you can do to change your spouse's reaction. Should you give up on the idea of counseling? That's your decision, of course; sometimes even one person going alone can get help for a troubled marriage. If you are thinking about a divorce, marriage counseling can help put it into its proper perspective. In fact, there's a whole new industry built around what's popularly called "divorce counseling," helping people make the tremendous adjustment from married to single life.

Whatever you want to call it, this type of counseling is going to cost money, and not a small sum if you pick a psychiatrist or a psychologist with an advanced degree. Marriage counselors with these, or similar, qualifications will charge anywhere from $25 to $75 an hour. And top-of-the-line help is even higher. Masters and Johnson charge as much as $2,500 for two weeks of concentrated sex therapy.

There are a number of ways to find low-cost counseling, however. You can start by calling your local family service agency; also check with your county health and welfare department. They may be able to refer you to counselors who will charge in relation to what you're able to pay, including free counseling for those who need it but can't afford it. (These are not all welfare cases. A good example is the browbeaten wife with no income of her own and with a husband who won't spend a nickel on marriage counseling. She is "destitute" and qualifies for free counseling, even though her husband earns a respectable salary.)

Any woman who finds herself in this situation, or who can't get her husband to a counselor, should contact her local woman's self-help organization. It can recommend counselors and sometimes even a few helpful hints on how to get around that recalcitrant husband.

Another good way for either spouse to find qualified marriage counselors is to contact the American Association of Marriage and Family Counselors, 225 Yale Avenue, Claremont, California 91711.

The AAMFC will supply you, at no charge, with the names of accredited marriage counselors in your area. The people recommended are well qualified, having at least a master's degree in a behavioral science, plus two years of clinical experience.

Preparing Yourself for Divorce

If, after all that, you can still say "Yes, divorce is the only answer," then you are ready to begin. One of the most important things to remember at this time is that you are not in complete control of your mental faculties. The business and personal decisions you make now will be "tainted" by your emotions. This is particularly relevant if you are a lawyer or accountant, because then you will believe you can advise yourself. The old adage that a lawyer who defends himself has a fool for a client was never more appropriate than in this situation. And the tax accountant who believes that he can remember all the financial advantages and pitfalls at this time is whistling in the wind. Once involved in a divorce, the inanities of your system of justice will drive even the most even-tempered person to fits of rage and tears. With all the worry and emotional problems, it is difficult to believe that *anyone* could make the right decisions, particularly since those decisions may affect you for the rest of your life.

An example of what can happen is illustrated by the case of a famous multimillionaire West Coast lawyer. After a couple of years of wrangling and trial separations, his wife kicked him out and filed for divorce. She hired one of the best female divorce lawyers available. Our friend, the lawyer, represented himself. It wasn't that he was incapable, but he would *never* do a divorce case for anyone else. Even considering that he had little experience in divorce cases and was personally and emotionally involved, he believed he was the best to represent himself. (During the initial hearings, it was rumored that the wife's accountants were awarded $75,000 just to determine his earnings and net worth.)

After several months passed, the front pages of the newspapers were full of pictures of him and his intended bride. He said he wanted to get his divorce finalized so that he could marry by the end of the year. His wife's attorney promptly said that there were many issues regarding the property settlement and spousal support that must be resolved before any divorce could be granted. In other words, if he wanted the divorce soon, he would have to pay through the nose! Was it over yet? No. His wife, a few days later, said she was thinking of withdrawing the divorce suit. Eventually she did. He had to begin the proceedings all over again himself. This meant an additional delay of another year or two. His major mistake, outside of representing himself, was not to countersue his wife for a divorce at the same time she sued him. Additionally, he should have kept a low profile until the divorce was granted, which is something even a mediocre divorce attorney would have advised him to do.

With these problems fresh in your mind, follow the advice here step by step. If you are uncertain of your spouse's reaction and the amount of "friendliness" in the upcoming divorce, then by all means pick a good lawyer and tax accountant to assist you. You will probably need both, since most attorneys who accept divorce cases are generally not as familiar with taxation problems as a good CPA. Their fees will be a small price to pay if you consider it as an investment in happiness for the rest of your life.

A word of caution: The tax laws affecting divorce change from state to state and sometimes from court to court. It is not possible to state unequivocally that the tax effect discussed in this section will always apply, or apply in your particular case. It is hoped that this section will provide you with numerous suggestions that you will find advantageous regardless of the tax consequences. If you are in doubt as to the tax consequences in your particular case or state, discuss them with your accountant or attorney. However, the tax advice should be correct in the majority of situations and will provide you with at least several areas to investigate.

Just about every year Congress changes the tax rates by giving rebates or refunds or by levying surcharges. Throughout this book, various tax computations are made which indicate how much it costs you in taxes to do a certain thing (like getting married). It is important to remember in reading this book that even if Congress does change the rates, the principles stressed won't change. This means that even though the savings or costs of a particular tax position may change, this book will be valid until Congress radically changes the tax laws so that there is no difference in the taxes paid by a person because of his marital status.

The following detailed chapters have been condensed into two checklists in Chapter 39, one for the legal and one for the tax-rate side of divorce. Used properly, you'll find them to be step-by-step guides to help you during your divorce.

One further word of advice! If you haven't yet started your divorce but are still planning and thinking about it, don't leave this book lying around for your spouse to find. Some of your best strategies may then backfire.

22

HOW MUCH DO YOU REALLY KNOW ABOUT DIVORCE?

I shall marry in haste and repeat at leisure.
—James Brauch Cabell

THE STATISTICS ON DIVORCE are staggering. For example, the United States passed the one million mark for divorces in one year, 1975. In California, there are two divorces for every marriage (although it's going to be tough to keep this rate up—statistically speaking, that is). And of those one-million-plus divorced people out there, 75 percent will remarry within two years after the final decree. Which just goes to show that not only do most people make mistakes, but they make the same ones over and over again.

Most of the people reading this section of the book will fall into one of three categories:

1. Those contemplating a divorce
2. Those already involved in a divorce action
3. Those whose divorces are finally over

Your "divorce sophistication" will range from incredibly naive (if you are in group 1) to embittered beyond belief (group 3). And after all the dust settles and resignation sets in, you'll go out and remarry and threaten to start the whole process over again.

Which is OK—at least life is never dull for you—but you ought to try to avoid the nasty habit of writing six different alimony and child-support checks each month. Divorce doesn't have to cost you an arm and a leg—if you know what you're doing.

> *Warning:* If you've been through one divorce already and are remarried, chances are you think that this time it's for good. Oh, yeah? Well, next to shoplifting and ladies of the evening, divorce produces more recidivists for our courts to deal with than any other segment of society. For those of you going through your second (or third) divorce, the temptation to think that you know it all is great. True, you are a battle-scarred veteran whom no one or nothing can surprise, but just remember this: Divorce is the only game in town where the ground rules change with each new opponent. While spouse number one was only interested in battling you for custody of the kids, spouse number two may only be interested in cleaning out your savings account. Don't be lulled into a false sense of security by telling yourself that you've seen it all. You haven't. Keep your guard up at all times. And just to make sure you're still on your toes, take the following quiz.

Your "Pop Quiz" on Divorce

This test was designed to measure your divorce ability. First, read the two sample divorces and then answer the multiple-choice questions at the end.

Case 1—Tuna on Toast

Mr. and Mrs. Charles Tuna live in a $250,000 co-op apartment on Park Avenue in New York City. They have been married for twenty-one years. Charlie is a successful TV star with an eye for cute young carps from the chorus line. Charlie's wife, Mabel, suspects his constant infidelity and consults a lawyer about a divorce. Unfortunately, Mabel picks a publicity-hungry attorney, Shyster Shad, to handle her divorce. Shyster informs her that there's still "big bucks" to be found in divorce, even in no-fault states.[1] On his advice, Mabel hires a private detective to trail Charlie. After three weeks on the job, Charlie is caught in *flagrante delicto* with a chorus-line cutie, and Mabel ends up with some very damaging negatives. In the suit for dissolution of their marriage, Mabel asks for custody of their two children, $3,000 spousal support per month, $1,000 a month in child support until the children reach eighteen, and all legal fees. The court grants her $5,000 a month temporary support. As the papers are being served on Charlie, Mabel has a locksmith change all of the locks on their apartment, and then hires two bodyguards to protect her in her own home just in case Charlie picks one of the locks. Now Charlie, who cannot gain access to his own home to get so much as a teaspoon, has to take a furnished suite at the Waldorf Towers. He also takes a divorced buddy's advice and hires a famous lawyer to protect what's left of his interest in the marriage. Angered by Charlie's impudence, Mabel escalates the hostilities by threatening to turn over the damaging photos of Charlie to a national tabloid. Charlie, whose career as the all-American albacore would be ruined by such exposure, decides to fight back. He hires his own private eye to see if he can get something damaging on Mabel for a countersuit. The detective trails Mabel for several months, but to no avail.

Charlie begins to put pressure on Mabel to get the di-

---

[1] New York's no-fault grounds are peculiar in that they still encourage fault-finding. See Appendix.

vorce over. But Mabel, in no hurry at all, is bent on exacting the last pound of flesh. She stalls, delays, and regularly drags Charlie into court to get her temporary allowance raised. Charlie regularly gets drunk and calls Mabel on the phone to harass and threaten her. What it finally amounts to is a Mexican standoff with each side raging at the other through their lawyers. After five years of going back and forth like this, and with lawyers, detectives, and accountants running wild, Mabel and Charlie finally arrive at an out-of-court settlement (called, for some perverse reason, an uncontested divorce). In the end, Mabel gets lifetime alimony, but at $1,000 a month less than she asked for. Child support is also lowered by $500. And, thanks to the changing times, the court orders Mabel to pay her own lawyer's fees. In order for her to do this, the co-op she gained in the divorce settlement must be sold. The real estate agent, anxious to sell the property, informs prospective buyers that the co-op must be sold at any price because of the divorce. As "distressed" merchandise, the apartment sells for $50,000 under the market value. The price of the Tunas' divorce:

Mabel's legal fees	$250,000
Mabel's detective fees	3,000
Mabel's bodyguards	2,500
Locksmith	150
Charlie's legal fees	200,000
Charlie's detective fees	7,500
Charlie's extra household expenses	20,000
Loss on the sale of the co-op	50,000
Real estate broker's fee	12,000
	$545,150

Case 2—Sweetness and Light

At the same time, three thousand miles away in San Rafael, California (a no-fault state[2]), John and Jane Doe have also come to a parting of the ways after ten years. While there are indiscretions and grievances on both sides, John and Jane are trying to keep their divorce amicable. They file for separation on the grounds of irreconcilable differences. John is the treasurer of an electronics firm. Jane has raised their two children. They buy a "how-to-do-your-own-divorce-in-California" book for $3.95. This shows them how, when, and where to file, and provides them with all the necessary forms. Then, John and Jane sit down and work out a settlement. Marin County, of which San Rafael is a part, has a set schedule that the court usually follows in awarding alimony and child support. John and Jane agree to follow the schedule, realizing the court deviates from the schedule only in rare circumstances.

John makes $20,000 a year after taxes and under the schedule will pay $600 alimony a month for the next five years (half of the years of the marriage) and $300 a month in child support until his children reach age eighteen. Jane will keep the family home and all the furniture and other personal property (minus what John will need to start another residence). John gives Jane a note for $20,000 for her equity in an apartment building they bought five years ago. In this way, John keeps the building but must make all the mortgage payments from now on. Jane has custody of the children, with liberal visitation rights accorded to John. Although they could probably file their divorce papers on their own, John and Jane visit Dave Cheapo, attorney at law. He draws up the papers for them and then files them.

---

[2] California really means it when it proclaims itself a no-fault state.

The cost of the Doe's divorce:

One divorce book	$ 3.95
Fees for filing for divorce in California	50.00
Lawyer's fee	100.00
	$153.95

Questions

1. The battling Tunas are more representative of divorce today because:
   A. All wives try to soak their husbands dry.
   B. All husbands are lying cheats.
   C. Even in a no-fault state, you can drag proceedings on forever and run up half a million dollars in attorney fees.
   D. It is not representative of divorce today.
2. The example of the Doe divorce is closer to the truth because:
   A. Men and women are more civilized toward each other than they were twenty years ago.
   B. You can't have a long-drawn-out divorce in a no-fault state.
   C. More and more couples are realizing they can keep a greater portion of their net worth if they exclude attorneys until the end.
   D. It is not representative of divorce today.

Answers

1. A. False. Many husbands try to do this, too.
   B. False. Eve created a terrible precedent.
   C. True. If you work at it.
   D. False. Unfortunately, these kinds of cases still dot the social pages of your local newspaper.
2. A. False. Ha, ha.
   B. False. If you're cunning and wily, you can, but it

takes an awful lot of time and energy.

C. True. They are not exactly a teeming majority, but they're around.

D. False. Do-it-yourself and one-lawyer divorces are on the rise.

What Does This All Mean?

If you missed one or both of the questions, you need to strengthen your divorce acumen. Read on.

If you answered both questions correctly, you either cheated or you've been through several divorces already. In the latter case, you are an incorrigible recidivist with a lousy memory. Two-time losers always forget all their previous divorce problems; that's how they have the strength to get married again. They are terrible risks and should definitely read on.

23

PRE-DIVORCE STRATEGIES

The test of a man or woman's breeding is how they behave in a quarrel.
—George Bernard Shaw

MANY VETERAN LTR PARTNERS and married couples have been lifetime devotees to their own version of the Friday-night fights. These are the couples who may view with considerable distaste our continuing advice to keep a low profile during divorce. Most people going through the trauma of divorce do not want to hear things like "Turn the other cheek" and "It is better to give than to receive," but those really aren't bad phrases to remember. Certainly, you should try to avoid fights, verbal rabbit punches, Chinese spouse torture, and the like.

In every instance your divorce proceedings will be much less traumatic and your postdivorce relationships will be much healthier (mentally) if you quit fighting.

But no matter how earnestly *you* attempt to take the high road, it will do you no good if your spouse wants a knock-down, drag-out divorce. It may be because you broke the news of your intentions in a callous or painful manner; it may be that you were caught cheating; it may be that your spouse is just a naturally vindictive person. Whatever the reason, you can't take the high road if your partner takes the low road. You'll inevitably end up having mud slung all over you (and slinging some back yourself) before the final decree is a reality.

If this is a possibility for your divorce, face up to it as soon as possible. Start your financial planning early, because chances are good that the proceedings will be long, costly, and very divisive.

Months or even years before a divorce, this kind of planning may seem out of the question. After all, you don't know for sure that your divorce is going to be a rough one. However, this kind of planning is essentially harmless, and if you're close to a divorce, the bills will come out of the community assets. In other words, it all works out in the end.

How to Raise Money Without Your Spouse Knowing

Following are some financial hints you should consider before telling your spouse you want a divorce. It's not possible to cover every financial situation or condition here, but the tips will get you started, and your fertile imagination should produce more.

Both men and women can raise money by using the family credit cards and accounts to pay for personal items. For example:

1. Have your car fixed and charge it. Chances are that fixing the car will add very little to the value assigned to it when you divide the property, but the liability will be counted in full as a joint liability.

2. Buy some new clothes. You'll need them. Be sure to charge them.
3. Go to the dentist and the eye doctor and make sure that all the "repair" work you need is done. This might be the time you want to spring for contact lenses. Remember to charge them.

How do you keep from paying these bills? Well, you don't, not completely, but since they are charged to family accounts, they naturally become part of the family debt. This means that when the financial declaration is made for the divorce proceedings, all debts and assets of the family must be listed. Obviously, you will not list your new eyeglasses or wardrobe as assets to be distributed equally, but you will list the debt you incurred to buy them. When the house and other assets are sold or divided, the proceeds will be used first to pay off the family debt before any is available to be distributed to the couple. The effect of the above planning is to get your intended ex-spouse to pay half of the cost of your new wardrobe or medical bills. That is better than you can do in any store sale. In addition, your morale will be considerably higher with your new appearance.

Taking the Low Road

You will need all the dollars you can scrape together if your divorce is contested. Unhappy marriages usually lead to the same kinds of divorce. Be prepared for a slugfest; take advance steps to protect your property and financial assets.

When a divorce degenerates into continuous name-calling and mudslinging, you are in for a long and arduous fight. You need to have every point in your favor. In a contested divorce, you can only turn the other cheek for so long before it begins to affect your mental stability. If your spouse discovers that it is easy to walk all over you, it may take years to get a final decree. It may end up costing you in excessively high alimony and child support. Or you may lose almost everything in the property settlement.

Don't be afraid to hit back. A show of strength is sometimes the only way you have of finishing the divorce. Remember, too, that if you are the one who's going to end up with the children, you'll have to protect their rights and financial position as much as your own.

With this in mind, here are some strategies for women, and then some for men.

Sneaky Strategies for Women

Since the assumption in this case is that the male is the major breadwinner, a woman will want to be familiar with all the items of income that her spouse has.

First, how familiar are you with your tax return? If you have done nothing over the years except sign on the dotted line, get a copy of your last joint tax return and study it while reading Chapter 19. This is of vital importance to you. Finding out what your income was last year and discovering other assets and liabilities will give you a good idea of what to expect in the property settlement and the setting of support payments.

If your husband doesn't keep previous years' tax returns on file, contact your family accountant or lawyer. If that turns out to be a dead end (i.e., he's hiding the returns from you), then simply write to your local IRS center and give them your names and social security numbers and the tax years needed. They will request a copying fee from you, but that's all you have to do to get a copy of that illusive joint return.

> *Note:* A word of caution about obtaining copies of tax returns. Remember the example of the ex-wife who suspected that her former husband's financial circumstances had changed after the divorce? She wrote to the IRS giving them the necessary information and

they promptly sent her a copy of his single tax return. If *you* are contemplating such a maneuver (after your divorce has been granted), you should be aware that you are probably violating several federal and state laws relating to invasion of privacy.

Checking for Hidden Earnings

If his salary raises have been consistent and of substantial amounts, and such a raise doesn't show up during the divorce proceedings, consider asking your attorney to put your husband's boss on the stand to find out if there have been any agreements made relating to deferment of his compensation until after the divorce. Usually, the threat to do this works wonders in getting concessions. Remember that your attorney can subpoena anyone who has knowledge of your spouse's financial affairs. Use this weapon sparingly, though, because it can backfire.

If he is a union or other nonsalaried worker and has always worked overtime, make sure the court is aware of it when it sets support payments.

For those whose husbands are self-employed (doctors, lawyers, etc.), don't take anything for granted—especially what he claims is last year's income. Of course he'll try to minimize it. Counter by requesting to see his returns for the last *three* years. If there's a sharp drop between those years, make sure your lawyer investigates it. You might ask your lawyer to go to court and obtain funds to hire a CPA to examine the returns.

Long-range Planning

Several years before a divorce actually begins, you will probably have some inkling that the marriage is failing. When you realize that divorce is the only eventuality, even though it may be years away, you will want to start "raising" your standard of living as high as you can. This is a polite euphemism for running up a lot of household bills. Why? Aside from the fact that you will probably get the house in a settlement, you want to show the court how much money you and your husband have spent in the last few years on nonessential items. This will give you a solid base from which to argue for high spousal and child support. In essence what you are saying is, "Look, your honor, we have been spending $1,000 a month on goodies for the last two years and I've become accustomed to this standard of living."

So start buying and charging as fast as possible. Keep your bank charge cards close to their limits. Have the house repainted inside and out. Install new carpeting or have major renovations made to the house.

Start a campaign for a new car, and one for your children if they're old enough to drive. Spend two weeks in Tahiti. Tell your husband how much you think he deserves that power boat he's wanted for so long.

Chances are this strategy will work if your husband is also thinking about divorce and is feeling guilty about it. Play on this submerged guilt as much as possible, especially when it comes to buying things for the kids.

However, if you're the only one contemplating divorce, you will have to be extra cautious around your unsuspecting husband. Don't start fights; try to compromise whenever possible and be as nice as you can.

You Too Can Be a Financial Wizard!

This is no time to be the dumb-but-innocent Hausfrau. You must discipline yourself and turn your orientation toward business. Start reviewing all the monthly bills if you don't pay them now. Balance the checkbook every month, even if your husband has already done this. If he's playing the stock market, find out what stocks and bonds you own and if he has a margin (credit) account. If he buys or sells options, find out what paper losses are really long-term gains. It may sound like a foreign language now, but you had better learn to speak it. What you don't know about your assets at the time of the divorce could end up costing you hundreds, or even thousands, in the property settlement.

One of the best all-round guides to the world of finances can be found in the business section of your daily newspaper. Especially helpful are the syndicated columnists like Sylvia Porter, Milton Moskowitz, and others. Another good all-round source is the *Wall Street Journal.* Once you have a feel for this subject, your local librarian can recommend beginner's books on finances and the stock market. You'll find this knowledge helpful not only during your divorce, but later on as well, when you're handling your own finances—perhaps for the first time in your life.

Sneaky Strategies for Men

One of the sad realities of divorce is that there's never enough money to go around. This is particularly true when one salary must suddenly support two households. There are no sneaky strategies for evading child support. Your children deserve your support, both monetarily and psychologically, and as much of it as you can realistically afford. Alimony is another matter. In a contested divorce, your wife may try to have an astronomical sum set for her support as a means of punishment. Many states which have recently enacted no-fault provisions still have the old fault grounds on the books. If your wife decides to sue, for example, on the grounds of adultery, you could end up paying "punitive" or high spousal support if the "right" judge (i.e., one sympathetic to wronged wives) hears the case. To retaliate, you will have to mask part of your income.

Postponing Increases

Before you decide to tell your wife about getting a divorce, it would be a good idea for you to approach your boss with certain special requests relating to your income. For example, if you are due to receive a bonus, or a raise, you might want to ask your boss to defer paying these increases to you until after the divorce is granted. Of course, you will want the back wages or bonus paid in a lump sum after that time to catch up to where you should be on the pay scale. You might point out to your boss that he will be saving interest on the payments as he gets the use of the money for that period of time.

"Lothar Is My Stockbroker"

Another approach to take in deferring your income would be to ask your boss to grant you a "phantom" stock option. This option is in essence an informal agreement between you and employer that you will have X amount of your company's shares of stock at current value, with the ability to purchase those shares at some later period of time at today's prices. In addition, some companies also credit the dividends earned on the stock during this period of time to the "phantom" account. If the stock goes down, you simply do not exercise your right to purchase the stock at the previously agreed price.

A word of caution in dealing with your boss: Remember your wife's subpoena power mentioned above. If she finds out about it and threatens to use it, you'd better be prepared to fight. Say it will cost you your job. However, if she is really tough, this won't matter. Be prepared to counteroffer something if she does go through with it. If your boss gets on the stand and says that you and he fixed up this little deal, you can bet you will get no sympathy from the court.

Union and Other Hourly Workers

If you are a union or nonsalaried worker, stop working overtime as soon as you've decided to get a divorce. Don't indicate *any* overtime pay on your financial statement.

For Self-employed Persons

Let's say that you run a small grocery store next to a vacant corner lot. Because business has been good, you'd like to expand the store and build on the vacant lot. Don't do this if you're contemplating, or already into, a divorce. The value of your store is a community asset, and once you start improving it, you'll only end up losing more at the time of the final decree. And this advice goes for all types of store owners.

For other service-oriented self-employeds (doctors, dentists, lawyers, accountants, etc.), you would do well to cut office hours drastically at least a year before filing for divorce. There is little point in working long hours to earn extra money. The higher income will result in your spouse getting higher support payments. If that happens, you will have to continue working the longer hours after the divorce in order to have sufficient money to live on. Or, if you are sure that the divorce proceedings will be of short duration, then consider deferring all billing to your patients and clients until after the final decree.

24

HOW TO TELL YOUR SPOUSE YOU WANT A DIVORCE

Breaking up is hard to do.
—N. Sedaka

THE MOST FATEFUL DAY of your marriage is the day you tell your partner you want a divorce. The way you handle it will set the tone for the entire divorce proceedings. If you're tactful and considerate, things will get off on the right foot. If you bungle it, then you may be in for the roughest ride of your life.

PROCEED CAUTIOUSLY

It is always a good idea to analyze your partner carefully to determine the potential reaction to the divorce request. If he or she is given to moments of rage, perhaps it would be better to have someone else break the news, or to do it by letter (the coward's way out). By all means, don't do it in the kitchen where there are a number of breakable, throwable, and sharp, pointed objects handy. A little caution and tact can go a long way. One unlucky fellow had been drinking with a friend to bolster his courage to confront his wife. When he got home, she was wearing a filmy negligee. He immediately put off telling her until the next morning. He was very lucky his wife was a poor shot because she missed him three times.

There Is Never "Someone Else"

From a planning standpoint, *never* admit that you love someone else. This can only cause a lot of hurt feelings without accomplishing anything. Knowing a spouse is involved in an adulterous affair is terribly painful, and usually encourages vengefulness. Make up some tale of incompatibility or possible mental breakdown or a total fantasy, like going off to hunt for Shangri-la.

Choose the time, mood, and place yourself. Make it firm. Don't get in any arguments now; there will be plenty of time for that later.

You should be able to discuss this in a calm, if somewhat unhappy, manner. When you and your spouse have the basic details straightened out, carefully choose the time and place to tell your children. Remember, they're the ones who are going to be most affected by all of this.

What to Do When There Are Problems

If you have closely analyzed your spouse and have concluded that he or she is going to react badly to the news, then you are going to have to take special, sometimes drastic, steps to see that everything proceeds with some semblance of order.

In most cases, it seems improbable that your spouse will not suspect your divorce plans. Indeed, when you broach the subject, the entire matter may be viewed as merely another attempt to "get your way." Be firm, don't give in, and don't tell your spouse until you are *absolutely* ready.

Tips for Especially Difficult Cases

For the male: Send your wife to visit her mother, or anybody. While she is gone, have the moving van in and move whatever you need to set up housekeeping in your new apartment. Don't forget, take *everything* you may want now or later (you can always give things back later if you like). In most divorce cases, the spouse with the possession keeps the possession. Call your attorney. Have him file the divorce papers. If you don't want to tell your spouse over the phone, tell her when she gets back. By then the papers should have arrived.

For the female: Pack his clothes and personal effects and put them on the front step. Be sure to have the locks changed so that he can't get in. And see if you can prearrange a place for him to spend the first night. This will assure that he stays out of the house, and it will also start his thought processes toward accepting the idea of divorce. Call your attorney to have the papers filed.

When You're Not the Major Breadwinner

If you are not the primary-income-earning spouse, you will be faced with the immediate question of alimony and child support. If the mood warrants, bring up the subject now. Often, the shock of the divorce will cause a person to agree to terms he or she would otherwise contest. Failing that, be prepared to ask your attorney to go to court immediately for temporary alimony and child support.

Use Your Counsel—That's What He's There for

By this time you should be working closely with your attorney and CPA. They will give you the best advice from a monetary standpoint. Rely on your friends for moral and emotional support.

One Final Note

The importance of good postdivorce relationships cannot be stressed too strongly. You will come into contact with your ex-spouse more than you can imagine, especially when you are parents. Things will go much more smoothly if you call a permanent truce at the time of the final decree. If you cannot be genuinely friendly and open with your ex-spouse, at least be civil and *fair*. Prolonging hostilities, trying to exact that last pound of flesh, will only cause you both a lot of grief and money. Grow up. It's cheaper.

25

THE LEGAL SIDE OF DIVORCE

It made our hair stand up in panic fear.
—Sophocles

GETTING A DIVORCE is like wandering through a dense forest of legal underbrush. You should know what to expect at each turn, how to protect yourself at all times and keep that embarrassing blank look off your face as much as possible. This is true even when you've hired a lawyer to handle your divorce. For one thing, knowing what's ahead means your lawyer will spend less time explaining various forms and court procedures to you, and the less time he spends on you, the less his fee will be.

Also, for those rugged individualists who want to do their own divorce, this chapter will give you a broad overview of what to expect. *Caution:* Not all states allow you to "do your own divorce." Don't attempt one on your own without a specially written book or prepackaged set of forms for your state. Check with a local bookstore or library or the classified ads to find out whether these aids are readily available in your state.

The first hurdle you will cross is something called:

1. The Petition to Show Cause

This petition is filed with the court. It stipulates a cause of action and denotes the action as being a petition for divorce. The petition (see pages 229–230) is the legal instrument that begins the proceedings and is generally filed with the county clerk or the county recorder.

The petition usually requires a residency period in both the county and the state. Some state courts, however, have taken the position that intent is more determinant than physical presence. This happened where one spouse moved to Nevada and obtained a divorce after six weeks without the concurrence of the other spouse. Accordingly, the home state ruled the divorce invalid and a subsequent marriage was bigamy.

Items 1 and 2 are self-explanatory. Item 3 requests that the joint property of the two parties be split according to the court's discretion. It probably will not be possible to list all the assets and their value at this time, so "unknown," or some such term, may be inserted here.

Item 4 is to list separate property. Item 5 is the section to request child and spousal support, although this particular petition does not have a place for specifying the amount.

Very important note: The petition must be signed under the penalties of perjury.

Name, Address and Telephone Number of Attorney(s)

Space Below for Use of Court Clerk Only

Attorney(s) for..

SUPERIOR COURT OF CALIFORNIA, COUNTY OF

In re the marriage of

Petitioner:

and

Respondent:

CASE NUMBER

PETITION (MARRIAGE)

1. This petition is for:

☐ Legal separation of the parties pursuant to
  ☐ Civil Code Section 4506(1)
  ☐ Civil Code Section 4506(2)

☐ Dissolution of the marriage pursuant to:
  ☐ Civil Code Section 4506(1)
  ☐ Civil Code Section 4506(2)

....has been a resident of this state for at least six months and of this county for at least
(Petitioner/Respondent)
three months immediately preceding the filing of this petition.

☐ Nullity of the marriage pursuant to:
  ☐ Civil Code Section 4400
  ☐ Civil Code Section 4401
  ☐ Civil Code Section 4425(   )

2. Statistical information:

a. Husband's social security number: .... Wife's social security number: ....

b. Date and place of marriage: ....

c. Date of separation: .... The number of years from date of marriage to date of separation is: ....years, ...months,.... .. days.

d. There are. ......children of this marriage including the following minor children:
(Number)

Name	Birthdate	Age	Sex

Form Adopted by Rule 1281 of
Judicial Council of California
Revised Effective January 1, 1972

PETITION (MARRIAGE)

California Newspaper Service Bureau, Inc.
Established 1934

3. **Property statement:**

☐ **There is no property subject to disposition by the court in this proceeding.**

☐ **All property otherwise subject to disposition by the court in this proceeding has been disposed of by written agreement of the parties.**

☐ **The following described property is subject to disposition by the court in this proceeding:**

4. **Petitioner requests that the following described property be confirmed as petitioner's separate property:**

5. **Petitioner requests that:**

a. ☐ Custody of children be awarded: ....
(Petitioner/Respondent/Other [Specify])

b. ☐ Support of children be awarded

c. ☐ Spousal support................be awarded..
(not) (Petitioner/Respondent)

d. ☐ Property rights be determined as provided by law

e. ☐ Attorney's fees and costs................be awarded.......................................
(not) (Petitioner/Respondent)

and that the court inquire into the status of the marriage and render such judgments and make such injunctive or other orders as are appropriate.

Petitioner declares under penalty of perjury that the foregoing, including any attachments, is true and correct and that this declaration was executed on...at ...., California.

(Signature)

....

(Attorney for Petitioner) (Type/print name)

A declaration under penalty of perjury must be executed within California. An affidavit is required if executed outside California.

Now we come to an item called:

2. The Response

After being served with the petition, it is imperative to enlist the services of an attorney. If you do not respond, you risk the danger of having the court declare a divorce by default. This means that support (child and spousal) and any property settlement will probably be what the petitioner is asking for. This is one good reason for being the person who files for divorce. One rule to remember: *Always try to be the plaintiff*. It will save you a lot of time in the long run.

In most states, a response (see pages 232–233) must be filed with the court within thirty days. However, the court will accept certain reasons for not filing, such as absence from the country, severe illness, etc.

Name, Address and Telephone Number of Attorney(s)	Space Below for Use of Court Clerk Only
Attorney(s) for..	

SUPERIOR COURT OF CALIFORNIA, COUNTY OF ....

In re the marriage of Petitioner: and Respondent:	CASE NUMBER RESPONSE (MARRIAGE)

1. This response is for:

☐ Reconciliation of the parties

☐ Legal separation of the parties pursuant to:
  ☐ Civil Code Section 4506(1)
  ☐ Civil Code Section 4506(2)

☐ Dissolution of the marriage pursuant to:
  ☐ Civil Code Section 4506(1)
  ☐ Civil Code Section 4506(2)

....has been a resident of this state for at least six months and of this county for at least
(Petitioner/Respondent)
three months immediately preceding the filing of this petition.

☐ Nullity of the marriage pursuant to:
  ☐ Civil Code Section 4400
  ☐ Civil Code Section 4401
  ☐ Civil Code Section 4425(   )

2. The statistical information in the petition is.................................. (If incorrect, complete the following)
(correct/incorrect)

a. Husband's social security number:.................................. . Wife's social security number: ....
b. Date and place of marriage:..
c. Date of separation:.. The number of years from date of marriage to date of separation is:................years,..............months,...........days.
d. There are....................children of this marriage including the following minor children:
(Number)

Name	Birthdate	Age	Sex

3. The property statement in the petition is........................ (If incorrect, complete the following)
(correct/incorrect)

☐ There is no property subject to disposition by the court in this proceeding.

☐ All property otherwise subject to disposition by the court in this proceeding has been disposed of by written agreement of the parties.

☐ The following described property is subject to disposition by the court in this proceeding:

4. The statement in the petition of separate property to be confirmed by the court in this proceeding is..................
(correct/incorrect)

Respondent requests that the following described property be confirmed as respondent's separate property:

5. Respondent requests that:

a. ☐ Custody of children be awarded:..
(Petitioner/Respondent/Other [Specify])

b. ☐ Support of children be awarded

c. ☐ Spousal support................be awarded....................................
(not) (Petitioner/Respondent)

d. ☐ Property rights be determined as provided by law

e. ☐ Attorney's fees and costs................be awarded....................................
(not) (Petitioner/Respondent)

and that the court inquire into the status of the marriage and render such judgments and make such injunctive or other orders as are appropriate.

Respondent declares under penalty of perjury that the foregoing, including any attachments, is true and correct and that this declaration was executed on....................................at...................................., California.

.... (Signature)

(Attorney for Respondent) (Type/print name)

A declaration under penalty of perjury must be executed within California. An affidavit is required if executed outside California.

Next up is something called the:

3. Order to Show Cause

The order to show (see pages 235–236) will set forth the requested spousal support and child support and will designate a date for a hearing limited to temporary arrangements for these items. In general, to support the order to show cause, the moving party will file a financial declaration. Although its only purpose is to validate the requested support, it is obvious that the declaration as to financial information will be utilized during all stages of the proceedings and *great care* should be utilized in its preparation.

If the parties can reach a voluntary agreement, the temporary-support order will provide for support.

However, if no voluntary agreement is reached, the court will consider each financial declaration and any testimony permitted at the hearing, and then enter its temporary-support order. This order is used to provide financial assistance to the separated marital unit (usually wife and children) until the final arrangements can be completed.

Temporary support should not be confused with a Decree of Separate Maintenance, which is a final disposition rather than a temporary order pending a final determination. For the spouse paying the support, it is imperative for tax-planning purposes that this decree be ordered by the court, or that if any voluntary agreement relating to support has been made, that such agreement be entered into in writing and signed by both parties. If this is done, then the temporary-spousal-support payments, if properly worded, are deductible as alimony during the year the divorce occurs.

Name, Address and Telephone Number of Attorney(s)

Space Below for Use of Court Clerk Only

Attorney(s) for..

SUPERIOR COURT OF CALIFORNIA, COUNTY OF ....

In re the marriage of

Petitioner:

and

Respondent:

CASE NUMBER

ORDER TO SHOW CAUSE AND DECLARATION RE CONTEMPT (MARRIAGE)

ORDER TO SHOW CAUSE

TO CITEE: ....
(Name)

You are ordered to appear in this court,

located at ....,
(Street address and city)

on .... at ....m., Department or Room No. ...., to give any legal reason why this
(Date) (Time)

court should not find you guilty of contempt and punish you for wilfully disobeying its orders, as set forth in the DECLARATION below

☐ and why you should not be required to pay, for the benefit of the moving party, the attorney's fees and costs of this proceeding

Dated..

....
Judge of the Superior Court

DECLARATION

The citee, ..., has wilfully disobeyed certain orders of this court as set
(Name of citee)

forth herein.

1. The citee had knowledge of the orders in that:

2. The citee was able to comply with each order when he disobeyed it. He.. .... been previously cited for contempt in this proceeding. (Specify prior citations) (has/has not)

Form Adopted by Rule 1285.60 of Judicial Council of California Effective January 1, 1972

ORDER TO SHOW CAUSE AND DECLARATION RE CONTEMPT (MARRIAGE)

California Newspaper Service Bureau, Inc. Established 1934

3. State each disobedience of an order separately:

(a) Orders for child support, spousal support, attorney's fees, and court or other litigation costs:

Date Due	Type and Date Order Entered	Payee	Amount Ordered	Amount Paid	Amount Due
			$	$	$

Recapitulation of orders for:	Total Amount Ordered	Total Amount Paid	Total Amount Due
Child support	$	$	$
Spousal support			
Attorney's fees			
Court/other costs			
Total	$	$	$

(b) Injunctive or other orders: (Describe each order and disobedience with particularity)

4. State other material facts, if any:

I declare under penalty of perjury that the foregoing, including any attachments, is true and correct and that this declaration was executed on .... at ...., California.

(Signature,

....

(Type/print name)

A declaration under penalty of perjury must be executed within California. An affidavit is required if executed outside California.

You can't have an order to show cause without a:

4. FINANCIAL DECLARATION

Filed by both parties, the financial declarations (see pages 238–239) call for detailed listings of all expenses, income, assets, and liabilities. However, the declaration does not reflect the tax-return income because of the special exemptions and deductions allowed for tax purposes.

The net-monthly-income amount shown on line c is the income the court will use in setting the amount of payment.

The only real areas of manipulation in the numbers occur in the income-tax calculation. The reason for this is that the setting of spousal support in a certain manner will transfer income to the support-receiving spouse, thereby lowering the income taxes. If the divorce doesn't occur by the year-end, however, the income isn't shifted and higher taxes are due.

Therefore, when preparing the statement, assume the worse and calculate the taxes as a married person filing separately. If the court awards support, and your spouse won't consent to file a joint return, that's just the tax rate you will have to pay unless you can finalize that divorce by year-end.

You will be asked to list your assets under the penalty of perjury. Obviously there are certain contingent assets which you might have, assets that would be available only upon retirement, for example. There is no requirement that these types of intangible assets be listed. They are not assets upon which you now have control. Do remember, however, that there can be severe penalties for perjury, and that the general rule of thumb is that assets in your possession discovered subsequent to divorce will go to the other spouse in total.

Be prepared to support your liberal estimate of the amount of income you need to live in the style to which you are accustomed.

Name, Address and Telephone Number of Attorney(s)	Space Below for Use of Court Clerk Only
Attorney(s) for..	

SUPERIOR COURT OF CALIFORNIA, COUNTY OF ....

In re the marriage of	CASE NUMBER
Petitioner:	☐ PETITIONER'S ☐ RESPONDENT'S
and	FINANCIAL DECLARATION
Respondent:	

Dated:

Husband:		Wife:	
Age:	Social Security No.:	Age:	Social Security No.:
Occupation:		Occupation:	

PART A: INCOME AND EXPENSE STATEMENT	Husband	Wife
(a) Gross monthly income from:		
Salary and wages (including commissions, bonuses and overtime) payable .... (weekly/monthly/etc.)	$	$
Pensions and retirement		
Social security		
Disability and unemployment insurance		
Public assistance (welfare, AFDC payments, etc.)		
Child/spousal support re prior marriage		
Dividends and interest		
Rents		
All other sources: (Specify)		
....		
....		
Total monthly income	$	$
Disability insurance		
(b) Itemize deductions from gross income:		
Income taxes (state and federal)	$	$
Social security		
Unemployment insurance		
Medical or other insurance		
Union or other dues		
Retirement or pension fund		
Savings plan		
Other: (Specify)		
....		
....		
Total deductions	$	$
(c) Net monthly income	$	$

Form Adopted by Rule 1285.50 of
Judicial Council of California
Effective January 1, 1972

FINANCIAL DECLARATION

(d) Total monthly expenses: (Specify which party is the custodial parent and list name and relationship of all members of the household whose expenses are included) ....

....

....

	Husband	Wife
Rent or mortgage payments (residence)	$	$
Real property taxes (residence)		
Real property insurance (residence)		
Maintenance (residence)		
Food and household supplies		
Utilities		
Telephone		
Laundry and cleaning		
Clothing		
Medical		
Dental		
Insurance (life, health, accident, etc.)		
Child care		
Payment of child/spousal support re prior marriage		
School		
Entertainment		
Incidentals		
Transportation		
Auto expenses (insurance, gas, oil, repair)		
Auto payments		
Installment payment(s) (Insert total and itemize below)		
Other: (Specify)		
Total expenses	$	$

Creditor's Name	For	Monthly Payment	Balance
....	....	$	$
....	....		
....	....		
....	....		
....	....		

(e) Other debts and obligations:

Creditor's Name	For	Date Payable	Balance
....	....	....	$
....	....	....	
....	....	....	
....	....	....	
....	....	....	

(f) All property of the parties known to me includes the following:

Cash on hand	$
Money in checking accounts	
Money in savings accounts	
Money in credit union accounts	
Money in any other accounts or deposits	

Retirement or pension fund	$
Life insurance cash value	
Value of any stocks & bonds	
Value of real estate	
Value of all other property	
Total property	$

Now we're getting somewhere. After all the financial declaration hocus-pocus and other legal mumbo–jumbo, we subsequently get around to ending the marriage with the:

5. Interlocutory Decree

The interlocutory judgment is the initial order of the court dissolving the marriage. This judgment may be entered either following a default or following a contested hearing. The judgment should also incorporate any final settlement, or if negotiations are unsuccessful, the court will include in this order a declaration of rights of the parties to the separate and community property and will also issue an order relating to spousal and child support. A default judgment occurs where one spouse cannot be found or has left the state or has not chosen to respond to the divorce petition.

Where the parties have agreed, one attorney can file the necessary motion, stipulating that the parties have agreed to the settlement. If this is true, the legal proceedings are perfunctory.

In most states, the interlocutory decree does not automatically result in a divorce. Unless positive action is taken by one of the spouses, the marriage will continue indefinitely. Usually, either spouse can file a final-judgment petition and the divorce is granted.

California Newspaper Service Bureau, Inc.
Established 1934

Name, Address and Telephone Number of Attorney(s)

Space Below for Use of Court Clerk Only

Attorney(s) for..

SUPERIOR COURT OF CALIFORNIA, COUNTY OF.

In re the marriage of

CASE NUMBER

Petitioner:

and

Respondent:

INTERLOCUTORY JUDGMENT OF DISSOLUTION OF MARRIAGE

This proceeding was heard on .... (Date) before the Honorable................................

Department No...........................

The court acquired jurisdiction of the respondent on........................ (Date) by:

☐ Service of process on that date, respondent not having appeared within the time permitted by law.

☐ Service of process on that date and respondent having appeared.

☐ Respondent on that date having appeared.

The court orders that an interlocutory judgment be entered declaring that the parties are entitled to have their marriage dissolved. This interlocutory judgment does not constitute a final dissolution of marriage and the parties are still married and will be, and neither party may remarry, until a final judgment of dissolution is entered.

The court also orders that, unless both parties file their consent to a dismissal of this proceeding, a final judgment of dissolution be entered upon proper application of either party or on the court's own motion after the expiration of at least six months from the date the court acquired jurisdiction of the respondent. The final judgment shall include such other and further relief as may be necessary to a complete disposition of this proceeding, but entry of the final judgment shall not deprive this court of its jurisdiction over any matter expressly reserved to it in this or the final judgment until a final disposition is made of each such matter.

Dated____________________________

____
Judge of the Superior Court

Form Adopted by Rule 1287 of Judicial Council of California Effective January 1, 1970

INTERLOCUTORY JUDGMENT OF DISSOLUTION OF MARRIAGE

Finally, at long last, we come to the closing curtain, the last of the ninth, the:

6. Final Judgment

The request for the final judgment is the last step in dissolving the marriage. The judgment usually requires a certain amount of time following the filing of the petition for dissolution (or the interlocutory decree), and until then the parties may not remarry. Under certain circumstances, state law permits a couple to waive this statutory filing requirement and such parties may remarry immediately. Your lawyer will know the amount of time in your state that you have to wait before remarriage can take place (see the breakdown of the various state laws in the appendix).

Even though it's all over, there may still be some extra trips to court to wrangle over various and sundry items. Remember the advice in the preceding chapter—the divorce never ends? Well some of the reasons why it's never over (even after the final decree) stem from:

Subsequent Issues and Changes

Often subsequent events affect the divorce determination. Sometimes the spouse who's paying support loses his job or takes a salary cut and cannot make the payments. Perhaps arguments arise regarding visitation rights.

All state courts jealously guard their jurisdiction over a couple in a divorce and will continue to maintain control as long as there are minor children or alimony payments.

If the property settlement was incorporated into the interlocutory judgment, or if the court made its own determination of property rights, the failure of either party to abide by these orders leaves them open to a contempt-of-court citation. They can be imprisoned, or other forms of coercion (garnishing wages) may be exercised to guarantee compliance with the court orders.

Name, Address and Telephone Number of Attorney (s)	Space Below for Use of Court Clerk Only
Attorney (s) for..	

SUPERIOR COURT OF CALIFORNIA, COUNTY OF ....

In re the marriage of Petitioner: and Respondent:	CASE NUMBER FINAL JUDGMENT (MARRIAGE) OF .... (LEGAL SEPARATION/NULLITY/DISSOLUTION)

The court acquired jurisdiction of the respondent on....................................by:
(Date)

☐ Service of process on that date, respondent not having appeared within the time permitted by law.

☐ Service of process on that date and respondent having appeared.

☐ Respondent on that date having appeared.

The court orders that:

☐ Pursuant to ☐ Civil Code Section 4506(1) or ☐ Civil Code Section 4506(2), a Judgment of Legal Separation and such other orders as are set out below be entered.

☐ Pursuant to ☐ Civil Code Section 4400, ☐ Civil Code Section 4401, or ☐ Civil Code Section 4425( ), a Judgment of Nullity and such other orders as are set out below be entered, and that the parties be restored to the status of unmarried persons.

☐ Pursuant to ☐ Civil Code Section 4506(1) or ☐ Civil Code Section 4506(2), a Final Judgment of Dissolution be entered, and that all of the provisions of the interlocutory judgment, which was entered on...................................., except as otherwise set out below, be made binding the same as if set forth in full, and that the parties be restored to the status of unmarried persons.

Dated... ....
Judge of the Superior Court

Form Adopted by Rule 1289 of
Judicial Council of California
Revised Effective January 1, 1972

FINAL JUDGMENT (MARRIAGE)

California Newspaper Service Bureau, Inc.
Established 1934

Unfortunately, one way ex-spouses get to see each other is to drag each other into court periodically for a custody battle or for a change in support. That change is termed by the court to be a:

7. MODIFICATION

This is generally a process whereby alimony or child-support payments are to be altered because of a change in financial circumstances of either the ex-wife or the ex-husband. The parties can make spousal support nonmodifiable in the agreement, but the court will retain jurisdiction over child support until the children reach majority, usually the age of eighteen, or when marriage occurs (especially important in the case of a female child).

CASE NUMBER:

SUPPORTIVE DECLARATION RE MODIFICATION

An order or judgment was made as follows:

Type of Order	Date Order Entered	Amount Payable	Payee	Date Payable
Child support		$		
Spousal support		$		
Attorney's fees		$		
Court/other costs		$		

Child custody/visitation:*

Other:

I have fully complied with the order or judgment except as follows:

The necessity for requesting this modification is:

I declare under penalty of perjury that the foregoing, including any attachments, is true and correct and that this declaration was executed on .... at ...., California.

(Signature)
....
(Type/print name)

*Specify, including date of each order.

A declaration under penalty of perjury must be executed within California. An affidavit is required if executed outside California.

Form Adopted by Rule 1285.30 of Judicial Council of California Effective January 1, 1972

SUPPORTIVE DECLARATION RE MODIFICATION

California Newspaper Service Bureau, Inc. Established 1934

Legal Definitions

Whether you are doing your own divorce or letting a lawyer handle it, you should have some knowledge and understanding of the words and phrases you are going to run into from now on.

Adultery is defined as the voluntary sexual intercourse of a married person with a person other than the offender's spouse. In some states, however, adultery does not apply unless the adulterer is a married woman having sexual relations with someone other than her husband. For the man to be considered an adulterer, he must be habitually cohabitating with a woman other than his spouse. This rule follows the old Roman and Jewish laws. In some jurisdictions, if one of the parties is married, both are guilty of adultery.

Alimony at Common Law means the sustenance or support of the wife by her divorced husband and stems from the common-law right of the wife to support by her husband. California has adopted the term "spousal support" rather than "alimony." Apparently this is to detract from the guilt feeling the term "alimony" arises in some persons.

Alimony Pendente Lite is an allowance made for support during the suit for divorce or separate maintenance.

Annulment is the state's ruling the marriage null and void. The effect of this is as if the marriage never took place. However, most states will grant an annulment only if the marriage has not been consummated.

Collusion is something couples are often forced into in states which have no no-fault provisions in their laws. Collusion is an agreement between a husband and wife that one of them will commit (or appear to commit) an act causing a divorce (adultery, for example). The purpose of this "fraud" is to obtain a divorce that both husband and wife want but cannot get because of strict state laws. Obviating the necessity for such fraud is one of the very best arguments for every state having at least one no-fault provision in the law.

Community property includes those items which are acquired by either husband or wife during the marriage. (Exceptions to this are gifts and inheritances.) The couple jointly owns all community property. Eight states are community property states: California, Texas, Nevada, Idaho, Washington, Louisiana, New Mexico, and Arizona.

Contempt means willfully disobeying the orders of a court of justice.

Divorce, or dissolution is the legal separation of a husband and wife by the judgment of a court totally dissolving the marriage.

The Decree of Separate Maintenance, called a *legal separation* in some states, allows a couple to live apart. Thereafter, their earnings will be separate property. However, they will still be legally married. For the tax effect of a legal separation, see Chapter 28.

The Interlocutory Decree is the initial order of the court dissolving the marriage. The decree usually lists certain items, such as spousal support. The interlocutory decree is not a divorce. For tax and legal purposes the couple is still married. Why the decrees are even granted or used in this day and age of high divorce rates is confusing. But you can't get a divorce without one, and they can usually be waived. Perhaps the states hope that the interlocutory decree will provide an additional breathing time for the couple to get back together.

No-fault divorce means that a marriage can be dissolved without pointing a finger at the "guilty" party. The "fault" —accusations, recriminations, damning evidence—has been removed from the divorce proceedings. If your state provides for divorce on the grounds of incompatibility,[1] living separate and apart, or irreconcilable differences (irretrievable marital breakdown), then you can get your divorce on no-fault grounds. By removing the burden of proving fault, the two parties involved in a divorce can sit down as equals and iron out a settlement with much less rancor. There is less apt to be an atmosphere of "penalizing" the "guilty" party by taking all the assets or asking for unusually high alimony.

Modified no-fault is starting to be enacted by some states where there are no safeguards or procedures for reconciliation in the present no-fault laws. A Missouri Court of Appeals adopted a modified no-fault law to prevent a divorce-seeking husband who no longer loved his wife from getting a divorce. As the court saw it, the problem was that the husband had to establish more criteria (her bad behavior, etc.) for the divorce than just that he had stopped loving his wife.

---

[1] Not all states view incompatibility as "no-fault" grounds. If your state lists this ground, check the appendix description carefully.

26

A FEW QUESTIONS AND ANSWERS ABOUT LAWYERS

The first thing we do, let's kill all the lawyers.
—Shakespeare

THERE MAY BE TIMES during your divorce when you feel the same way. Your lawyer will drive you to distraction; he won't return your calls right away, he'll counsel you to compromise and negotiate with your spouse when all you want to do is go for the jugular, and he'll often be seen fraternizing with the enemy, i.e., your spouse's attorney. After all of these injustices, just before you're ready to fire him, stop and remember that you are not in perfect control of your faculties at this time. Your view of the world (and of your lawyer's actions) will be distorted by the strain of the divorce. Before you go storming into that law office, take a moment to reflect on how the case is going. If you haven't been burned yet, chances are your lawyer is doing a good job.

How to tell when you need a lawyer and how to choose one are two of the most critical questions you'll face in your divorce proceeding.

When Do I Need a Lawyer?

Perhaps you might be wondering whether you should employ an attorney at all. Of course, it varies with each individual case. If your partner is amicable, you might be able to forgo legal counsel until the drawing up of the final papers at the very end of your divorce. However, in most divorce cases, not using a lawyer would probably be a mistake on your part. An attorney's fee will be a small price to pay for the peace of mind and assistance you will need in negotiations. This will be one of the most trying times of your life. You must compromise, negotiate, compute living expenses, deal with your spouse's attorney (whom you won't know), and be served a summons about which you don't know a thing. Don't risk years of unhappiness for a few extra bucks. Hire an attorney.

How Do I Choose a Lawyer?

There are numerous ways for you to select an attorney. It can be as simple as calling one listed in the Yellow Pages. Probably the best way is to choose an attorney recommended by one of your friends who has recently gone through a divorce.

Your area may have a "lawyer's referral service." This is usually nothing more than a legal clearing house where, for a fee, an attorney can get his name listed. Despite its respectable-sounding name, it is no more reliable than the Yellow Pages.

In most situations, it is unadvisable for both of you to use the same attorney. A reputable attorney will not represent both parties in a contested divorce. Some attorneys will, however, represent you both at the final stage of divorce when there are no matters such as visitation rights, spousal support, or the disposition of community assets to be decided. However, don't count on these items being nettled amicably. Be prepared for negotiations in order to settle the issues.

What About My Family Lawyer?

Don't be concerned if your family lawyer turns down a request to represent either you or your spouse in a divorce action. He probably doesn't want to become involved, or doesn't specialize in divorce. Divorce is a complicated process and not all attorneys are qualified to handle it.

Why Can't I Use My Company's Lawyer?

If you are an executive of a corporation that has a prestigious law firm representing it, your first reaction may be to ask the firm for help in the divorce case. In nine cases out of ten, the prestigious law firm will not want to represent the executive in the divorce action for two reasons: One, the firm does not specialize in divorce; and two, it might place the firm in the position of doing work for you, its client, for a fee lower than what it would charge a normal client. Also, there may be times when your own lawyer or law firm will appear to be as much an adversary as your spouse, and the corporate law firm does not want to risk your possible wrath for its inability to move things along in the divorce action. Naturally, the firm wants to keep all its clients happy, so it will want to represent you only in business matters.

Should I Choose a Divorce Lawyer of the Opposite Sex?

Let's assume you expect your negotiation proceedings to be long and difficult. Consider, then, selecting an attorney of the opposite sex who specializes in divorce. Often this person has generally superior knowledge of the ways of his or her own sex. It seems probable, for example, that a woman attorney will have represented primarily women. She will have greater knowledge of their feelings and desires and may be more adept at negotiations. Don't feel that you will be discriminated against because of your sex by your own attorney; this would be unethical. A good attorney will not generally feel this way.

What Happens When I Have Problems with My Lawyer?

As we have already pointed out, many times you'll find yourself in an adversary position not only with your spouse, but with your attorney as well. For example, Adam hired an attorney to institute a divorce suit against his wife. His wife failed to respond to the divorce action within the required period of time. Technically, this could have resulted in a default judgment against his wife, with the divorce being granted forthwith with no consideration for support. Adam wanted his attorney to go through with the default-judgment proceedings, but Adam's attorney refused, citing "unfairness" should they do it.

What Adam probably didn't know was that once long ago his own attorney forgot to reply in time to the other attorney, and because of their friendship, the other attorney did not pursue this advantage when it was available. Remember that your attorneys will continue to deal with each other and with the courts long after your particular divorce has been granted.

Another case involved Elizabeth, who was suing her husband for divorce. Because of the long drawn-out negotiations and the complexity of splitting the family property, Elizabeth became very incensed at the lack of action by her own attorney. She called his office almost daily with new offers of settlement which her attorney knew would never be accepted. Finally he stopped returning her calls.

This infuriated her. One day Elizabeth said to her estranged husband, Carl, that she was considering bringing suit against her attorney for malpractice. Carl, tired of the long negotiations to determine the property settlement, happily volunteered to testify on behalf of her attorney. He believed her demands were unreasonable, and he believed her attorney felt so and was not striving to terminate the marriage because of her unreasonableness.

There is a lesson to be learned here. Attorneys (and judges) are human. They don't want to sit and listen to a couple fighting over the sofa or whether the kids are to be brought home at seven-thirty in the evening rather than seven. So often, opposing attorneys will simply sit and wait until the warring couple decides it's time to end the hostilities and come to terms. Once they agree, the attorneys will quickly find an open court date and the divorce will be granted. If you can't agree on a settlement, and the court is forced to make all the decisions, you can count on the divorce dragging on for at least two years, which will cost you that much more in fees. Obviously, the courts set contested hearings for the last possible calendar date. One other point: You are not your attorney's only client. Don't expect him to jump every time you have a query or complaint.

Should I Tell My Lawyer Everything?

The legal profession has always promoted the idea of being completely truthful with your attorney and telling him everything. But this is not necessarily wise, particularly in the case of a divorce. The major reason is that your lawyer probably won't want to know it all. Of course, respond to all of his questions truthfully. Failure to do so may be most embarrassing when you are in court and want the judge's sympathy. But there is no point in telling your attorney that your ailing maiden aunt is about to die and leave you $5 million. He's human and won't be very sympathetic when you want to fight over some personal property. Your potential inheritance will not enter into the court's determination of spousal support and property settlement. (However, be careful. After you receive the inheritance, your higher income may constitute grounds for a modification of the support payments.)

How Can I Save Money When Using an Attorney?

When asking questions of your attorney, be as precise and succinct as possible. Plan your visit or phone conversation in advance so as not to waste his time. It will save you money, and your attorney will appreciate your businesslike approach. He doesn't want to hear whining. Of course, if something crucial happens—say, the support payments aren't coming on time—tell him. He'll call the other attorney and threaten to bring contempt proceedings.

When it is impossible to talk directly with your spouse, send letters to your attorney with the suggested format of any offers of settlement that you wish to make. This will enable him to represent you better and to obtain your desires in the settlement and, at the same time, cut his own participation and fees to a minimum.

If both spouses have retained attorneys, it is unethical (prohibited) for one attorney to talk to the other attorney's client. Therefore, be prepared for misunderstandings when offers have to go through two additional persons. Where one spouse refuses to negotiate directly with the other spouse, the settlement drags on at a snail's pace.

What's the Best Way to Change Lawyers?

Your lawyer is on the same footing as your doctor. If, during the proceedings, you do not like him or have insufficient rapport, tell him so and switch to another lawyer. During this trying time, you should be as comfortable with your attorney as possible.

In order for you to change lawyers once you have hired one and he has started proceedings, you will have to get him to send a letter to the opposing attorney specifying that he is withdrawing from the case. The court should be notified in the same manner. You will then be asked to substitute yourself or a new attorney for his place in the court proceedings.

How Much Is All of This Going to Cost Me?

The cost of using an attorney varies from state to state and depends upon settlement negotiations and the value of the property to be distributed. In most circumstances, you can probably figure between $350 and $750 for an uncontested divorce, with the usual personal property. Some lawyers will quote you an hourly fee, usually around $50 at the minimum. Where stock options, retirement benefits, stocks, bonds, and other assets are concerned, negotiations will be somewhat more complex and the fees will range higher. For wealthy people involved in a contested divorce, the fee may be a percentage of the settlement or net worth, which may run into thousands of dollars. Remember, too, that your fees will be considerably higher if the attorneys have to get involved in deciding who gets the sofa.

Can I Go Bargain-hunting for a Lawyer?

There is considerable pressure upon the American Bar Association to allow competitive bidding and advertising among lawyers concerning fees. At the time of this writing, this is not fully in effect, but it should ultimately result in lower divorce fees.

We Want to Do Our Own Divorce—Do We Still Need a Lawyer?

That depends on what state you live in. California and New York have thriving "do–it–yourself" entrepreneurs who sell everything from how-to books to packets containing all the legal forms and instructions you'll need to file your own divorce. (For an idea of what's involved, see Chapter 25.)

Even those people who have truly uncontested divorces use at least one attorney to file the necessary papers. They don't have the time or the patience to fill out all the necessary forms. When there are significant amounts of income or property at stake, always use at least one lawyer. The small amount you might save in attorneys' fees will be more than offset by what you lose in future tax and financial considerations.

In general, don't do your own divorce unless you can meet all of the following requirements:

1. There is little or no community property.
2. There is little or no community debt.
3. There are no children.
4. The marriage was of short duration (not longer than five years).
5. Neither partner wants any payments or support from the other.
6. The state allows you to obtain your own divorce.
7. You do not care whether or not you pay additional income taxes for the year of divorce.
8. You have the time to do it.

While this book is not intended to provide jobs for lawyers or accountants, most divorces require at least one attorney (and usually two) to achieve the best possible financial and legal settlement for both partners. If nothing else, a divorce attorney should be able to give you a feeling of security and guidance and reassure you that you are doing the best thing for your own interest. This peace of mind will be of great benefit to you.

Can I Deduct My Legal Fees on My Tax Return?

Although there has been a slight liberalization in the deductibility of legal fees, the general rule is that the legal fees incurred in a divorce are not deductible. However, that part of the legal fee which is given as tax advice and/or to receive income (such as alimony) can be deducted. Therefore, ask your attorney to submit an itemized bill to you for the legal fees, indicating in it those charges for the advice which relate to earning income (alimony) or the tax affects of paying alimony or child support.

If you pay your spouse's legal fees, however, none of the payments is deductible, even that part for tax advice. Therefore, make some other arrangement to cover this reimbursement.

Stay Close to Your Lawyer

One word of advice for cost-conscious people: Don't move away until the divorce is final. A move will tremendously complicate your ability to communicate with your attorney and to represent yourself in negotiations. Your attorney may be reluctant to have you fly back for an appearance in court for what may be a relatively minor issue forced by your spouse. This puts you at a tremendous disadvantage and gives your spouse additional leverage in the negotiations.

Beware of Shysters

Unfortunately, some lawyers are not the most ethical persons around. Take the case of Mary. She went to a lawyer who she had heard was real tough in a divorce settlement. She told him that she thought her husband did not have any hidden cash or assets that she did not know about. However, the shyster convinced her that there might be and said she should find out. Her husband was subsequently inundated by a blitz of questionnaires, financial declarations, and subpoenas, all of which produced nothing but higher fees for the shyster. The word of advice here, of course, is to keep your wits about you when you deal with your attorney. Don't be sidetracked from your intent to settle the divorce fairly, quickly, and cheaply.

What's It Like to Appear in Court?

For persons who have never been in a courtroom before, the thought of testifying can be frightening. However, don't be afraid. Divorce cases, like traffic cases, are usually dispensed with in about ten minutes. Of course, if the court has to rule on who gets the sofa, the hearing will take more time. You and your attorney will go over what questions are likely to be asked, and what your response should be. After all, your attorney does not want any surprises from you while you are testifying. Therefore, the better prepared you are, the better chance you will have to obtain a favorable decision.

27

WHEN YOU NEED AN ACCOUNTANT

The world knows nothing of our greatest accomplishments.
—An anonymous CPA

NOT MANY PEOPLE consider using a Certified Public Accountant in a divorce proceeding. They could be making a big mistake. A CPA who specializes in income taxes has a valuable contribution to make regarding the tax consequences of any proposed property settlement and support payments. For starters, your attorney may not be as experienced in the tax area as the CPA, who specializes in income taxes.

A good reason for obtaining the assistance of a CPA can be illustrated in the following examples. Assume that, in the divorce settlement, Alice keeps the family home, which has a fair market value considerably in excess of its cost. Her husband, Alex, took stocks worth approximately as much as the equity in the house. If Alex does not buy a new house within eighteen months after moving out, he will have to pay taxes upon his half of the gain between the tax basis and the fair value of the house that he gave to Alice in the settlement. If the stocks given to Alex were joint property and had a fair market value in excess of tax basis, then Alice will have a taxable gain upon the market value over her basis in the stocks given to Alex. This means that both Alex and Alice have taxes to pay and no money with which to pay them, i.e., they have taxable gain without selling anything. The result is somewhat different if they live in a community-property state. There, Alice doesn't have a gain but Alex will. Although they may still have gone this route in the distribution of the property, at least an accountant could have told them of the consequences of this settlement.

OK, got all that? Well, if not, don't worry. Most people have difficulty grasping our convoluted tax laws. However, it does illustrate the value of a good tax practitioner, because the above example is not a difficult problem for a good tax CPA. The real problems—and they're lulus—occur in the areas of dividing your property by selling your part to your ex-spouse or vice-versa.

If you find yourself facing any of these situations, with a great deal of money at stake, you would be foolish not to obtain the services of a topflight tax CPA.

Help with Your Tax Return

Another major advantage to engaging the services of an accountant is to have him look at your tax return. This is particularly important for the spouse who has no particular financial aptitude or doesn't understand the extent of the other spouse's financial holdings. The CPA will quickly spot the items of income and other transactions which will perhaps point out hidden or forgotten assets that may not be listed in the Financial Declaration. In most cases, when the CPA finds any such hidden assets, he will have immediately earned his fee several times over.

Estate Planning

Other tax-planning devices that the accountant can employ in assisting the attorney in the settlement lie in the area of estate planning. He can assist in setting up a trust for the children's education at the least cost with respect to either spouse. He can advise upon the particular tax effects of life insurance and the relative benefits of dependency and alimony deductions. In short, he can use his skills to parlay the settlement to the best possible financial advantage to both spouses while at the same time minimizing the impact of federal and state income taxes.

How to Find a Good Tax CPA

Keep in mind that not all CPAs specialize in these matters. As is true with attorneys, you should choose a CPA who specializes in the tax effects of financial planning and divorces. How do you find one? Well, if you choose a large national accounting firm, it may have such a specialist on its staff. In a smaller, local practice, you would just have to ask. Get any recommendations you can from friends who have used local accountants for divorce or estate-tax planning. If all else fails, try to find a tax accountant who's been through a divorce; nothing can match that sort of firsthand experience.

While a CPA is under the same ethical prohibitions against representing two spouses as an attorney is, he will have greater latitude in the divorce negotiations because, in general, he will only be compiling facts or rendering tax opinions.

Cost for Tax Advice

In general, a CPA will not have a set fee for working on a divorce case. His fee will be determined largely by the amount of time that he spends on your case. A good estimate is about $50–$75 per hour for a tax specialist from one of the prestigious national CPA firms, and about half that for a local CPA. You should be able to find out all you want to know about your income-tax return in an hour. However, figure twice that for advice concerning tax consequences of alternative property settlements and support payments. The fees will range considerably higher if there are extensive property holdings or if the couple has lived in different states.

28

THE DECREE OF SEPARATE MAINTENANCE

There's gold in them thar hills!
—A Forty-niner

DON'T OVERLOOK this great tax-planning device!

The Decree of Separate Maintenance, called a legal separation in most states (both terms are used interchangeably here), is extremely important because of the particular language of the tax law, which reads as follows: "An individual legally separated from his spouse under a decree of separate maintenance shall not be considered as married." The intent of the tax law is to give the same tax status as single persons to those who obtain legal separations from their spouses, but who, because of religious or personal reasons, do not want a formal divorce. In other words, they are single for tax purposes, but they are still legally married.

WHY IS IT BETTER THAN DIVORCE?

The major advantage of a legal separation is that, unlike a divorce, there is usually no waiting period before one can be granted. To illustrate how it can be used most effectively, assume that John and Mary split up in August for a trial separation. They are not sure whether they want to get a divorce, but they want to maximize their tax savings if they do. Being astute tax planners, John and Mary draw up a written statement that says that John is going to pay $500 per month spousal support for Mary and any children they may have. By putting it in writing, they ensure that these support payments will be deductible as alimony.

At this point, their current tax status is this: Although the payments being made by John qualify as alimony, he and Mary are still legally married for tax purposes. If they file a joint return, the alimony payments are ignored and have no effect on their return. If they file separately, John can deduct the alimony payments and Mary must report the amount as income, but they will have to use the "married filing separately" tax rates, which will cost them more money than if they file a joint return. So far, their written separation agreement has provided no benefit. John and Mary have to be able to file as single persons to save the aforementioned marriage tax. However, unless they go to the Bahamas for a quickie divorce, there is not enough time to get a regular state divorce before year-end. However, they have plenty of time to get a legal separation.

How to Do It

Unfortunately, most attorneys know little about the legal aspects of a Decree of Separate Maintenance, or legal separation, because they have never done one. Usually, if a couple wants a trial split, the attorney will invariably advise them to stay married so they can file a joint return. Except in extremely rare tax circumstances, this advice will cost the couple a lot of money. On the other hand, he will suggest that the couple might as well petition for a divorce if their intent is to separate permanently. The first recommendation is wrong from a tax standpoint, but the second is okay, provided there is enough time to get the divorce before the year-end so that the couple can file singly. If not, a Decree of Separate Maintenance should be obtained. However, both spouses must consent to the terms of the legal separation or it will be just as hard to obtain as a divorce decree.

John and Mary agree that since it is too late in the year to obtain a final divorce decree, they will file for legal separation instead. However, they have not decided on how to split their property, or whether the temporary support is going to change, or for how long it is to be paid. No matter, they can decide all these questions later on, since none of them is a requirement for the decree.

The sample California legal separation decree reproduced on page 266 contains language that gives both spouses and the court the ability to modify the terms of the separation agreement just as they could in case of a divorce.

John, Mary, and their attorneys appear in court and the decree is granted immediately. In the usual case, they simply meet in the judge's chambers, as the appearance is a mere formality and the hearing will last about ten minutes. Getting the decree should not cost much more than $200, unless you have to spend some money for your attorney to learn about legal separation agreements.

Since John and Mary are now single for tax purposes, they can file as single persons for the year, thereby avoiding the "marriage tax." If Mary has any children at home, she can use the head-of-household rates and save even more. The savings in taxes over what they would pay if they filed a joint return are these:

Name, Address and Telephone Number of Attorney (s)

Space Below for Use of Court Clerk Only

Attorney (s) for..

SUPERIOR COURT OF CALIFORNIA, COUNTY OF....................

In re the marriage of

Petitioner:

and

Respondent:

CASE NUMBER

FINAL JUDGMENT (MARRIAGE) OF

LEGAL SEPARATION

(LEGAL SEPARATION/NULLITY/DISSOLUTION)

The court acquired jurisdiction of the respondent on Dec. 27, 19 by:
(Date)

☐ Service of process on that date, respondent not having appeared within the time permitted by law.

☒ Service of process on that date and respondent having appeared.

☐ Respondent on that date having appeared.

The court orders that:

☒ Pursuant to ☒ Civil Code Section 4506(1) or ☐ Civil Code Section 4506(2), a Judgment of Legal Separation and such other orders as are set out below be entered.

~~☐ Pursuant to ☐ Civil Code Section 4400, ☐ Civil Code Section 4401, or ☐ Civil Code Section 4425(--), a Judgment of Nullity and such other orders as are set out below be entered, and that the parties be restored to the status of unmarried persons.~~

~~☐ Pursuant to ☐ Civil Code Section 4506(1) or ☐ Civil Code Section 4506(2), a Final Judgment of Dissolution be entered, and that all of the provisions of the interlocutory judgment, which was entered on................, except as otherwise set out below, be made binding the same as if set forth in full, and that the parties be restored to the status of unmarried persons.~~

Upon request of both parties and pursuant to provisions of Section 4800 of the Civil Code, the Court expressly reserves jurisdiction hereafter to determine and make appropriate orders concerning the custody and support of the minor children of the parties, and the property rights of and spousal support rights as between the parties; Attorney's fees and costs not having been requested none are awarded to or against either party.

Dated December 28, 19

....
Judge of the Superior Court

Form Adopted by Rule 1289 of Judicial Council of California Revised Effective January 1, 1972

FINAL JUDGMENT (MARRIAGE)

California Newspaper Service Bureau, Inc Established 1934

John's Taxable Income	*Savings*
$10,000	$1,235
20,000	2,468
30,000	3,377
40,000	4,812

To be fair, this tax savings should be split equally between both partners.

By using the divorce laws to lower their taxable income to equal amounts, John and Mary have obtained the maximum benefits from income splitting by using the single-return rates for him and the head-of-household rates for her.

After the Decree Is Granted

Once the Decree of Separate Maintenance has been granted, all earnings and separately purchased property will remain separate, and either party may have it converted to a petition for divorce at any time. On the other hand, if John and Mary decide they want to go back to filing jointly, they can petition the court to vacate (terminate) their legal separation.

You may be wondering why all married couples don't get a Decree of Separate Maintenance. Well, probably because most married couples don't know that they're paying extra in taxes, and even those who do know are unaware of the advantages of a legal separation. Also, they may feel that this only works when there is an actual physical separation. Well, let's go one step further in the case of John and Mary and assume that a few months after their separation, they decide to move back together in an attempt at reconciliation. Not wishing to pay more income taxes, they leave the legal separation decree in effect. From time to time, they modify their written support agreement so that John pays Mary just enough alimony to equalize their income for tax purposes. They judiciously maintain separate bank accounts so they can support their purchases, deductions, etc. Of course, if they desire, they can purchase their home or other property as joint tenants, just as any other couple can.

Is This Legal?

This is a question that most people ask at this point. Does all this stand up for tax purposes? Technically, yes. The fact that John and Mary may "cohabit" after the decree is granted is of no tax consequence. As is true of "foreign" divorces, until the state declares the decree void, the couple is single for tax purposes.

The major problem in this situation is a legal one. For example, one New York woman sued to have a legal-separation agreement set aside after she and her husband had resumed marital relations for a period of two months. The court disagreed with her, deciding that her husband had no intention of returning to the marriage. As in marriage, a legal separation can be set aside only if both parties agree to it. Those couples who reside in common-law-marriage states may have a harder time keeping their Decree of Separate Maintenance in effect for tax purposes because "cohabitation" probably makes them automatically married again.

Suppose that John and Mary did not physically part in August, but simply obtained a legal separation and prepared a written support agreement. Thus, they have met the requirements for filing as singles, but their state court may balk at granting them a decree. They do not legally intend to separate. To be absolutely safe on this point, you should consult an attorney on how your state may rule on cohabitation with your spouse after obtaining legal separation. For tax-planning purposes only, read the section on what constitutes separation in Chapter 34.

Remember, You Are Not Really Single

One point to keep in mind about the Decree of Separate Maintenance is that while you enjoy single tax rates, you are still legally married. This will cause no problems if you are happily married and have obtained the legal separation for tax purposes only. In the case of an actual separation, however, this could put a cramp in your dating style if you wanted to get serious about another person. Most of the time, however, it will probably serve to bail you out of numerous sticky situations. It's like being on parole—you're out on the street, but not permitted to do much mischief.

How to Send Your Kids to College Free

Unfortunately, the cost of going to college is skyrocketing beyond the means of many families. Bert and Helen are a typical couple caught in this bind. Bert makes $20,000 a year, and Helen, who has just started back to work, earns $10,000. This combined income of $30,000 puts them in the "high" bracket that Congress and the President ignore when they pass out tax-refund goodies. For Bert and Helen, though, $30,000 is not enough. For one thing, the marriage tax takes its toll; they would have much more after-tax income if Bert alone earned the $30,000 and Helen did not work at all. Another problem is their lack of savings. What money they had saved went to pay enormous medical bills last year and for food the year before, when Bert was temporarily without a job. Now their oldest son, Bert, Jr., has finished high school and wants to go on to college, and there is no money to help him. Bert, Jr., applied for a scholarship and was turned down for two reasons: His grades were only above average and his parents' income was too high!

Bert and Helen solved their problem by obtaining a Decree of Separate Maintenance (Legal Separation). Bert agreed to pay Helen alimony under terms and conditions that would give them the biggest reduction in their federal and state income taxes. Bert, Jr., then reapplied for a financial scholarship, listing only his mother's earnings and the support she was receiving from Bert, Sr. With this reduction in income, Bert, Jr., easily qualified for the scholarship, and as an extra bonus, Bert and Helen had extra money left over because they were no longer subject to the marriage tax.

Now, before you follow Bert and Helen's tactics, check on what the scholarship requirements are for your intended college. Some states, for example, require that Bert's income would have to be added to Helen's if they lived together when Bert, Jr., made his application. Also, some states (and some universities) require that alimony, but not child support, be counted in determining family income. In that case, it is obvious that Helen will have to be given custody of the children so that only her income will be counted.

29

WHAT CONSTITUTES DIVORCE FOR TAX PURPOSES?

Things are seldom what they seem,
skim milk masquerades as cream.
—W. S. Gilbert

DIVORCE—in some states, like California, it's called dissolution—is the process by which a marriage is ended. While the means of obtaining a divorce vary from state to state, the result is the same: the dissolving of the marriage. While some states recognize the legality of common-law marriage, no state has adopted procedures to allow common-law divorces. Therefore, once married, you are forever married until such time as you are divorced. The states of being separated, legally separated, or separated with an interlocutory decree are nothing more than variations on the state of being married.

THE IRS DEFINITION OF MARRIAGE

As stated by the Internal Revenue Code: "The determination of whether an individual is married shall be made as of the close of his taxable year; except that if his spouse dies during his taxable year such determination shall be made as of the time of such death; and "an individual legally separated from his spouse under a decree of divorce or of separate maintenance shall not be considered as married."

Married vs. Single Rates

Up until 1969, when the high tax rates on single persons were finally reduced, most couples wanted to file joint tax returns to save money. Therefore, January was the month in which most divorces were granted, to enable couples to file joint returns for the previous year. Unfortunately, all too many people still believe that a couple should do everything possible to file jointly for as long as possible. This is a costly mistake if both couples work (see the marriage tax chart in Chapter 16). The truth of the matter is that a working couple should try to file separately (as single persons) as soon as possible. By proper planning, they can save enough in federal and state income taxes to pay for their lawyers and have enough left over for a nice vacation.

What Divorces Are Valid

For the most part, the IRS takes the approach that whenever a divorce is granted in a particular state or country, that divorce is valid for federal income-tax purposes. For example, if a divorce is granted in Nevada or Mexico, it's valid for federal tax purposes until the state where the couple *legally* resides declares the divorce invalid. Remember, the IRS can't bring a suit to declare the divorce invalid —only one of the spouses can do that. Therefore, the IRS is legally bound to accept the divorce as legal. However, recently the IRS issued a ruling that took the position that if a couple obtained a divorce in the Bahamas for tax purposes and then later remarried in January, such divorce was a sham and would not be recognized. This stance will cause considerable litigation in the future; *all* of the court cases to date have been against the IRS and it is difficult to believe the IRS's position will prevail.

The Tangled Web

Where and how you get your divorce is of crucial importance. The only divorce that you can be sure of is one that both spouses agree to and obtain in the state in which they legally reside. When you get an out-of-state (or out-of-country) divorce, many, many things can go wrong. The following nightmare is an example.

Charles and Elizabeth were married in Pennsylvania in 1945, lived in Connecticut, and separated in 1962, at which time Charles moved to New York and Elizabeth remained in Connecticut. In 1964 Charles obtained a Nevada divorce without Elizabeth's consent. (Remember, they are now legally divorced for tax purposes.) Four years later, Elizabeth obtained a decision from the Supreme Court of New York that she was still Charles's legal wife. Earlier, Charles had married Amy in California, where they lived until Amy's death in 1969. In this case, the primary question was whether Amy was legally Charles's wife for estate-tax purposes. The tax court sided with the IRS and said that because of the New York decree, Elizabeth was still Charles's wife.

Pity poor Charles: Not only is he guilty of bigamy, but since Amy was not his wife, it was illegal for him to file joint returns with her for all those years he thought they were married. This resulted in Charles owing the IRS substantial back taxes and penalties on his tax returns which had not been closed by the Statute of Limitations. Fortunately, the state decided not to charge Charles with bigamy.

Foreign Divorces

Perhaps the best way to explain the current status of foreign divorces is by the following example. Suppose a person goes to Puerto Rico to get a divorce and properly obtains such a divorce under Puerto Rican law. Further, this person returns to the United States, establishes residence in another state, and subsequently remarries. Is the marriage legal? The answer for federal income tax and legal purposes is yes, until one of the states declares the divorce invalid.

One woman obtained a Mexican divorce and subsequently remarried. When her new husband met with an untimely death, she went to the New Jersey courts to overturn her Mexican divorce. The New Jersey Court set aside her divorce and declared that she was still legally married to her first husband. Since he had remarried, he thought this was somewhat unfair. However, after suitable arrangements for spousal support were made, he was able to obtain a valid divorce from his first wife.

You can be reasonably sure that any state court will overturn a foreign divorce (i.e., one obtained outside the United States) upon petition of either party if one of the persons did not consent to the divorce in writing. The courts have generally taken the position that if both husband and wife consent to a "quickie" foreign divorce, then the divorce will be legal and will withstand any subsequent challenge by either party. A word of warning, therefore: Be extremely careful when you obtain a one-sided divorce outside your state of residence. However, if our Bahamian couple discussed earlier had simply not remarried, they would have had the best of tax-planning opportunities. They would be legally divorced for federal and state tax purposes, but their foreign divorce could be set aside at any time by either party.

What About Gay Divorces?

Can there be such a thing as a gay divorce? From a tax standpoint, gay divorces provide the same tax-planning opportunities as do heterosexual divorces. Unfortunately, there is little case law to refer to, to determine how states will react to a legal petition for divorce between persons of the same sex. It will be interesting to see how they handle it.

Taxes and the Gay Divorcee

Now for the tax side. Let's assume that after five years of marriage, John and Jay decide to split and want to make the best deal from a tax standpoint. John realizes that Jay has forgone earnings to care for the house, and he wishes to provide an amount for Jay so he can readjust to the working world. John agrees to pay Jay $500 per month for five years. Do the payments qualify as alimony? That's right, alimony. The real question for gay couples of whether alimony is deductible or not is whether the alimony is paid pursuant to a marital relationship. The tax laws do not specifically define what a marital relationship is other than referring to it in terms of husband and wife, and the law specifically provides that "husband" and "wife" are substitutable for each when reading the Internal Revenue Code. Once a state court grants John and Jay an "uncontested" divorce, the IRS would have a very hard time sustaining an allegation that the payments are not being made pursuant to a marital relationship. Therefore, if the payments meet the same criteria for heterosexual couples, they will be deductible by John and taxable income to Jay.

Suppose that John and Jay decided to live together after the divorce was granted and John continued to make the payments to Jay. Would the payments still qualify as alimony? Yes. There is nothing in the tax law that would deny alimony treatment for payments made pursuant to a divorce decree if a couple decides to live together subsequent to the divorce. In other words, as with heterosexual couples, there is no requirement that John and Jay must live apart after their divorce to have the payments qualify as alimony.

HOW MUCH WILL I HAVE TO PAY– OR HOW MUCH CAN I GET?

Don't count your boobies until they're hatched.
—James Thurber

IT'S IMPOSSIBLE TO COVER all situations in all states. However, all courts agree on one thing. No matter how desperate the wife's needs or how many children there are, they have to leave the husband with enough to live on and enough incentive to continue working. The primary intent in all states is to assure that the wife and children do not become "wards" of the state. If they set the amount too high, they may drive the husband out of the state or country and all would be lost.

Most counties throughout the United States have developed some sort of informal guidelines about how much to award for spousal and child support. As an example, the following chart was set up by one county in California to give lawyers some idea of what sums the court would accept as "equitable" for alimony and child support. The chart is based on what the husband's net monthly income is

County Rules of the Superior Court

Guidelines for Temporary and Permanent Support
Guidelines for Temporary Support Orders

Net Monthly Income	*Wife Alone*	*Wife and One Child*	*Wife and Two Children*	*Wife and Three Children*	*Child Support Only (per child) (The total not to exceed amount in Column 5)*
$400	$100	$100	$100	$100[1]	$50– 75
500	200	200	200	200	75–100
600	250	300	300	300	75–100
700	300	350	375	400	75–100
800	325	400	425	450	100–125
900	375	450	475	500	100–125
1,000	400	500	550	600	100–150
1,200	475	600	650	700	100–150
1,400	550	700	800	850	125–175
1,600	650	800	900	950	125–175
1,800	750	900	1,000	1,050	150–250
2,000	800	1,000	1,000	1,150	150–250
Above 2,000	40%	40% plus $150–200			Court's discretion

[1] As you can see, at the lowest income levels the court awards the same amount of support whether there is one dependent or four.

after all federal and state income taxes.

Although it uses the term "wife" in referring to the supported spouse, California and most states grant alimony to either husband or wife. The court usually gives special consideration for a handicapped spouse or child.

Agreed Support

The usual situation is that the attorneys will show the couple a similar schedule for their county or area and hope that they can avoid having to go to court and get the judge to set the amount. The attorneys usually argue that unless there are special circumstances, the chances of the court varying significantly from the established norms are not high. Unless you really do have special circumstances, agree to the average for your family income scale. You will save a lot of headaches and attorney fees plus an appearance in court. You will want the amount agreed to in writing or ordered by the court so you can deduct the payments as alimony. For more information on this, see the next two chapters.

Court-ordered Temporary Support

If you and your spouse can't agree on the amount, the court will award a temporary amount of spousal and child support until the divorce is granted, which will set permanent support. One word of advice: Once a couple has agreed to an amount or has had the court set temporary support, the court will probably make the temporary-support amount permanent in the final decree. Usually it will vary only if either spouse's income has changed substantially during the divorce period or the couple themselves agree to a new amount.

How Long for Child Support?

The general rule for child support is it must be paid until

the child reaches eighteen years of age (twenty-one in a few states). Usually the wording in the divorce agreement provides child support until the child reaches the age of "majority." This is an interesting concept and one you should keep in mind. In Texas, for example, a woman who is legally married has attained the age of majority (regardless of her biological age) and presumably is not entitled to child-support payments after her marriage.

Alimony

In general, most husbands and wives agree between themselves about the amount and for how long the payment of spousal support will be made. The reason for this is that they have finally realized that in a contested divorce the courts are not even going to listen to them except as a last resort, and only after several months or years have passed. With this in mind, they sit down with each other and their lawyers and begin the tough task of negotiating the amount and the time. The attorneys will try to work things out to the best interests of their clients. Remember, though, that most states are moving quite rapidly toward ending the concept of permanent alimony. The rule seems to be that for marriages under twenty years in length, alimony will be granted for half the length of the marriage. This is usually increased if there are small children involved and the wife has no readily marketable skills. For marriage over that length, alimony for life is rare except in cases of hardships, or where there is a considerable difference in earning capacity.

A Word of Caution About Taxes

If you are the recipient of spousal support, you had better pay attention to the wording used in the divorce decree. The Tax Courts have been quite liberal in deciding that all of the payment constitutes alimony income unless the language is expressly clear that a certain amount is for child support, which is not taxable. To see how clear the language must be, read the section on child support in Chapter 31.

Chances are that you have been involved with the divorce for several months, and you probably haven't been concerned about the tax effects of the support you are receiving. The reason for this is that you are continuing to file a joint income-tax return with your husband. His withholding or tax deposits have gone to cover the taxes due, and you have not had to concern yourself with the problem.

Suppose you are being paid $500 per month spousal and child support, and that this amount has been made permanent by the divorce decree. Assuming you have one child, you are going to owe $432 in federal income taxes on the alimony plus some more for state taxes on your first separate tax return. This will pose quite a hardship if you have become accustomed to living on $500 per month. Without doubt, many women get burned in this situation because of the tax effect of their support payments after the divorce is granted.

Conversely, a shrewd wife can turn the above problem to an advantage. She simply doesn't take any steps to get the divorce over with unless her husband agrees to increase her permanent-support payments by an additional amount necessary to cover her income taxes.

Here's the reason it works. Until she meets someone, or for other personal reasons, she has no incentive for agreeing to any of her husband's divorce terms. She probably has the house, the kids, and his support payments without any tax effect. In addition, he has to plead with her to get her to file a joint income-tax return with him. Until she is good and ready to negotiate to end the thing, you can probably bet that the divorce proceedings will just drag on.

For the husband, this tax rule is the major reason your

spouse is not all that interested in getting the divorce finalized. Of course, if you can get her to agree to a legal separation, you will have effectively removed about 90 percent of her teeth because now you can file using the single rates. For more information on its effect, read Chapter 28.

31

HOW TO SAVE MONEY ON ALIMONY AND CHILD SUPPORT

He that hath wife and children hath given hostages to fortune; for they are impediments to great enterprises, either of virtue or mischief.
—Francis Bacon

ALIMONY, or spousal support, is generally considered to be payments by the primary-income-earning spouse to the other spouse for support, sometimes for life. Others have characterized alimony as the high cost of loving and leaving. Whatever term one uses, the very concept of alimony is going through a considerable change. Most states are now moving toward a system which provides for no lifetime alimony except under certain limited circumstances. The view is that alimony should be only a transitional vehicle, giving the spouse who receives it time in which to readjust and develop a separate life and separate income.

For convenience only, in the following discussion, the person paying alimony will be called the husband, and the terms "alimony" and "spousal support" will be used interchangeably.

Tax Benefits

The major importance of alimony in any divorce proceeding is that it can be adjusted to benefit both parties. If a divorcing husband and wife can sit down and amicably discuss the subject of alimony payments, then they can fiddle with the amounts and the length of the payments until they reach the maximum tax savings. After all, if alimony has to be paid, why not get Uncle Sam to foot as much of the bill as possible? Alimony is deductible to the person paying it and must be reported as income by the person receiving it. Because of this deductibility, the higher-income-earning spouse, with greater after-tax income, can afford to pay his wife substantially more than would be possible in the case of a nondeductible payment.

Alimony has not always been deductible by the husband nor income to the wife. However, in the Revenue Act of 1942, Congress expressed concern that the alimony-paying spouse might not be able to afford both the alimony and the high tax rates. To correct the situation, Congress provided for the taxation of alimony and similar payments made under separate-maintenance agreements.

Lump-sum Payoffs

The ongoing debate about spousal support also concerns how it should be paid: lump sum or periodic payments. There are crucial tax differences between the two methods, so pay attention!

Consider the case of Flo T., a famous singer, who was also the primary-income-earning spouse in a very bad marriage. As they were breaking up, Flo made an offer to her husband, Mario, an unemployed painter, of a lump-sum of $25,000 in order to be relieved of all future payments relating to spousal support. Her reasoning was that she did not want to be bothered with paying alimony for something which was of no future value to her (there were no children involved). However, this was the worst thing she could have done from a tax standpoint. In Flo's tax bracket, she loses the biggest tax advantage of paying support to Mario.

Why? Because she can't deduct it. Lump-sum payoffs are *not deductible.* Therefore, Flo's paying her support in *after-tax* dollars, which means that it's not deductible to her and not taxable as income to Mario. If she must pay alimony (and Mario threatened to go to court to get it), then it should be *termed* alimony or spousal support so she can deduct it on her tax return. Remember, too, that Mario is unable to sell any of his paintings and thus, with no income, can receive up to $2,950 in alimony per year without paying any federal income taxes on it.

Get Every Deduction You Can

Although the concept of paying alimony or spousal support is repugnant to many persons, don't let this feeling cloud what should essentially be a business decision on how to save income taxes. It should be kept in mind that if you can save $10 in income taxes, it is like earning $10 tax-free. Here's another way to look at it: To have $10 in your pocket when you're in a 50 percent tax bracket, you have to earn $20. So don't pass up those tax-saving opportunities just because you don't like to make out a monthly support check.

This kind of alimony planning is available to almost everyone. You don't have to earn astronomical sums of money to take advantage of it.

To illustrate this financial impact, let's assume that you earn $30,000 per year, which puts you in the 50 percent tax bracket for federal and state income taxes. Now you're getting a divorce and you agree to pay your wife $500 per month for five years (that's $30,000) in lieu of a lump-sum payment of $25,000. Over the five years, you will save $15,000 in income taxes and will have $10,000 left over after you pay your wife the extra $5,000 for making the payments over five years instead of all at once. On the other hand, your wife (assuming no other income) will have paid $3,140 in income taxes and will still have $1,860 left after that. This arrangement will save you both $11,860.

Since the amount of savings fluctuates greatly, it is important that both of you put personal animosity aside and work out the best deal possible. A word of advice: When you are getting a divorce, obtain an alimony schedule from your attorney (or use the guide in Chapter 32) on how much spousal support will have to be paid and start adjusting the support amounts to obtain the most tax savings.

To compute the savings possible, grab a tax-rate schedule and find your tax due by deducting, and not deducting, the alimony.

Income	*His*	*Hers*
1. Enter salaries, interest, etc.	$	$
2. Alimony to be paid	( )	+
3. Exemptions	(750)	(750)
4. Standard deduction (use itemized if you prefer or 16% of line 1 @ $750 each	( )	( )
5. Children's exemptions @ 750 each	( )	( )
6. Taxable income (add or subtract where applicable lines 1 through 5)	$	$
Tax from table	$	$

In finding the tax due from the tables, use single rates for him and head-of-household rates for her if she has custody of any children (or vice versa).

By moving the amounts paid for spousal support between husband and wife, it's possible to see the tax cost of shifting the payments. The maximum savings occur when the taxable incomes are identical, but it is not always possible to achieve this because rarely will the support payments be that high.

THE TAX DEFINITION OF ALIMONY

The Internal Revenue Code defines alimony as payments made under a decree of divorce or separate maintenance, and which are received after such decree is executed. The payments must be for the discharge of a legal obligation by the paying spouse because of a marital or family relationship. They are to be considered as income by the receiving spouse and as a deduction by the paying spouse. The term "alimony" has also been extended to include payments made under written separation agreements voluntarily entered into by a couple.[1] Payments received as spousal support are taxable income to the recipient under the following three categories.

1. Decree of Divorce or Separate Maintenance. If a wife is divorced or legally separated from her husband under a decree of divorce or separate maintenance, the wife's gross income includes payments received after such decree was granted or under a written instrument incidental to such divorce or separation.
2. Written Separation Agreements. If a wife is separated from her husband and there is a written separation agreement, the wife's income includes amounts received after such agreement is executed, provided

[1] See the chapter on Written Separation Agreements for more details.

the husband and wife do not file a joint income-tax return.

3. Decree for Support. If a wife is separated from her husband, her income includes payments received by her from her husband under a court order requiring the husband to make the payments for support, provided the couple does not file a joint income-tax return.

Note: In the latter two instances, the payments qualify as alimony even though a couple is still legally married. The tax-planning opportunities are so important under the Decree of Separate Maintenance and the Written Separation Agreement that they are discussed in detail in separate chapters. Unless a couple fits into category 1, they will have to file as "married filing separately" or file a joint return. The tax rates are so high on marrieds filing separately that they should avoid this if they can.

Payments Made to Your Ex-roommate

When a couple splits after a long period of living together without benefit of marriage, the court sometimes awards support payments. However, such payments do not constitute an alimony-type settlement and are not taxable to the recipient nor deductible by the payer because these payments are not the result of a marital relationship. However, if the court refers to a "family relationship" when setting the support, this would probably qualify the payments as alimony and therefore deductible.

How to Insure Deductibility

The payments must be "periodic." Alimony payments are not taxable to the receiving spouse nor deductible by the paying spouse unless they are periodic. In general, a payment of cash or property in a single lump sum is not taxable or deductible. Payments are periodic in *any* of the following cases:

1. A fixed amount each period for an indefinite time
2. An indefinite amount for a fixed or an indefinite period
3. Installments, when they are stated as a lump-sum amount, if the period of payment specified is more than ten years
4. Installments under a period of ten years, if the payments are subject to a contingency such as death or remarriage, or a change in the economic status of either spouse

There is no requirement that the periodic payments be made at regular intervals. For example, if a spouse has been in arrears and pays the arrears in a lump sum, the lump sum is deductible by the payor in the year paid and is reported as income by the receiving spouse when received. For the long-suffering spouse who suddenly receives such an "in arrears" alimony payment, there is always the device of income-averaging to reduce the income taxes due on such a large payment.

Some of the various tax problems that crop up when alimony is being paid are illustrated in the following examples:

1. Suppose a divorce decree obligates one person to pay another person $300 a month for as long as the other person lives. The payments are for an indefinite period and thus qualifies as alimony payments, deductible by the support-paying person.
2. If a divorce decree obligates one person to pay a certain percentage of his monthly income to his spouse as long as that spouse lives, then the payments qualify under the indefinite-period clause and are deductible as alimony.
3. Should the support be paid in a lump-sum settlement,

it will not qualify as a periodic payment, since it is a definite amount and is not payable over a period of more than ten years. (From a tax standpoint, lump-sum payments are extremely costly.)

4. If a divorce decree obligates a husband to pay $20,000 in spousal support within five years, then such "principal payment" will not qualify as a support payment. This is because the sum is to be paid over a period of less than ten years. However, if the decree states that the $20,000 is to be paid at $150 per month, then the sum is stretched to eleven years and thus all the payments are deductible.
5. If the decree calls for alimony for a period of less then ten years, the payments will qualify as alimony provided they are subject to any contingencies, such as: you are not obligated to pay it in the event of your death, or hers, or if she remarries.

Important Note: Let's assume that you're the wife, and in your divorce proceedings, you were very shrewd and obtained a decree that provided for periodic payments to you for a span of less than ten years and did not mention any contingencies such as your possible remarriage. These payments may nevertheless become taxable to you if your ex-husband goes back to court because of a change in his circumstances or some other reason and has the decree modified in some way. You should always be aware of this possibility. Most states take the position that they can always modify the terms of the divorce decree because of a change in circumstances. When the Tax Court has found this to be true in a particular state, it almost always concludes the payments are *alimony* because they are subject to a contingency.

If you have any doubts, you should know that most courts will go to great length to find that payments are alimony. They change their mind only if the payments are really a division of the couple's property.

Must Some of the Alimony Payment Be Designated "Child Support"?

An august body called the U. S. Supreme Court has ruled that if the spousal support payments do not specifically fix the amount of the child support, then the entire amount of the payment shall be construed to be alimony.

The problem, of course, is that the recipient wants the highest amount set for child support because it is not taxable, and the payor wants the big alimony tax deduction. As noted many times, what they really need to do is work together to minimize taxes and maximize what they both get.

In the above Supreme Court case, the question relating to whether the entire payment was alimony depended on the interpretation of the wording in the divorce decree. The decree said that "in the event that any of the three children of the parties hereto shall marry, become emancipated, or die, then the payments herein specified shall be reduced in a sum equal to one-sixth of the payments which would thereafter otherwise accrue."[2] The IRS did a little calculating and said that since three-sixths of the payments would cease when the children were grown, then half of the payments must be for child support. There does seem to be a certain logic to the IRS's approach. However, the Supreme Court looked at the reason Congress made alimony income to the wife in the first place and noted that Congress said that "the wife, generally being in a lower-income-tax bracket than the husband, could more easily protect her-

---

[2] For you doubting Thomases, read J. Lester (U. S. Supreme Court), 366 U. S. 299.

self in the agreement and in the final analysis received a larger net payment from the husband if he could deduct the gross payment from his income."

The Supreme Court went on to discuss the fact that no matter what you called the payments, once they are made to the wife, she may or may not spend that amount on the children. The agreement must *specifically fix the amount* of support to be allocated for child support. It would appear from the Supreme Court's language that if you have to compute *in any way* the amount which would accrue for child support, then all of the payment will be called alimony.

A Sample Support Agreement

Under the Supreme Court's interpretation, in order to qualify the entire payment as alimony, the following statement in the divorce decree should suffice:

> Pursuant to agreement or order of the court, ______________ (first party) hereby agrees to pay ______________ (second party) the sum of $__________ per month spousal support which will be reduced to $__________ per month at __________ (specified date) until __________ (child one) is 18 years of age at which time the support payments will be reduced to $__________ until __________ (child two) is 18 years of age after which time the support payments will cease. In the event second party remarries, such spousal support payments will be reduced to $__________ monthly until __________ (child one) is 18, and $__________ monthly until __________ (child two) is 18 years of age, at which time the support payments will end.

The reduction of the support payment at the remarriage date signals the end of the time for paying alimony. However, payments made after that date may still qualify as alimony. Read on.

From a legal standpoint, most local courts seem very willing to go along with the above language. Their primary concern is that the wife and children are being supported with adequate funds, and if that support has been increased because the couple has structured their agreement to take maximum advantage of the tax laws, so much the better.

Does the Payment Still Qualify as Alimony After She Remarries?

There is an interesting New Jersey case involving the Links and this question. Their divorce decree provided for no reduction in the spousal-support payment in the event of remarriage. Apparently, what happened was that a provision for deletion of support in the event of remarriage was simply left out of the decree. In this case, the Tax Court ruled that although the payments were being paid to a married person, they still qualified as alimony, because the husband had not yet gone back to his state to petition the court to have the payments reduced on account of the marriage. It is not certain what impact this particular decision will have; it could be limited in the future by the Tax Court or could be reversed altogether.

Most states do not have requirements for spousal support if the wife has remarried. It has always been felt that the remarriage created an automatic termination of support requirements and that the payments made after that were for child support only. However, the Tax Court noted in a New Hampshire case that "under the New Hampshire law, the taxpayer's obligation under the divorce would not terminate because the rights of a child were involved. While the presence of the child may have been the sine qua non of the taxpayer's husband's continuing obligation to pay under the divorce decree, it did not follow that such payments were child support. New Hampshire does not view child support and alimony as separate and distinct provisions unless the decree specifically provides that they be such; a decree is read in its entirety. The fact that the Court could have modified the decree to designate the payments to the taxpayer as being solely for the child was irrelevant."

Wow! After reading that and the earlier Supreme Court decision on what constitutes the difference between spousal and child support, perhaps all fathers should take the position that any child-support payments made after their wife's remarriage will still qualify as alimony. They will save taxes doing this if their child-support payments are greater than the dependency exemption (currently $750) they get for each child. Even if you lose a subsequent battle with the IRS on this, your tax return can always be amended to claim the children as dependents. And note that the sample wording earlier mentioned will probably hold up in court so that child-support payment would qualify as alimony even after remarriage.

Payments Made in Error

Suppose your ex-wife did not immediately inform you that she remarried. Don't despair. Just about all states will make her give the payments back to you if you can catch her. Or you can adjust future payments to make up for your loss. Of course, unless you have a talkative child living with her, it might be difficult to find out about any remarriage if she lives in a distant state.

California has a provision, and a few other states have adopted similar rules, that if your ex-spouse cohabits as husband or wife with someone else, then you are off the hook for alimony payments. It takes more than a one-night stand, however, to qualify. Still, you should be on the alert and keep tabs on where and how your ex-spouse is living.

Set Amounts

Be very careful in agreeing to given or set amounts for alimony.

Here's one reason why: When installments of a stated or determinable lump-sum amount are payable over more than ten years, payments in any year are periodic only to the extent that they don't exceed 10 percent of the principal sum. The excess over 10 percent isn't taxable to the receiving spouse and is not deductible by the payor.

Let's say that Mr. Smith's divorce requires him to pay his wife $100,000 in installments of $15,000 a year for five years, and $5,000 per year for the following five years. In this particular case, Mr. Smith may deduct only $10,000 per year as deductible alimony (10 percent of the principal sum, $100,000). The excess cannot be carried over to another year; it is not taxable to Mrs. Smith, and it is not deductible by Mr. Smith. However, if the installments are subject to any of the contingencies, such as remarriage or death, the 10 percent limit doesn't apply and the full amount is periodic.

These are just some of the kinds of knotty tax problems with which family or divorce lawyers are not usually familiar. Mr. Smith definitely needs a good tax adviser.

Beware of Extras

Don't agree to open-ended support agreements for medical or dental care. It could be that your children will end up visiting the doctor for every ache and pain, no matter how trivial, or getting expensive braces when they don't need them, or lying on a psychiatrist's couch twice a week for all sorts of real and imagined disorders. Open-ended provisions are bad because they are so frequently abused. Don't let this happen to you; it could wind up costing you far more than you ever imagined.

Eternal Vigilance Is the Price of Reasonable Alimony Payments

Don't be naive or wishy-washy when the amount and character of your alimony payment is set. If you are going to be paying the support, try to get the court to set the lowest possible payments, making sure that these payments are clearly termed "alimony."

Conversely, if you're the one receiving the support, try to get the court to set both temporary and final support payments as high as possible. Also, try to get your lawyer to insert some language in the divorce decree that will change the bulk of the payments from alimony to child support. Remember that although you can't count the children as dependents, any money you receive for child support is not taxable to you.

If you are going to receive alimony for less than ten years, play it cagey and see if you can get the following language inserted in your divorce decree. "The parties incidental to the divorce decree do hereby agree that __Mr. X__ shall pay the sum of __$ Y dollars__ per month to __Mrs. Z__ regardless of death, remarriage, or change in circumstances." That way, without a contingency, you do not have to report the alimony as income on your tax return.

Alimony Trusts

Some spouses who are to receive alimony and child support may feel safer having a trust set up to provide for that support. The alimony trust is not considered a useful tax-planning device. Its primary function is to ensure that there are adequate funds to make the support payments.

Generally, support payments made to the wife by the trust are taxable in full to her. In addition, the husband does not get a deduction for the alimony payments made by the trust. In addition, he may be taxed under certain circumstances when he contributes any property to the trust.

Alimony trusts should be considered only by very wealthy people and only after considerable discussion with a tax adviser.

Is There Alimony After Death?

Whether he goes to heaven or not, you can ensure that those support payments will continue in the event of his death. When a deceased spouse's estate is bound to continue periodic payments after death, the estate may deduct those payments for income-tax purposes, and they are income to you.

One of the best ways to ensure after-death payments is via life insurance. Talk to your lawyer, tax adviser, or estate planner about this. If you have children, especially young ones, you owe it to them to make sure the support continues after your ex-spouse is gone.

Life Insurance Policies

When one of the settlement provisions of the divorce contains a stipulation that your ex-husband must maintain a life insurance policy, what are the tax consequences? The premium payments will be considered alimony (income) to you, provided that you yourself own the policy. The ownership of the policy can be determined by whether you have the ability to name any beneficiary so desired. This is how you want it. Otherwise he can change the beneficiary, or the amounts the beneficiaries are to receive, and you won't even know it. The taxes you will have to pay on the small amount of premium which is counted as alimony income will be a good investment for your peace of mind alone. If you make the premium payments yourself, obviously you have already absorbed the income as alimony and the payment has no tax effect.

If your ex-spouse dies, you can elect one of several options to determine how the insurance company pays you the proceeds. The important thing to remember is that no matter how you receive the money, *none* of it will be taxable as alimony income to you.

Alimony and the House

In many cases, the wife will continue to live in the house after the divorce is final and may be concerned about the tax consequences.

Suppose that your ex-husband owns the house after the decree is final and he provides it to you rent-free. His ownership of the house could have come about because it was his separate property to start with, or he might have bought your interest in it at the time of the final decree. However it's done, he cannot deduct the fair rental value as an alimony payment. (Your rent would then be considered income to you.) But if your husband actually pays the rent for you (say, on an apartment), then those payments qualify as alimony.

When a husband is required to make the mortgage payments on the house, the tax treatment of his payments depends upon how the title to the property is held. If the wife owns the house, then the payments qualify as alimony. If the husband and wife continue to hold the property as tenants in common, following separation or divorce, one half of the payment made by the husband would be alimony and he could deduct part of the other half as interest on the mortgage. In the case of joint tenants, usually the husband can treat half of the payment as alimony and deduct the interest expense from the other half.

Keogh Plans and Alimony

Keogh Plans, which are discussed in more detail in Chapter 20, provide that a person may contribute up to 15 percent of earnings from self-employment to an account at a savings-and-loan institution and take a tax deduction for the contribution. The tax law defines earnings from self-employment as income derived by an individual from any trade or business carried on by such individual. However, neither the law nor the regulations provide a definition of what is meant by a trade or business. This is so because no one definition can possibly apply to all situations. The IRS, based on court decisions, has defined a trade or business as "a pursuit carried on for livelihood or for profit."

Now, take the case of Amelia. She concluded that her "pursuit" of her alimony check each month from her former husband, Richard, was a "pursuit carried on for her livelihood," and her "business" was to see that the alimony was paid each month. In addition, Amelia felt that she earned every dime she collected. Since Richard paid her $500 per month ($6,000 per year), she promptly deposited 15 percent or $900 each year in her Keogh Plan at a local savings-and-loan institution and deducted the $900 on her tax return, which saved her $153 in income taxes.

But will Amelia's case stand up if the IRS should examine her? Who can say? People who make $6,000 per year are very rarely audited by the IRS, and this issue has never come up in a court case. Possibly the IRS thinks it might lose its case against her (and it might), and the resultant publicity would start a mad rush to the banks or savings-and-loan associations by everyone receiving alimony to open their own Keogh Plans. The IRS would then be faced with having to ask Congress for a change in the tax law, usually a very unpopular move. Without doubt, ex-wives are discriminated against in too many situations as it is. To deny them the privilege of protecting themselves in their own retirement when their ex-husband's are covered by their own company plans or their own Keoghs is patently unfair.

From a technical standpoint, since the issue has never been challenged by the IRS, or discussed by Congress when they passed the Keogh tax provisions, a person who sets up a Keogh Plan based on alimony received will be doing nothing more than taking an "aggressive" tax position. The worse that could happen in a subsequent IRS exam would be that the taxpayer would have to pay the taxes plus interest on the disallowed deductions.

High-bracket Alimony

For those of you in stratospheric income brackets, you might want to consider the tax approach being taken by Rosie. The tax law provides that there will be no more than a 50 percent maximum tax rate levied on *earned* income versus a maximum 70 percent rate on *all other types* of income. However, this law went into effect in 1971, so it's relatively new and there aren't many court cases to follow. Rosie feels that the alimony she receives qualifies as "earned income," and she intends to fight it to the death.

What are her chances of success? It's hard to say. As with Keogh Plans and alimony, the issue has never been challenged or litigated. Note, however, that the tax-law definition of earned income for Keogh Plans is the same one that's used for the maximum rate. Rosie felt she "earned" her alimony payments just as much as did Amelia above. It's easy to see why Rosie is interested in getting this rate. Suppose she has $50,000 of taxable income, after deductions, all of which is from alimony. She will save $990 in federal taxes alone, which is about 5 percent of her total tax bill. To qualify for this preferential treatment, though, you must have at least $38,000 in taxable income.

ALIMONY—THE HOT POTATO

It's not hard to see why alimony—and the way it is paid—is of tremendous importance to both the payer and the recipient from a tax standpoint. This is one of the reasons why it is often the most emotional aspect of a divorce. Always pay close attention to any discussion that concerns spousal and/or child support. Surely, if more than just a small sum is involved, you both would do well to check with a competent tax accountant or attorney for help in determining the best approach to take in this matter.

32

HOW TO COLLECT—OR AVOID PAYING—ALIMONY AND CHILD SUPPORT

Charity is indeed a noble and beautiful virtue. But charity must be built on justice. It cannot supersede Justice.
—Henry George

UNFORTUNATELY, chapters like this are necessary because so many spouses (especially those raising children) are cheated out of the support payments they deserve, and also because there are still a lot of primary-income-earning villains around who feel they have no obligation to support anyone, not even their children. This latter group is wrong, of course, but it is surprising how many of them think they can get away with it.

On the other hand, some wage earners lose their jobs or pay excessively high support when it's not needed. There should be some relief for them as well.

How to Collect Support

We now have a uniform spousal-support agreement among all states. This means that no matter what state your ex-spouse ran off to, it won't help any more, because any state housing a delinquent alimony payor can collect spousal support from him for you. Before this agreement was enacted, lots of ex-spouses were skipping out to other states to evade the jurisdiction of the primary state. Needless to say, they moved in order to escape paying support.

Unfortunately, the system for collecting back alimony is operating at a snail's pace. The major reason is usually that one of the spouses has moved to another state. In some cases, both have moved. In order to begin the proceedings for collection, the action must be initiated in the primary state with original jurisdiction. This means that if your ex-spouse hasn't paid you, and you have moved out of the state where you got your divorce, you will have to retain an attorney in your former state to sue for you. If your ex-spouse has also moved out of state, your problem is compounded because his or her new state must now receive copies of any delinquency notices, etc., from the first state. All of this legal shuffling takes a lot of time. But still, it's better than having no retrieval system at all.

Before the enactment of the agreement, a lot of lawyers were reluctant to accept a case involving the collection of delinquent alimony unless their client paid a healthy deposit in advance. They knew that the legal problems were time-consuming and the collection doubtful. Now, however, once a delinquent ex-husband is caught, he can be made to pay your attorney fees as well as the back support, which has encouraged many lawyers to accept these cases. If your ex-husband hasn't moved out of the original state, you can nail him quick and easy.

When You Lose Your Job

Take the case of Al, who was very diligent in sending his support payments until he lost his job. For several months he was out of work and slipped several support payments behind. His ex-wife sued for the payments. The court was sympathetic to Al, but it couldn't do anything about the back payments. What Al should have done was immediately sue to have the payments lowered as soon as he lost his job and before he became delinquent. The court lowered his future payments until he got a job, but couldn't do anything about the delinquent payments. Soon Al wound up in jail for contempt of court because he couldn't raise the money to make the back payments. While he was in the pokey, he couldn't find a job. Finally, Al and his ex-wife worked out a deal that would allow him to get out of jail so he could go look for a job. Apparently, his ex-wife realized that she had no hope of getting *any* back payments (or future payments) until he found a new job. She thought that Al had learned his lesson and wouldn't trifle with her rights anymore. Bear in mind that the *only* debt a person can be thrown in jail for in this country is for nonpayment of alimony and child support.

A New Life

Take the case of Jack, who may be a little more clever than Al. Jack, when he got his divorce, simply moved to another state and legally changed his name. Jack and his ex-wife had no children, so he felt he had no reason for any further contact with her and he didn't think she was entitled to the court-ordered alimony. Jack knew about the uniform spousal-support agreement that was signed by the various states, and he knew that they traced the ex-husbands through their social security numbers. Therefore, when he set up his new identity, he simply got a new social security number to give to his employer. A new social security number? That's right. It's not as bizarre as it sounds. People sometimes lose their social security cards and have to reapply. Unless they want the IRS to run their number down with its computers, they simply fill out a

ID: CN: DO: 100

DO NOT WRITE IN THE ABOVE SPACE

APPLICATION FOR A SOCIAL SECURITY NUMBER

See Instructions on Back. Print in Black or Dark Blue Ink or Use Typewriter.

Form Approved OMB No 72-R0571 No social security number may be issued unless this form is completed (26 CFR Part 31 6011(b)-2)

1	Print FULL NAME YOU WILL USE IN WORK OR BUSINESS	(First Name) (Middle Name or Initial—if none, draw line ———) (Last Name)	
2	Print FULL NAME GIVEN YOU AT BIRTH		6 YOUR DATE OF BIRTH (Month) (Day) (Year)
3	PLACE OF BIRTH	(City) (County if known) (State)	7 YOUR PRESENT AGE (Age on last birthday)
4	MOTHER'S FULL NAME AT HER BIRTH (Her maiden name)		8 YOUR SEX MALE ☐ FEMALE ☐
5	FATHER'S FULL NAME (Regardless of whether living or dead)		9 YOUR COLOR OR RACE WHITE ☐ NEGRO ☐ OTHER ☐
10	HAVE YOU EVER BEFORE APPLIED FOR OR HAD A UNITED STATES SOCIAL SECURITY, RAILROAD, OR TAX ACCOUNT NUMBER?	NO ☐ DON'T KNOW ☐ YES ☐ → (If "Yes" Print State in which you applied and Date you applied and Social Security Number if known)	
11	YOUR MAILING ADDRESS	(Number and Street, Apt. No., P.O. Box, or Rural Route) (City) (State) (Zip Code)	
12	TODAY'S DATE	14 NOTICE: Whoever, with intent to falsify his or someone else's true identity, willfully furnishes or causes to be furnished false information in applying for a social security number, is subject to a fine of not more than $1,000 or imprisonment for up to 1 year, or both	
13	TELEPHONE NUMBER	Sign YOUR NAME HERE (Do Not Print)	

DHEW, Social Security Administration
Form SS-5 (5-78)

☐ RESCREEN ☐ ASSIGN ☐ DUP ISSUED

Return completed application to nearest SOCIAL SECURITY ADMINISTRATION OFFICE

new form SS-5 and they will get a new number.

A word of caution, however. Notice that under item 14, Jack might have to ante up a fine or go to jail if he is ever caught. However, the charge is a misdemeanor and is levied only against those who attempt to collect social security payments to which they are not entitled. It is interesting to note that this is a social security form, and unlike most IRS forms, it does not require a signature under the penalties of perjury. Apparently, Jack figured the $1,000 fine was cheap compared to the alimony he was ordered to pay, and the odds of ever having to pay were very slim. Lately, however, the social security types have said they are going to get tougher in issuing new numbers.

Without spending an awful lot of money for private detectives (who still may not find Jack), it looks as if Jack's ex-wife will have to make do on her own. Jack also preserved his old social security card just in case it might come in handy in the future when he wanted to obtain his maximum social security retirement benefits. Actually Jack intends to make up some story about finding his "old social security card and not realizing that the numbers would be different. As a practical matter, if Jack is ten years or more from retirement, he can forget whatever benefits he has from the earlier years because those benefits would affect his retirement checks very little.

What are Jack's chances of success? Who can say? Since there are over 100 million social security numbers out, the chance of running Jack down with a new name and new social security number must be very slim. On the other hand, Jack was prepared to pay any price to keep from having to pay his ex-wife. Perhaps before anyone takes a step like this, he ought to be prepared to do the same.

How to Collect Child Support

Is there any way to avoid paying child support? No, not legally anyhow. If they are *your* children, you should support them. You owe it to them to provide as nice a life for them as you can possibly afford.

But you do not have to pay extremely high child support that would provide luxuries for your children while you exist near the poverty level. First, a practical approach. Many fathers, in the first few months after a separation, shower their offspring with lavish gifts in the hope of ensuring their love. No doubt the father feels guilty because he is subjecting his children to the trauma of a broken home, and he wants to make it up to them. The children, sensing this, often react the same way. They take as much as he will give. Ultimately, the father realizes his mistake and he adjusts his giving accordingly. He should be saving his money, because and probably for the first time, he is giving his children something they have wanted more than gifts: his time. When he takes his children for the day or weekend, they have his undivided attention without any outside interference.

However, be aware of your financial circumstances. If you lose your job or have to take a significant cut in pay, go back to court immediately to see about getting your child-support payments reduced. After all, if you were still married, your children would have to suffer the decreased income with you. There is no reason to shield them from the real world now. People do lose their jobs, and children should learn of the hardships of making a living. Therefore, don't try to shelter your children at all costs when you suffer financial hardship. Be aware, however, if you go back to court frivolously to have your support lowered, the court may take a dim view and increase it. Most judges are very reluctant to lower amounts for child support without strong evidence of a change in financial circumstances.

If you are married to a previously married woman with children, those children are not your responsibility. You have no legal obligations to support them. Should you get divorced, the court cannot order you to pay support for them.

If you adopt your wife's children from a former marriage, you may be in for trouble. Some states take the position that you have assumed the father's legal obligation to support the children. Should you become divorced after the adoption, you may get stuck with child support. The decision to adopt is potentially expensive, and you should discuss the matter very carefully with an attorney before you proceed.

The Parent-Locator System

Another way to find delinquent parents is the Parent-Locator System run by the Department of Health, Education and Welfare. The Parent-Locator System traces delinquents on a nationwide basis by using their social security numbers. If you have custody of the children and you can't get the court-ordered child support from your ex-spouse, contact your county welfare department. They know how to put the Parent-Locator System to work for you.

When the Check Is Always Late

When your child (or spousal) support is chronically slow, see about getting the court to order your ex-spouse's employer to deduct the child support from his paycheck and remit it directly to you. You will find that some courts are sympathetic and will order it done. Usually, a threatening letter, from your attorney to your ex-spouse, that says you are going to ask the court to order his employer to make the deduction will work wonders.

Most husbands don't want the employer involved in any way.

Beating the Rap

A few words to those of you who are negligent in your support payments. Don't try to skip out of the country to avoid paying alimony or child support. Some foreign countries have spousal-support treaty agreements with the United States. Anyway, your ex-spouse can obtain a court order which will levy a lien upon any income and assets you have or will inherit. Therefore, you can never return to the United States or have any property in the United States because your ex-spouse can merely attach it until you decide to fork over the back alimony or child support.

Alimony is a distasteful subject for all involved. However, it is a necessary evil. To make the best of the situation, read and follow the advice in Chapter 31. At least you will get Uncle Sam to help share the burden. To those who will receive it, be open minded. If you work with your ex in planning the support payments, you can wind up with more money as well. This will weigh a lot easier on your conscience and in any further dealings you have with your ex-spouse.

33

EFFECT OF INCOME EARNED AFTER SEPARATION

Money never cometh out of season.
—Thomas Draxe

Community-property Status

INCOME EARNED after separation in most community-property states continues to be community income until the couple's divorce is final. Therefore, it will usually be advisable for the primary-income-earning spouse to compute the tax effect of allocating half of his income to his spouse and filing a separate return using the higher "married filing separately" tax rate. However, only in very rare circumstances will this method save money over filing a joint return. But it's something to remember if she won't sign the joint tax return. Of course, if your divorce is granted before the end of the year, you can't file a joint return, but will file as a single person.

To illustrate the effect, let's assume that Ted and Carol lived in Texas and filed for divorce in January, and the divorce was final in November. Let's assume that Ted earns $18,000 per year and that Carol does not work, but stays at home to care for their two children. Since Texas does not require Ted to pay alimony, only child support, Carol has no income from alimony. When Ted files his return for this year, he allocates half of his income to Carol through *November* and is able to count the children as dependents. Ted will report $9,750 in taxable income, and Carol must report $8,250. Assuming Carol has no itemized deductions and can count only herself as a dependent, she will owe $797 in federal income taxes. If they have two children, Ted will owe $852. Since Ted's employer has been withholding on Ted based upon his $18,000 annual salary, he will have a nice fat refund. Pity poor Carol.

It is somewhat of a travesty that the federal tax laws treat Carol this way, but it is due to the Texas law. Carol, no doubt, probably needed all the support she was receiving from Ted to care for herself and the children. To discover that she owes $797 in federal income taxes for the year the divorce is granted must be shocking. California, recognizing this burden, changed its laws in 1972 to follow the rule of the non-community-property states. That is, the earnings are separate from the date of separation and not from the date the divorce was granted. Remember, though, that Carol will have this problem only in the year the divorce is granted. All payments made after that date are child-support payments and not alimony income.

Separate-property States

If we take the same example and put Ted and Carol in New York, the result is somewhat different. And Ted's earnings are his separate property. He will have to pay alimony to Carol, which she must report as taxable income. Using the New York informal guidelines for his income and the fact he has two children, Ted will pay $700 per month support, of which $400 is for alimony. Ted will report the alimony as a deduction and claim the two kids as dependents. He will owe $1,597 in federal income taxes, or $745 more than if he lived in Texas. Carol will report $4,800 in taxable income and pay taxes of $236, $561 *less* than if she lived in Texas.

In non-community-property states, earnings are generally separate property to begin with, so there is no division or particular legal impact when the couple begins divorce proceedings.

Interim Management of Property

One of the primary areas of contention between husband and wife during the divorce proceedings is how to manage joint property such as their stocks, bonds, rental property, etc. It would be wise for the couple and their attorneys to sit down as soon as possible after the first motions have been filed and divide the property that requires management. Subsequent gains and losses on the property as well as income would then be separate and belong to the individual spouses.

34

WRITTEN SEPARATION AGREEMENTS

Beneath the rule of men entirely great,
the pen is mighter than the sword.
—Edward Bulwer-Lytton

A MARRIED COUPLE does not have to be divorced to have spousal-support payments qualify as alimony. Keep this in mind if you are planning a divorce or legal separation. It will save you a good deal in income taxes. Here's why.

The tax law provides that alimony will be taxable to the recipient only if it is received pursuant to a written agreement or imposed by order of the court. In addition, only payments made after the execution of the written agreement or court order qualify as alimony.

Assume John and Jane separate in January, and John orally agrees to pay $500 per month for spousal and child support. In January, Jane files for the divorce, but because she is already receiving temporary support from John, it is not necessary for the court to award support. If the divorce is granted in September, John will be able to deduct only those payments made after the divorce is granted, i.e., in September. However, if John and Jane had prepared a written agreement regarding the $500 support when they separated, John could deduct the payments from January on.

The written agreement which should suffice for tax purposes is as follows:

Written Separation Agreement

Date ____________

Because we have decided to separate pursuant to a divorce, I, ________________________, hereby agree to pay ________________________, the sum of $____________ per month spousal and child support effective ________________________.

This sample agreement, illustrated, appears deceptively short and simple. The major problem is that neither the tax law nor any applicable state laws define exactly what a written separation agreement is. The IRS regulations merely provide that support payments will be treated as alimony if the husband and wife are separated and living apart and they do not file a joint income-tax return, and the payments are made pursuant to a written separation agreement. The regulations also provide that payments made under a written separation agreement after a divorce has been granted will continue to be taxed as alimony.

If your spouse won't sign this statement when you separate, make no support payments until you are ordered to do so by the court. The reason? The court-ordered payments qualify as alimony, too. Suppose Jane wouldn't sign the written agreement. Since John refused to pay support voluntarily, when Jane sued for the divorce in January she also petitioned the court for temporary support, and the court granted it. No matter when the divorce is finally granted,

John can deduct the payments from January on as alimony.

There are two important things to remember about written support agreements. First, don't be lulled into a false sense of security by the words "temporary support." It often becomes the final amount in the divorce decree, so be certain that you can afford it when it is first set. Second, it is important not to confuse a Written Separation Agreement with a Decree of Separate Maintenance or a legal separation. The latter two are defined very clearly in state laws and have certain legal implications. However, the legal definition of a written separation agreement can only be inferred, although the tax law does provide that the agreement doesn't even have to be enforceable under state law. With this in mind, it seems that almost any language referring to a separation and specifying support payments will qualify under the tax law to make the payments alimony from the date the agreement was executed. But remember, *it must be in writing.*

Texas Wives: Beware of the Coyotes

A word of warning to Texas wives: Don't consent to a written separation agreement! The reason is that this will qualify the temporary-support payments as alimony in Texas. Under the Texas community-property laws, you are already required to report and pay income taxes on half your family income to the date of the divorce, not the date of separation.

To illustrate the effect of this, assume that Jane doesn't work, and that John earns $18,000 through September, the date the divorce was final. Jane will have to report $9,000 of John's earnings as her separate taxable income. If she had also signed a written separation agreement in January to receive $500 per month spousal support, she would also have to report those payments received through September as alimony income. In other words, her taxable income is $13,500, while John's is $4,500. John will make out like a bandit. In addition, unless the terms of the written separation agreement are changed by the Texas divorce decree, the payments will continue to be taxed as alimony to Jane. This is probably desirable in any event because Jane will have much lower income taxes on the alimony than John, and he can afford to pay her more as a result.

John can't use the ploy of not paying support until ordered to do so by the court if Jane won't sign the written separation agreement, because under Texas law, the court can order only child support and this won't fit the tax definition of alimony. Therefore, unless Jane consents, John can't get alimony treatment in Texas for his support payments. But John might be interested to hear the story of a Texas fellow who deducted his temporary-support payments as alimony because he read where the Tax Court, in another state, allowed alimony treatment for temporary-support payments made under an *oral* agreement which was enforceable under state law. Who knows, maybe this is a leak in the dam.

However they do it, John and Jane should definitely work out some arrangement to qualify the payments as alimony, because they can save a bundle in taxes.

What Constitutes Separation?

As noted above, the law provides that when a wife is separated from her husband and there is a written separation agreement, the wife's gross income will include alimony payments received after the agreement is executed and which were made under such agreements, because of a marital or family relationship.

However, the tax law does not define what "separation" between husband and wife means. The marital status of the husband and wife for federal tax purposes is determined as of the last day of the taxable year. If this rule were to carry over to separation and the parties were "separated" at the end of the year, presumably they would qualify under the tax law and the alimony payments for the year would be deductible.

Suppose that John and Jane continue to live together until the divorce is granted in September. They stipulate that they were not "cohabitating" as husband and wife. Could the IRS assert that they do not qualify under the written separation agreement provisions and that the payments through September do not constitute alimony? It's hard to say; this could put the IRS in the dubious position of having to allege that the couple was not having sexual relations. Actually, the IRS would be forced to follow state law in determining whether a couple is separated.[1] Most state laws have decided that in situations in which the couple was not having sexual relations, they were to be treated as being separated. Most southern states use the "bed and board" concept. Therefore, she must be separated from his board as well as his bed to qualify as being separated.

Married and Separated at the Same Time

When two households are maintained, or the husband has a residence elsewhere, there will be no problem in supporting the alimony deductions. However, if a couple obtains a legal separation, there is no requirement that they have to live apart for support payments made under a written separation agreement to qualify as alimony. Therefore, those of you who are very tax-aggressive should con-

---

[1] Subsequent to the original writing of this section, the IRS disallowed the alimony deductions for a couple who continued to live together, and the Tax Court agreed! However, the Tax Court was overturned by the Court of Appeals which said it was all right for a couple to continue to live together.

sider entering into a written separation agreement coupled with a Decree of Separate Maintenance or legal separation. This will give you the ability to equalize your income, pay taxes using the single rates (head of household, if you have any children), still live together, and be legally married. Although these procedures technically qualify under the tax law, you will have to determine if you can be legally separated in your state and still live together.

Payments Made Prior to a Separation Agreement

Suppose, in our earlier example, John and Jane drew up their separation agreement in September. Can they make any payments made during the first part of the year qualify as alimony? No. The tax law provides that only payments made after the written separation agreement is executed qualify as deductions.

After the agreement is signed, however, John can make a lump-sum payment to Jane of alimony for the back months of that year, and the entire amount would be deductible, provided the written separation agreement specified that the payment was made pursuant to an oral agreement.

35

COMMUNITY-PROPERTY AND NON-COMMUNITY-PROPERTY STATES

For a man's house is his castle, et domus sua cuique tutissimum refugium.
—*Sir Edward Coke*

THERE ARE EIGHT primarily community-property states: California, Nevada, New Mexico, Arizona, Idaho, Washington, Louisiana, and Texas. Most of these original community-property states have a French or Spanish background, and it is through those systems of legal jurisprudence that the wife's community interest in the property was based rather than upon the common-law doctrines of the English system.

A couple's rights concerning property in a marriage are fixed by state law. Where the state's highest court has made a determination as to the ownership of the property interest, that decision will control in the federal courts for federal income-tax purposes. (This rule also applies to non-community-property states.)

In the non-community-property states, if a couple has

been married and the husband was the primary wage earner, the wife has certain inchoate (rudimentary) rights to her husband's property. This will be granted to her in the form of a property settlement at the date of divorce. This, in effect, results in a transfer to the wife of a portion of her husband's separate property in a manner similar to what occurs in community-property states. Unfortunately, the tax agents leap upon this transfer in non-community-property states and say that if the assets transferred have a fair market value greater than cost, the husband has a gain for tax purposes. Imagine the husband's plight when he not only gives his spouse the property but has to pay a tax on the transfer.

Property Acquired Before Marriage

In general, both real and personal property acquired before marriage retain the character of separate property in any divorce split. Also, the status of property is determined as of the date of acquisition, and separate property will continue to be separate property throughout all sales and exchanges as long as the transactions and the funds used can be traced. However, the method of treating the income *arising* from separate property varies in different states.

In Texas, earnings on separate property are community income, whereas in California the earnings continue to be separate. The earnings in the non-community-property states attach to the status of the property. However, where the earnings are *commingled,* they will probably lose their character as separate property.

The community-property states that recognize income from separate property as community income are Idaho, Louisiana, and Texas. In other words, income from separate property after marriage is community income. This is known as the "Texas rule." In Idaho the statute provides that if the conveyance of separate property to the wife specifies that the income shall be for her exclusive use and enjoyment, the income from such separate property does not belong to the community.

The "California rule," for Arizona, California, Nevada, New Mexico, and Washington, is that income from separate property remains separate property. It should be emphasized that one of the major problem areas in a divorce is the tracing of a particular piece of property through a marriage.

One word of advice to those couples who have been married and who have resided at one time or another in a community-property state: Any assets accumulated during marriage from community funds during those years will constitute community assets, and the move into a separate non-community-property state generally will not change the character of those assets. This is because states recognize that when a couple enters a particular state, the character of the property that they each own at that time will be decided by the state they resided in when the property was acquired. In other words, if the property was acquired and constituted community property when they moved into a separate-return state, that state will honor the other state's rules relating to accumulation of property (and vice versa).

For those community-property states under the "Texas rule," during the year a divorce occurs the community income will be divided equally between the spouses for the amount of time they were married. In other words, if the divorce was final September 30, half of the community income up to that date would be allocated to each spouse. The income earned after the date of divorce would be separate income. If a spouse files a separate return during the divorce proceedings and reports half of the community income, 100 percent of the community property is liable for the taxes on the income so reported.

Under the "California rule," the individual earnings are separate property from the date of separation.

SOME NOTES ABOUT COMMUNITY-PROPERTY DECISIONS

California has generally supported agreements, whether written or oral, between husband and wife that earnings of the husband or wife are to be treated as their separate property. In the Lee Marvin decision, the California Supreme Court applied this rule in the reverse to a couple who lived together. That is, the court upheld as valid an oral commitment made by Mr. Marvin that all earnings after the date they started living together would be community income. Accordingly, the IRS has ruled that the income earned by either the husband or the wife for personal services pursuant to a valid agreement under California law will be treated as the separate property of the earner and not as community income.

It has generally been ruled that if the husband's business income is earned primarily by personal services, the part attributable to the personal services will be community income. This is true even though the husband owned the business before marriage.

In California, there is a presumption that where separate and community properties are commingled, the whole will be treated as community property in the absence of proof to the contrary.

An interlocutory decree will have no effect upon the division of community income for a particular year. This is because an interlocutory decree is not a final decree of divorce, and the couple is still legally married by state law.

If it is important to you to prove that certain property is separate property in a divorce settlement, it should be noted that the presumption is that the property will be community property unless otherwise proved to the contrary. Therefore, it behooves each individual in a marriage to keep separate records, checks, invoices, etc., for as long as the marriage lasts in order to support the contention that certain property was acquired by separate funds.

Arizona laws follow California's relating to oral or written agreements concerning the ability to specify community income as separate property. The tax court has followed these oral agreements and will abide by those decisions of the Arizona courts.

Louisiana laws state that any stock owned by either party prior to the marriage will always be separate property unless there is an agreement to the contrary. Therefore, any subsequent increase in value will belong to the particular spouse.

Texas laws state that income from separate property becomes community property when received. This is true for gifts as well, unless a contrary intention is expressed by the donor.

Dividends on corporate stock owned separately by one of the spouses in Texas is community income for federal income tax purposes and becomes community property under Texas law. However, this does not apply to a stock dividend.

As in California, a Texas couple may agree to a division of community property. Although it is not stipulated, it seems that this could be made for a particular year, like the year of the divorce.

It's not hard to see why community-property states pose additional problems for a couple trying to work out divorce settlements. Oral agreements to shift the income to one spouse or the other can result in significant tax savings for the year of divorce (or significant litigation as to who said what). Properly used, the agreement can save considerable taxes by equalizing the tax rates between the couple.

36

TAX EFFECT OF SELLING AND SPLITTING YOUR PROPERTY

Stop, Look, and Listen.
—A financial spokesman for the bankrupt Penn Central Railroad

WITHOUT DOUBT, no other area of the tax law is as fraught with danger to a divorcing couple as is the tax law applicable to property settlements.

As a general rule, property divisions between husband and wife caused by a divorce decree result in either a gain or a loss to the transferrer. The nature of the gain or loss will depend upon the character of the property. This also determines whether or not the loss is deductible. For example, the transfer of income-producing securities at a loss would be deductible, unless the property is transferred while the couple is still married. However, a loss on the transfer of a personal residence (your home) would not be deductible under any circumstances. Within reason, provided you aren't splitting a fortune in gold coins or jewels, you can divide your personal property any way you like and not worry about the tax consequences.

Transactions Between Spouses—Non–Community Property States

The tax law that generally applies to transactions between related parties is that any gain is treated as ordinary income and losses are not deductible. This part of the Internal Revenue Code is pretty clear, and it's difficult to sidestep its application. For example, assume that you sell your wife (or your brother) your General Motors stock at a loss of $1,000. The tax rule quoted above denies you the ability to deduct the loss. Suppose you sold the property to your ex-wife? The loss would be deductible. Ex-wives, and couples separated by a legal separation decree, do not fit the category of related persons.

OK, now let's assume that you sold the stock at a $1,000 gain to your wife. This is an exception to the ordinary-gain rule quoted above. The sale of a security such as stocks or bonds will be taxed at capital-gain rates. Therefore, the ordinary-gain rules apply only to the sale of a depreciable asset to a related party.

In a property split, it is immaterial whether the property is transferred in exchange for cash, for other property, or for the release of marital rights. If all or part of the consideration is for a release of marital rights such as for support or inheritance, the gain will be measured by the differences between the basis (original value) of the property for tax purposes and its fair market value. For example, if a husband transfers his separate property to his wife in the divorce, and his tax basis is $1,000 and the fair market value is $3,000, he will realize a taxable gain of $2,000.

In a typical example, suppose that pursuant to a property

settlement, Betty transfers her undivided one-half interest in jointly owned real estate to her husband, Bill. Incidental to that, Betty releases any and all marital rights she may have in respect to her husband's separately owned property. Suppose the real estate is worth $40,000, with a tax basis of $20,000. This makes Betty's one-half interest worth $20,000 with a basis of $10,000. In return for the transfer of the real estate, Bill transfers securities to her worth $50,000 and $30,000 in cash. The securities have a tax basis of $10,000. Under these circumstances, Betty has a gain of $10,000 on the real estate, since she received more than its value in cash and securities. She has no gain on the release of her marital rights in Bill's separate property. Bill has a gain of $40,000 on the transfer of securities. His basis in the real estate, after the transfer, is $30,000, which is the $20,000 market value of the half interest acquired from Betty plus his original $10,000. Betty's basis for the securities received is their fair market value of $50,000. Here's how their situation looks:

	His	*Hers*
Securities @ FMV	($50,000)	+$50,000
Cash	(30,000)	+ 30,000
Real estate	+20,000	(20,000)
Effect before taxes	($60,000)	$60,000
Taxable gain	$40,000	$10,000

The IRS ought to be very happy with this example. Both Bill and Betty have gains. If the transfer occurs before their divorce is final, the gain on the real estate is taxed as *ordinary* income. Remember capital-gains tax rates are about half those of ordinary gains, such as salary income. Bill and Betty, though, being astute tax planners, delay the exchange above until after their divorce is final. Then, along comes the IRS and asserts that their gains were ordinary because the intent to exchange was formulated during the time they were married, and the Tax Court agrees with the IRS! (With luck, Bill and Betty will win their appeal.)

What Should Be Done?

All right, what should they have done? Note the effect of the cash given to Betty in the exchange. She got $30,000 in cash but her gain recognized for tax purposes is the $10,000 gain on the transfer of the real estate. Therefore, if Bill had given her $50,000 more cash instead of the securities, her gain would still be only $10,000, but Bill would have avoided the $40,000 gain on the transfer. Betty now has $80,000 in cash and $10,000 in taxable income. Bill would be wise to do it this way even if he has to borrow the additional cash to pay Betty. He can use as collateral the stock he would have transferred. Even if he decides to sell the stock in order to obtain the necessary cash, a sale to an outsider would surely generate capital gains, while a direct transfer to Betty may not.

Can Betty avoid the $10,000 gain? Probably not, but she can postpone it. Under the facts given, the IRS would probably say the $10,000 gain is ordinary. If Bill and Betty decide to own the property jointly for some time after the divorce, her subsequent sale to Bill would probably cause the gain to be taxed at the more favorable capital-gains rates. Of course, Bill and Betty might feel they would want to take an even more aggressive stance with the IRS and state in their divorce decree that Betty agrees the real estate was Bill's separate property. Therefore, she would have no gain at all to report, since she didn't own an interest in it, and she couldn't be taxed on its transfer to Bill for release of her marital rights. If the divorce decree contains this kind of language, the IRS will usually go along with the terms of the decree for tax purposes.

If Betty's name had been on the title to the property,

however, she might have a harder time saying it was Bill's separate property, unless they had an oral agreement that it was Bill's, and that only for convenience or personal reasons did they take title to the property together. Perhaps an easier way would be to show that Betty did not have sufficient separate income to purchase the property, or that her funds were used for other purposes. Whichever way she chooses, the IRS would have a difficult time proving otherwise. The IRS doesn't really lose its tax money, because after all of this, Bill has a lower tax basis and he will have to pay additional taxes should he decide to sell. However, this may not be as important to Bill if he really wants the divorce over with or intends to hold the property for a long time.

As can be seen from the above example, when it is necessary to split the property incidental to a divorce, cash is the safest way to "purchase" the other's interest. Additionally, it is highly advantageous to provide in the divorce decree that the property retained is, and was, separate property.

Community-property States

In community-property states, an exception to the above tax law has developed when the parties simply make an equal division of community property, even where one spouse receives all the assets and the other receives only cash. In addition, there is no requirement for an actual division of each item of community property. That is, he can take some items and she can take some. If the property being divided is more or less equal in value, then no gain or loss will be recognized by either spouse. The tax basis of the property in the hands of the individuals will carry over and be the tax basis of such property to whichever spouse winds up with the property.

A similar rule has been applied to a division of jointly acquired property under Oklahoma law and property held by husband and wife as tenants by the entirety under Florida law. However, both of these states are not community-property states.

A word of caution: Even in community-property states, unequal division of jointly owned property may be viewed as a taxable sale or exchange. For example, if Bill and Betty (from our previous example) had lived in a community-property state, the tax effort would have been the same because their division of property was not equal, and Bill was transferring his separate property to Betty.

How to Handle the Sale of the House

Unlike other property in a divorce settlement, any gain on the sale of the house receives special tax treatment. Pay particular attention to the following discussion. Probably no other area of the tax law can be so dangerous to a couple getting a divorce as what happens when they sell the house.

Suppose that a couple sells their house to an outsider and they realize a gain on the sale. Here are the general tax rules applicable to all persons: In order to defer the recognition of the gain, they must replace the old residence with a new residence within a period of eighteen months before or after the sale, and the new residence must cost at least as much as the old one. If the couple is getting a divorce, they each must purchase a new residence equal to or greater in value to half of the selling price of the old residence in order to avoid paying taxes on the gain on the sale of the old house. For example, assume Tom and Mary purchased their house for $20,000 and sold it for $40,000 in the divorce. Each must purchase a home costing $20,000 for the recognition of gain on the sale of the old residence to be deferred.

The major problem for divorcing couples is the tax law regarding the replacement period. Suppose, in our earlier example, that Tom had moved out of the house six months ago and rented an apartment, and the house is now sold, or given to Mary in the divorce. Has he effectively been denied the reinvestment privilege, and must he report the gain on the sale of the house? Yes, probably.

The tax law specifies that in order to defer paying taxes on the gain of a house, certain rules must be followed. One of these is that the residence sold must be a couple's (or a person's) principal residence. Another is that the same couple who sold the house must be the same couple who purchases a new principal residence(s) within the required time. In our example, Tom has effectively converted his principal place of residence to his apartment. Once he has done this, he cannot thereafter purchase a new home and expect to escape paying taxes on the sale of the old residence.

If the IRS should assert a tax on Tom in this case, he should maintain that the apartment was not his principal place of residence, that he intended to move back to his house, and that he left a lot of his things there and was looking for a new place to buy. Tom should also prepare to borrow the money to pay the tax deficiency, because it will be hard for him to prevail with his argument, particularly if the divorce has been granted and he did not in fact move back.

What Tom should have done was to buy a place as soon as possible after moving out. When a couple (or a person) sells a house in a city and moves to another city, the tax law provides a "reasonable" time to find a new home in the new location. In other words, they could rent a room in a motel or a temporary apartment, while they are looking for a place to buy, but neither place must become their "residence." The test of this is a subjective one, and the IRS will look at all the facts and circumstances. In Tom's case, he will try to prove that he was talking to real estate agents, making applications for loans, using a post-office box for his mail, and anything else he can think of to show that he was living in the apartment only temporarily while he was buying a place.

So, what if Tom loses? What will he owe?

That depends.

Assume that Tom earns $15,000 a year after his alimony payments to Mary. He will owe an additional capital-gains tax of $2,000 on his $10,000 gain on the sale of the house.

Note, too, that if Tom signs the house over to Mary in the divorce, that qualifies as a sale and he will have to pay taxes on the difference between his part of the cost and the fair market value of the house. Tom can get an appraisal on the house to determine its value, or he might be able to use the property he received in lieu of his interest in the house. For example, if he received stocks and cash worth $20,000 for his half of the house, they would mean the house was worth $40,000.

Another problem to watch for is that the IRS may take the position that the transfer of the house to Mary generated *ordinary* gain to Tom because the house was a depreciable asset. Although there is only one Tax Court case on point, the IRS is technically right. But take heart; the IRS has been very lax about asserting taxes on persons involved in a divorce when they sell their houses at a gain. After all, perhaps IRS agents also occasionally get divorced.

Here is another problem to watch for: Suppose you are single and you plan to get married and buy a new home. If you sell your present residence and take title jointly with your new spouse in the new home, you probably will have to pay taxes on the gain on the sale of your old residence. As noted earlier, the same person(s) who sells the old home must be the same person(s) who buys the new home(s) in order to avoid paying taxes on the gain on the sale of the old house.

Unfortunately, the law relating to the deferral of paying

taxes on the gain on the sale of a house was written forty years ago when the living situations of most people were considerably different from what they are today. However, this is one of the bad parts of the tax law that affects persons getting a divorce, and this won't be changed until Congress decides to do so. Without doubt, paying taxes on the "sale" of a house without the ability to reinvest in a new residence because he moved to an apartment is a very terrible burden to inflict on a husband during a divorce. It is similar to the married-filing-separately penalty problem, in that both of these "penalties" generally apply only to the husband, because the wife usually stays in the house until it's sold and her custody of the dependent children allows her to avoid the married-filing-separately problem. What Congress has done is to encourage wayward husbands to stay at home and not seek divorces, by punishing them alone with heavy tax penalties. However, if the wife moves out and leaves her husband with the house and children, the same harsh rules apply to her.

One Tax Court judge said: "This case epitomizes the difficulties in which taxpayers often find themselves when a marital relationship turns sour and one or the other of the parties thereto finds himself or herself caught in the web of tax consequences flowing from the more equable period of such relationship or the rules applicable during the unraveling period. More often than not, the trial of the tax case which ensues reflects the rancor and antagonisms that are inevitably involved. Although it is not always easy to do so, the court must avoid the not unnatural human instincts to look behind the tax facts and to allow its approach to decision to be influenced by its conception as to who is to blame for the marital discord. We have steadfastly adhered to the requisite judicial neutrality in this regard as far as these cases are concerned." And another judge wrote: "We sympathize with the taxpayer's dilemma in these years before he obtained a final divorce, but many taxpayers suffer from the web of tax consequences which endure throughout the unraveling of an unsuccessful marriage."

It is clear the courts are sympathetic, but Congress must change the law that taxes people differently because of their mutual status before we can say that everyone is treated fairly by the IRS.

37

HOW TO FILE YOUR TAX RETURNS AFTER SEPARATION AND DIVORCE

Robin: On Tuesday I made a false income tax return.
All: Ha! Ha!
1st Ghost: That's nothing.
2nd Ghost: Nothing at all.
3rd Ghost: Everybody does that.
4th Ghost: It's expected of you.

—*W. S. Gilbert*

Filing a Tax Return While Separated

SEPARATION, by itself, has no effect upon your marital status for federal income-tax purposes. However, some states (like California) do not allow you to file a joint return if your estranged spouse resides outside the state.

When to File the Last Joint Return

Marital status is determined as of the end of each December 31. If a couple is divorced at any time during the year, they are considered as being divorced and single for the entire year. Conversely, when a couple is married on the last day of the year, they are considered to be married for the *entire* year and may file a joint return. However, since it is possible to be divorced during the year from one person and married to another person before the end of the year, you can still file a joint return, but in this case with your new spouse, not your old.

Points to Remember

Once a divorce is decided upon, you want to get into single status as quickly as possible so as to avoid the "marriage tax." Although the marriage tax is usually defined as affecting primarily families where both spouses work, it will cost you in a divorce situation even if only one of you works, because through the shifting of income via alimony, you can save a bundle.

Problems with Joint Returns After Separation

A lot of divorce actions take more than one year, in which case you will be faced with having to file a tax return during the proceedings. About 90 percent of the time you should file a joint return, meaning that both you and your spouse will have to get together with your receipts, medical bills, and so on. Obviously, this contact can lead to all sorts of problems. For example, one wife, after she got the completed return from her husband to sign, turned the return over to her lawyer. He began to question various tax deductions and positions taken on the return. Unfortunately, he took too much time and the deadline for filing passed. The husband thought that his wife had signed the return and sent it in. He was somewhat surprised at the subsequent penalties he had to pay for late filing. Another husband thought he had it made, however. On the pretext that he and his wife were at the deadline for filing and that the accountant would have to send the forms in at midnight, this husband got his wife to sign a blank form. He copied the blank page, filled in the tax-return numbers he wanted her to see, and sent it to her. She, not believing her copy of the return to be real, sent for a copy from the IRS. Alas, the battle rages on.

Only legally married couples can file a joint return. Therefore, if you have obtained a "quickie" divorce in the Bahamas, you are single for federal tax purposes. If your spouse then goes into court and gets the quickie divorce overturned, you are back to being married for federal tax purposes. This makes things rather complicated if you have already filed a tax return as a single person. However, one of the nice things about the tax law if this happens to you is that if the IRS comes along later and disputes your return, you can go back and file a joint return with your wife (if she agrees). The rule doesn't work the other way—if you once file a joint return, you cannot then go back and file separate returns.

Interlocutory Decrees

An Interlocutory Decree does not make you divorced. As long as the *final* decree has not been entered, you can file a joint federal income-tax return.

A Decree of Separate Maintenance, or a legal separation as it is called in most states, makes you single for federal tax purposes. These can be quite useful when properly used by a divorcing couple.

Married Filing Separately

Unless you have obtained a Decree of Separate Maintenance, you will want to file a joint return until your divorce is final. The reason for this is that you will have to use the rates for marrieds filing separately, which are about 20 percent higher than single rates.

The married-filing-separately rates almost never result

in any benefits. Their primary function is a sort of penalty tax for the errant spouse. The penalty ranges from zero at very-low-income levels to 24 percent at $25,000 of taxable income, and 1 percent at amounts of $100,000 or more. It is obvious the rate hits hardest where it would affect the most people. For those with a very high income, the more favorable maximum rate (50 percent) on earned income cannot be used to figure the tax.

Why would anyone use this tax rate? You wouldn't unless your spouse won't sign the joint return. If you run across this problem, plan to beg a lot.

Take the case of Al, who lives in Illinois. Al makes $25,000 per year, and Ann, his wife, takes care of their one child at home. After they separated, Al agreed orally to send Ann $800 per month (their divorce petition was silent on the amount of support). Later, Ann decided that she wanted more money, a cash settlement, and the house, but Al balked. When he refused to give in, Ann said she would not sign his dirty old tax return. This forced Al to file, using the married-filing-separately rates. In other words, he paid $7,030 total taxes, or $1,864 more, because Ann wouldn't sign the return. Ann had a potent bargaining force and she knew it.

What Al should have done to solve the problem was *not* to have paid Ann anything unless she signed a written separation agreement or until he was ordered to do so by the court. For tax purposes, this changes the $800 per month to alimony, which Al can deduct. Even though he still has to use the married-filing-separately rates, he will owe no more in taxes. Ann, on the other hand, now has an additional $9,600 taxable income and will have to file her *own* tax return and pay the tax. Just by smart tax planning, Al could have changed the clout in favor of himself. Of course, Ann may go back to court and plead she was misled by Al and request more money for taxes, but the court may not be very sympathetic when it finds out she (at first) refused to sign the joint return.

Plead Temporary Insanity on Any Forgery Raps

When you don't want to do any of the above, you might do what one fellow did. He just signed his wife's name to the return, used the joint return rates, and sent it in. The IRS has no choice; it must accept the return as filed. Only the wife has any standing in court to sue her husband for forgery. It is puzzling that when these cases have come up, the IRS has not pursued the issue of signing the return under the penalties of perjury. However, the courts only look to see if the wife filed a separate return, or would have signed the joint return had she been properly informed. By the time the IRS gets around to examining these returns and questioning their intent, most divorces are final and most ex-wives don't want any more hassle, so they invariably say, "Yes, the joint return was okay." Zap goes the IRS's case.

Always, always remember this cardinal rule: You both must work together to save the maximum in income taxes—otherwise Uncle Sam comes out the winner in any marital dispute.

Filing After the Divorce

As was noted earlier, if you are divorced on December 31, you are considered divorced for the entire year. This means that all your earnings are yours and that you file a separate tax return, using the single rates. If you have custody of a child, you may use the head-of-household rates. However, there are some problems that arise when splitting the taxable income in the year the divorce is granted, particularly in Texas. For more information, you should read Chapter 33.

Qualifying for Head-of-Household Status

An individual who qualifies as a head of household is taxed at rates that are halfway between those applicable to joint returns and those for single persons. To qualify as a head of household, a person must be unmarried at the end of the year and maintain a home for himself with at least one child. It is not necessary that the child (or certain other dependents) can be counted as a dependency deduction in order to qualify the custodial parent as the head of household.

Dependency Exemptions After Divorce

The general rules relating to dependency exemptions are these: When the support-paying ex-parent contributes at least $600 toward the support of a child, and the divorce decree provides that he is to receive the dependency exemption, he gets the exemption regardless of the amount of support the custodial parent provides.

There is usually trouble and confusion when the divorce decree does not mention which parent gets the dependency exemption. If the parent paying support provides $1,200 or more in child support per child and the parent who has custody of the children cannot clearly establish that he or she provided the greater amount of support, then the parent paying $1,200 or more is entitled to claim the dependency exemption.

Note: Remember that the parent with custody has an extremely difficult time in proving the amount of support spent for the children. It is easier for the noncustodial parent, simply because all his payments are for child support. For a parent with custody to be able to claim the dependency exemptions, each amount specifically expended for food, clothing, shelter, etc. per child must be proved and the amount must be greater than such amounts contributed by the ex-spouse paying support.

For example, assume that the amount expended for a child was $2,200 and that the noncustodial parent contributed $1,200. He gets the exemption regardless of whether the $1,200 was directly spent on the child's support or not. Remember, when the noncustodial parent pays at least $1,200 per year in support, the custodial parent can pretty well forget about getting the dependency exemption.

How to Report Alimony on Your Form 1040

The Tax Return Act of 1976 allows the payer of alimony to deduct the payments even if he uses the standard deduction. For those in the lower-income brackets, this provides a welcome tax break. On the other hand, if you are the one receiving alimony, include those amounts as income on line 12 of Form 1040.

Subsequent Examinations of Old Joint Returns by the IRS

One of the areas to be particularly concerned about is this one. What does happen if one of your prior joint tax returns is examined and the IRS asserts a deficiency? Well, for starters, the IRS can attach the assets or income of either spouse, after the divorce, to settle this deficiency. If you are the spouse who does not have control or adequate knowledge of what's in the tax return, have your attorney put a clause in the divorce agreement to relieve you of any responsibility for tax deficiencies. Although this may not stop the IRS from attaching your paycheck, at least you can get it back from your former spouse if he has anything left.

38

THE SAFEST TAX SHELTER— U. S. SAVINGS BONDS

Merrill Lynch is bullish on America
—from a recent advertisement

DON'T LAUGH—in certain circumstances U. S. Savings Bonds, Series E, can save you a bundle. Here's how one person decided to handle a particular monetary problem.

Mimi and Rudy were about to get a divorce. Before the papers were filed, Mimi's old aunt sent her a birthday gift of $1,000 cash, which Mimi wanted to salt away without telling Rudy.

This is not as easy as you might at first think. For example, if Mimi hides it in a sock or in her car, there is a good chance that Rudy (a very distrustful character to begin with) will find it anyway. And any husband or wife under such circumstances just might well immediately go through his or her partner's belongings, looking for just such a stash.

Mimi can't really put it in a safety deposit box, either, even if she got a new one under her maiden name. Why?

Well, the bank will most likely want her address and will probably send her a note of thanks for opening the account. Can you imagine what Rudy would think if he were the first one to open the mail? Now, she could pay for the box in cash and use a false address, but this costs her a tax deduction, and more important, any sharp lawyer will just ask all the banks in the area if they have an account for her if he suspects any hidden assets.

If Mimi finds a place to bury her $1,000, she will always wonder if she can remember exactly where it is, or if the rats have chewed it up. And if the rats don't get it, inflation will.

What now? Well, perhaps Mimi could leave her stash with a friend. This could be foolish; her best friend may be having an affair with Rudy.

Mimi can't invest the money in the stock market or a savings-and-loan institution, because any dividends or interest have to be reported to the IRS, and Rudy's attorney can get copies of any tax returns.

> *Very important note:* Don't mess with the IRS while you are getting a divorce; it's not worth it.

Fortunately for Mimi, the U. S. Government, in its wisdom and generosity, *has* provided the perfect vehicle for keeping money safe and secret. Uncle Sam will even pay interest on it! Mimi simply took her aunt's gift down to the bank and purchased U. S. Savings Bonds, Series E. The interest earned on Series E bonds is not reported for income-tax purposes until she cashes them in (by that time she'll be single). Mimi doesn't need Rudy's permission to purchase them, only cash. The bank asked for her name, social security number, address, and who she wanted to be the beneficiary or co-owner (she chose her children equally). Mimi may cash the bonds in at any time in the future by herself. And if she doesn't trust anyone to hold the bonds for her, she can just memorize the serial numbers in case she loses the bonds.

Even if the bonds are somehow discovered, there's a good chance that Rudy can't get half of them, since Mimi made her children co-owners of the bonds. It's very possible that she may be able to argue successfully that the savings bonds are not her assets and need not be listed in the financial declaration of the divorce pleading. If Mimi wants to maximize this opportunity, she should list her children as the owners of the bonds, with herself as the "or" person. In addition, she should obtain social security numbers for her children and file tax returns for them with the following statement: "Taxpayer hereby elects to report the interest earned on the U. S. Savings Bonds, Series E, currently." This statement proves the bonds belong to her children. Remember, however, being the "or" owner, Mimi can cash them in herself without any signature or agreement from the children. The tax effect of the election statement merely means that the accumulating interest is taxable each year to her children. However, they will owe no tax on it unless the interest earned exceeds $2,200 per year, and will not even have to file a tax return again if the yearly earnings are less than $750. There will be no tax due on the accumulated interest when the bonds are subsequently cashed in by the children.

Buy Bonds Now!

Series E bonds can be bought for as little as $18.75 or as much as $10,000. The nice thing about them is that they currently yield 6¼ percent interest when held to maturity (seven years) and 5½ percent thereafter. If you own them individually, you can defer paying taxes on the interest until you cash them in. This means that if you are going to save for a period of ten years, and you expect your income to be significantly lower when you cash them in or retire, you will probably make more money investing in U. S. Savings Bonds than in a savings-and-loan account. The reason for this is that you have to pay taxes currently on the interest you earn on your savings account but not on any Series E bonds. It's definitely an investment worth your serious consideration.

39

THE DIVORCE CHECKLISTS

Be Prepared.
—Scouts of America

THESE CHECKLISTS are intended primarily to help you remember things during your divorce. You may think some of the suggestions are rather harsh and unfair to your spouse, and perhaps they are. After you have obtained your divorce, and if you still feel the same way, send your ex-spouse a check in sufficient size to make you happy. If your divorce is one of those made in heaven, great. If not, at least you will have protected yourself and not have burned all your bridges behind you.

In the following checklist, tick off each step as you come to it. *Don't skip any steps.*

When Your Divorce Is Still in the Future

1. Squirrel away some pocket money. You'll need it. The more time you take between your decision to get the divorce and the time you tell your spouse, the

better. This will give you time to tap different sources without raising suspicions. Remember that at some point in the proceedings, you will probably be asked (under penalties of perjury) to list all your assets. (See Chapter 26 for money-squirreling-away hints.)

2. Remove your personal things:
   a. Tax records. Take copies of all your old tax returns, expense vouchers, support for deductions, cost basis of stocks you've acquired, etc., and put them in a safe place. (One wife threw out her husband's support for his travel deductions and he had to pay taxes on the disallowed deductions. The court also threw out his argument that the loss of the documentation was a casualty loss.)
   b. Personal letters, books, pictures, etc., in some cases you will have to remove these items slowly so as not to raise suspicious until you are ready to move.
   c. Photo albums. These are not replaceable, and the chances are that when you want to see pictures of your children when they were little, you will not be able to unless you take action now. Alternatively, consider taking the negatives if you saved them.
   d. Sporting equipment, various household items, etc. Don't take any chances. If you don't take these now, you probably won't get them at all.
3. Get your financial investments in order. During the time the divorce proceedings are in effect, you may not be able to sell any stocks or bonds unless your spouse (and the attorney) agrees. This may cost you a fortune by not being able to sell in a declining market, or to use your margin account to purchase if you suspect a rise. Indeed, you may not be able to even sell or exercise a warrant before it expires. Consider reducing your account to cash or investing in long-term convertible securities. The latter ought to give

you some participation in a rising market and protection downside. Discuss this particular issue with your lawyer and heed his advice if it is a problem in your state.

4. Job benefits. If you are entitled to a bonus or stock option, you might consider asking your employer to delay these until after your divorce is final. It is more difficult for your ex-spouse to participate in these then. If you are the nonworking spouse, get out and look for a job now. This will give you an idea of what your skills are worth. If you're going to have a résumé done, be sure to have it finished before the proceedings start. However, before you take any job, ask your attorney what the consequences will be. A new job could result in lower support payments.
5. Consider selling the house. It's much easier to sell a house when both spouses are living together. Who has not heard a real estate agent talk about a couple having to sell because they are getting a divorce and must accept any offer? Face it now, the chances are good that you will have to sell the house anyway. Besides, it is much easier to get all the community bills paid if there is cash available from selling the house. Convincing your spouse to sell before the divorce will take some acting, though.

As It Gets Closer

6. Select an attorney. Read the section on attorneys before you choose one. See him before you do anything else. Have him prepare the divorce papers. Make sure you have a certain measure of control over the suit which allows you to make motions as a plaintiff and not as a defendent. Plaintiffs have a much easier time requesting speedy trials, for example.

7. Select an apartment. If you are the male, prepare to move. Chances are that she will get the house or it will be sold. It's best to find a place while you have the time to look. It's very difficult to sign leases when you are carrying your suitcases and have no place to stay.
8. Bank accounts. Close the accounts and withdraw all the money. For those items which must be paid, pay them from your own separate account. Also clean out the safety deposit box, transferring the items to your separate one.
9. Credit cards. Both men and women should know exactly what to do in the case of credit cards. Do not hesitate on this subject. Cancel all cards and charge accounts. You'll probably have to steal your spouse's cards, however, to effectively close the account, because most card companies will continue to accept small purchases. Get your own separate charge cards now; you'll need the credit over the next few weeks as temporary-support payments are fixed.
10. Decide how you want to tell the other spouse. This is a very critical time in the divorce proceeding; a slip here can be costly.
11. Special planning hints for the male. (Note: Although these points for the male and female have already been mentioned elsewhere, they certainly bear repeating here.) It is not possible to cover every financial situation or condition here. The following tips will get you started, and fertile imagination should produce more:
    a. If you are the major breadwinner of the family, it should not be too difficult to find a few bucks here and there. This is true even if the savings is generated by debt of the family, as the family assets will be used to pay off the family liabilities.
    b. Have your car fixed and charge it. Chances are that fixing the car will add very little to the value

assigned to it when you divide the property, but the liability will be counted in full as a joint liability.

c. Buy some new clothes. You'll need them. Be sure and charge them.

d. Go to the dentist and the eye doctor and make sure that all the "repair" work you need is done.

12. Special planning hints for the female. These are pretty much the same as for the male, but there are a few winkles.

   a. Buy yourself a new wardrobe. You'll find it absolutely necessary once you're on your own. Don't be afraid about charging the items even if you have to set up a new charge account. The liability will be added to the other family debts. If you are going to wind up with the kids, make sure that they have new wardrobes, too.

   b. If you have your own car, it is likely that you'll get it in the division. So if it's in need of repairs, do it now.

   c. Get your medical, dental, and eye doctor checkups now. This is especially important for the children in case child-support payments are not enough to cover costly items like orthodontia.

13. Once the first papers have been filed and your divorce is finally rolling, get out and meet new people to get your mind off the proceedings for a while. Be sure, though, to check all new sleeping arrangements with your lawyer until the final decree. A slip here could be very costly.

The Divorce Tax Checklist

The following checklist, set up as a question-and-answer summary, is designed to assist you in determining what steps you should take in your divorce to save you the most in income taxes. Ideally, a couple will use the checklist together and will forget their personal animosity in the interest of saving income taxes. A good rule to adopt at the start is to split the savings equally, or if there are children involved, give more to the parent who has custody. Better to let the children get the benefit than the government.

While the steps do have some explanations contained in the checklist, the checklist is intended to be a synopsis of the tax procedures discussed throughout the divorce section. Therefore, if you need more detail, consult the particular chapter.

1. Should I Try to Get Divorced Before the End of the Year?

Absolutely. This is true in about 99 percent of the cases. The reason for this is to shift income from the higher-earning spouse to the other via the payment of alimony. This shifting of the income will allow the receiving spouse to take full advantage of the low-income allowance, standard deductions, etc., allowed all persons but particularly beneficial in the lower tax brackets. For those folks who can't manage to get divorced by the end of the year, consult item 3 on the effect of a Decree of Separate Maintenance.

2. How Can I Get the Maximum Tax Benefit from the Spousal-support (Alimony) Payments?

First, obtain an idea of the amount of support that must be paid. This can be done by securing a schedule of the amounts your county usually awards. Once you have this amount, you can begin adjusting the support payments via the alimony route so as to generate the maximum savings in federal and state income taxes. After the maximum savings are determined, split the amount with your spouse under the aforementioned schedule.

Unfortunately, since most couples can't agree to do the

above, following are some suggestions to use in an adversary situation:

If You Are Going to Pay Support

For the person who is going to be paying alimony, the very first thing that you must do is to obtain a written agreement specifying the amount of support. This is important because in the year the divorce is granted, support payments made up to the date of the divorce may be deducted as alimony on your tax return *only if the payments are made pursuant to a written agreement or a court order.*

For example, assume Al and Leonore separate in January, and Al agrees to pay her $500 per month spousal and child support. In January, Leonore files for the divorce, but because she is already receiving support from Al, it is not necessary for the court to award support. If the divorce is granted in September, Al will be able to deduct only those payments made after the divorce is granted. However, if Al had executed a written agreement with Leonore about the $500 support when they separated, he could deduct the payments from January on. This sounds silly, but this is the tax law.

If your spouse won't sign the written temporary-support agreement when you separate, make no payments until you are ordered to do so by the court. If the court orders you to pay support, your payments will be deductible as alimony from the date the court ordered the support.

If You Are Going to Receive Support

There are two possible ways for you to proceed in the area of alimony. You can work with your spouse to obtain the maximum tax benefit and the most in support, or you can be stubborn and use all the power and energy you have for a bloody siege. Always remember to use this power carefully, or you may end up saving a few dollars in taxes and miss an important opportunity for more of the property split or higher support payments.

In the case of the husband, every dollar he can shift from his higher tax bracket to his wife in the form of alimony saves him taxes. Of course, she must report every penny in taxable income. However, the tax law allows her to receive up to $3,200 of alimony income *tax-free,* and she gets an additional $750 tax-free for each child in her custody.

One word of advice to the payer. Before you pass the extra money on to the government in higher taxes because she is stubborn and won't sign the agreement, or the court won't order it in the most beneficial form, do one thing: *Offer her all of the tax savings.* You are no worse off, and you may benefit indirectly because some of the money will be spent on your children.

If your spouse is encouraging you to sign the Written Separation Agreement, and he is not being fair to you in the amount of support being offered, don't sign it. Even if you have to go to court for temporary support, you will come out better because the amount set for child support is going to be nontaxable to you. If you point this out to your spouse, he will probably quickly reconsider his poor offer.

3. Should I Get a Decree of Separate Maintenance?

This piece of paper is an extremely valuable document because it allows a couple to file as single taxpayers. The Decree of Separate Maintenance is usually called a legal separation in most states and is usually easily obtained. Unlike a divorce, there is no waiting period, but it does require the consent of both spouses. The settlement of the property and other matters can usually be carried over and determined at a later date either by the parties themselves or by the court. (Indeed, most states will allow the *final* divorce decree to be granted, even though the family property has not yet finally been determined or divided.) The Decree of Separate Maintenance can be converted to a petition for a divorce decree by either spouse. Remember, however, the Decree of Separate Maintenance means you are still legally married, even though you are single for tax purposes.

4. What Is the Tax Effect of Selling the House?

When you sell your house to an outsider, you must replace the house with one equal to half the value within eighteen months. This means that if you sold your house for $80,000, you and your ex-spouse must each purchase (within the time limit) a house or other dwelling costing at least $40,000 to avoid paying taxes on the gain.

The eighteen-month limit referred to above also applies to the purchase of a home made *prior* to the time you sell your old house, if you establish the new home as your residence. It is not necessary to be divorced at the time of purchase for the eighteen-month rule to be effective. However, for those persons who move out before they sell the house, beware. You may be faced with having to pay taxes on the gain if you have changed your residence.

5. What About the Tax Effect of Splitting the Personal Property?

Generally, there is no problem when a couple splits and one takes a certain amount of the household furnishings and personal property and the other one takes another amount. Within reason, provided you aren't dividing a fortune in jewels, you can split your personal effects any way you like and not worry about the tax effects.

6. What About Stocks, Bonds, and Other Securities?

The general rule for these is that if one member purchases the other member's interest in any securities for cash, the person selling the securities will have a taxable gain based upon the difference between their cost basis for the securities and the cash received.

Chapter 38 discusses some of the problems in this area, but it is highly recommended that you consult with a competent tax adviser whenever you and your spouse agree to buy or sell stocks and bonds pursuant to a divorce agreement.

7. Can I Designate All Support Payments As Alimony?

The answer is yes. And the reason this question is so frequently asked is that spousal support is deductible and child support is not. The U. S. Supreme Court has ruled that if the support agreement does not specifically provide a separate amount for child support, all of the payment is for alimony. Very few courts will specifically request that a certain amount of the payment be designated as child support if the total payment is large enough so that it is obvious that the children are benefiting from it. See Chapter 31 for the exact wording you should use on the decree to qualify all of the payment as alimony.

8. Should I Pay for the Children's Medical Bills?

It depends. From a tax standpoint you should pay for their medical expenses only if you are entitled to count them as dependents. Otherwise, the medical expenses are not allowable as a deduction to you. The usual case is that the custodial parent does not get to count the children as dependents and therefore does not get a deduction for the medical bills. If you are bargaining for an amount to cover the children's medical expenses, have it added to the alimony award, as discussed in item 6. In this way, the custodial parent can claim the kids as dependents *and* get their medical bills deducted. Upon remarriage, however, you will lose this privilege.

9. What Is the Tax Benefit Gained by Paying for the Medical Expenses?

Assuming that you qualify to count your children as dependents, the amounts you spend for their medical expenses are deductible only to the extent that they exceed 3 percent of your adjusted gross income. The usual effect of this limitation is to reduce your medical-expense deduction to zero. If you want to make a rough calculation, take your salary, subtract your alimony payments, and multiply by 3 percent. Any medical expenses paid over this amount can be added to your other itemized deductions.

10. What Does It Take to Get the Dependency Deductions for the Children?

The tax rule for getting the dependency is this: The divorce decree must specifically provide for child-support payments, and the spouse who provides more than half the support gets the deduction.

There is a special rule for noncustodial parents. If they provide as much as $1,200 per year for the support of each child, they automatically get the exemption deduction unless the custodial parent can prove a greater amount spent on support. For most practical purposes, the custodial spouse has a very hard time getting a dependency deduction if support equals $1,200 or more per year for each child. The major problem in proving support is that you cannot simply divide your household expenses, claim a prorated part for yourself and the number of children in your care, and have this count as proof. You must actually keep an accurate record of such things as toothbrushes and clothes purchased, food eaten, etc. This is the amount that must exceed the $1,200 (or more) paid by the noncustodial parent in order to qualify you for the dependency deduction.

11. What Are the Tax Effects of Life Insurance Policies?

If you are the spouse paying child support, then by all means obtain a life insurance policy to ensure adequate funds to care for your children in the event of an untimely demise. The cheapest way, from a tax standpoint, is to have your former husband or wife own the insurance policy and make the payments. When you arrange the policy this way, the proceeds from the insurance will not be included in your estate whenever you die and will thereby escape an estate tax on the proceeds. Of course, your ex-spouse will own the policy and may spend the proceeds on anything he or she wishes. If this is of concern to you, simply take out enough additional insurance to cover the estate taxes and set up a trust for your children. When you die, the insurance proceeds will be paid to the children's trust. You can restrict the disbursements from the trust to assure support for your children, which is, after all, your main intent.

The life insurance premiums that you pay are not deductible by you, nor will they be income to your children or your former spouse. If your spouse owns the policy and he or she makes the payments, he or she will not get a deduction for those payments either. However, if you increase the spousal-support amount equal to the premium being paid, you will get a deduction for this and your ex-spouse will have to pick up this amount in income.

It's nice to know that any funds received on an insurance policy because of the death of your ex-spouse will not constitute taxable income either for federal or state purposes. Since there is no deduction allowed for the premiums, the government allows you to receive the money without taxes (other than the estate taxes noted above).

12. What About Lump-sum Settlements Rather Than Paying Spousal Support?

The general answer is no. Although this may appeal to you most of all, you have to weigh the fact that you will be losing an opportunity to have the U. S. Government pick up part of your divorce cost. For example, suppose that you have the choice of paying $25,000 in cash to your former spouse in a lump-sum settlement rather than paying him or her $600 per month for a period of fifty months. In the first case you will not get to deduct the $25,000 lump-sum payment, nor will it be income to your spouse. (Read the note below to see what may happen if you transfer property.) Getting rid of the requirement of paying monthly alimony may appeal to you, but it's costly in tax dollars. Look at it this way—since you have to pay it, you can get a certain amount of pleasure in knowing that it's *income* to him or her while you get to *deduct* it. Under the second alternative, the $30,000 paid over fifty months will be deductible by you as alimony and taxable to your ex-spouse. In any sort of tax bracket you will be getting the government to pay a significant amount of the support, plus you get the use of the $25,000. This means a considerable savings to you over the lump-sum payment.

A Note on Property Settlements

The Supreme Court ruled that a husband who transferred his separate property to his ex-wife (in exchange for her release of marital claims) owes taxes on the gain in value of the property over its original value. (Original value is also known as "basis.") On the other hand, the IRS has ruled that a wife who exchanges her marital rights for separate property realizes no gain or loss on such property. The rationale for this is that her rights are taken to be equal in value to the property received. The wife's tax basis of the property so acquired by her is its fair market value at the time she acquires it from her husband. She never has to report what its original value was.

It's clear in this case that the husband has ended up with the short end of the stick. For those of you who are involved in giving your spouse your own separate property in a divorce settlement, beware!

To be fair, the IRS also treats wives unfairly whenever it gets the chance. Take the following case:

Walter and Eva were married for several years and owned a business that they had built together. They decided in the divorce decree that she would sell her interest in the business to Walter. They agreed to the amount of the sales price, and so on, before the divorce was granted. After the divorce was granted, Walter purchased Eva's interest.

Now the tax rules in this situation are such that a gain on the sale of property between *related* people is taxed at ordinary-income rates while there is no deduction allowed for a loss.

Accordingly, believing she was no longer related to Walter, Eva reported the gain at capital-gain rates in her tax return. The IRS levied an extra tax on Eva and said the gain was ordinary income even though the transaction took place when they were no longer married. The IRS reasoning in this case was that Walter and Eva formulated the sale during the time they were married and that's what counted. And the Tax Court agreed!

Under this holding, it is going to be difficult for any husband or wife who wants to transfer property as part of a divorce settlement to escape paying heavy tax penalties. Probably the only answer at this time is to divide the property relatively equally, or be extremely cautious about the price of what is purchased.

In the first case, the hopeless husband, and any future transferrors, should give only separate property with a fair market value that is less than cost. This way they at least get a tax deduction for the loss.

14. What Is the Tax Effect of Company Stock Options?

Stock options which are separate property are treated much the same way as separate property. However, if the stock options are community property and they have a fair market value to the employee in excess of their original value, then a settlement payment to the other spouse will constitute a taxable transaction. The other alternative is to split the stock down the middle and let each have half. The latter case is usually impractical because the employer will not usually agree to such a split, especially if the right to the option is predicated upon future employment.

From a tax-planning standpoint, the best position is to place a very low fair market value on any options not yet exercised. If your spouse feels they are worth a greater amount, let her purchase the options from you or give them to her in the settlement. Perhaps she will have a vested interest in seeing you stay on with your employer, which may be advantageous to you in future negotiations. (This might be particularly useful if you have decided to leave your employer anyway.)

15. What About "Bunching Up" or Prepaying Alimony?

The general rule is that lump-sum payments for *past* alimony obligations may be deducted when paid. Conversely, the ex-spouse receiving such payments must report the alimony as income whenever it's received.

The general rule is that you can deduct prepayments of alimony provided the prepayment doesn't exceed 10 percent of your total alimony obligation. For example, if you were ordered to pay $500 per month for seven years ($42,000), you could prepay $4,200 at any time and still get it deducted.

A useful tax-planning device is to make your lump-sum alimony payments on December 31, using certified mail in order to prove that you actually disbursed the funds during the year. Since the receiving party did not receive the payment until the following year, he or she doesn't report the payment in income until then. This gives you a current deduction and your ex-spouse a delayed income item for the next year. Be sure and keep adequate records to prove when the payments were made, and when they were received, to support your position on the tax return.

Note: If only partial-support payments are received, the amount received is applied to child support first before anything can be allocated to alimony.

16. What About an Alimony Trust?

In general, these are of no value to either the wife or the husband in the event of divorce. The payor usually will not get a tax deduction for the amounts being paid by the trust for spousal support and indeed may have a taxable consequence if he transfers separate property to the trust. Alternatively, the recepient will have taxable income as alimony from the amounts received from the trust.

Recommendation: Ignore alimony trusts for tax-planning purposes. However, if you are afraid he will not have or maintain sufficient funds to make the support payments, ask your attorney about having him establish a nonrevocable trust with sufficient funds to make your support payments over the time period agreed to.

17. The Divorce Is Not Yet Final— What Tax Status Do I File Under?

Until the divorce decree is final, or you have a Decree of Separate Maintenance (legal separation), you are still married and will have to file under one of two categories: jointly, filing with your spouse, or married filing separately.

If you are a custodial spouse and living apart from your husband, you may use the head-of-household rates, and you do not have to file under the table "married filing separately." But to qualify, you have to have provided more than one-half of the support and a home for at least one child. If you are the noncustodial spouse you will have to use the rates for marrieds filing separately and pay the penalty tax.

If your divorce or separate maintenance decree is granted before the end of the year, you cannot file a joint return for that year and will have to use the rates for single persons, except in those cases when you are the custodial parent with at least one child and you can use the more favorable head-of-household rates. This is true even though you do not qualify to count your child as a dependent.

18. What About Liabilities for Unpaid Income Taxes or Future IRS Exams?

Caution: If you do not have it specifically stated in your divorce decree, any subsequent extra taxes levied by the IRS on your old joint returns may be charged to you. There is a provision in the tax law that an innocent spouse may be spared the penalties and interest, but you have to be *very* innocent.

Therefore, if you aren't that innocent, have your attorney put a clause in the divorce settlement so that if any extra taxes are levied on prior tax returns, your ex-spouse will have to pay them. Although the IRS can still collect from you for taxes owed on any joint return you signed, at least you can collect from your former husband or wife.

19. What Happens if I Deduct One Sum and She Reports Something Else as Income?

This is one warning to heed. The IRS is very fond of examining the first- and second-year tax returns of recently divorced people. Apparently, the IRS has geared its computers to automatically kick out these returns for examination by its agents. There are many, many cases of opposite positions being taken on taxable-income items by an ex-spouse. If the returns are at variance, the IRS will examine both returns and will pursue the spouse with the weaker case. Obviously, they want to disallow the deduction on one and require its inclusion as income on the other. The best protection would be for you and your spouse to agree in writing to exactly what will be taxable income on her side and the deduction on yours. Unfortunately, this is a utopian situation which seldom occurs in real life.

If you think an item is a legitimate deduction to you, send your ex-spouse a Form 1099 (with a copy to the IRS), reporting the amount as income to him or her. This puts the IRS on notice that he or she is supposed to report the amount on his or her tax return and may give you a leg up on the deduction. Of course, you can imagine how happy it will make your ex to receive such a form from you.

21. What About Deducting Legal Fees?

Any part of the legal fees you pay in your divorce for tax advice is deductible by you. Be sure to get an itemized statement from your attorney. Some courts have even allowed a deduction for the part of the legal fee that applies to the generation of alimony.

Note, however, that there is no deduction whatsoever for any payment made by you for your spouse's legal fees. In order for you both to take advantage of the tax law, simply pay (or obtain) an additional amount of alimony so that each spouse will pay his or her own legal fees and get the maximum tax deduction allowable.

22. What About Any Tax Refunds?

In general, most courts have held that tax refunds due from the last year a joint return is filed belong equally to both spouses. This is not necessarily so in the non-community-property states, as the refund may be generated because of the effect of income from separate property.

If you think you are entitled to part of the refund, refuse to sign the joint return until your ex-spouse agrees to let you have your part. Don't forget any state refunds as well.

APPENDIX

LTR LAWS FOR THE FIFTY STATES

ALABAMA

Living together

Cohabitation: varying fines and prison sentence depending on conviction

Fornication: no penalty

Marriage

Common-law marriage recognized: yes

Community-property state: no

Divorce

Grounds:

1. irretrievable breakdown of marriage
2. adultery
3. abandonment for one year
4. imprisonment for two years
5. conviction for crime against nature
6. habitual drunkness and/or the use of drugs
7. incompatibility
8. incurable insanity

Residency requirement: six months

Special note:

Warning: It takes only one partner to get a decree of legal separation changed to a divorce, providing the separation has been in effect for more than two years.

ALASKA

Living together

Cohabitation: a crime punishable by a maximum $500 fine and/or a one–two year sentence

Fornication: ambiguous law

Marriage

Common-law marriage recognized: no

Community-property state: no

Divorce

Grounds:

1. marriage not consummated
2. adultery
3. felony conviction
4. willful desertion for one year
5. cruel and inhuman treatment
6. personal indignities
7. incompatibility of temperament (no-fault)
8. mental illness
9. addiction to drugs or alcohol

Residency requirements: If marriage took place in the state no waiting; otherwise one year residency required.

ARIZONA

Living together

Cohabitation: a felony—maximum three-year sentence
Fornication: no penalty

Marriage

Common-law marriage recognized: no
Community-property state: yes

Divorce

Grounds:

1. irretrievable breakdown of the marriage

Residency requirement: ninety days

Special note:

You can get a legal separation from the court by:

1. meeting the proper residency requirements
2. proving the marriage is irretrievably broken
3. having both parties agree to the separation
4. making proper provisions for child custody and support

Before this, however, you must file a petition for

conciliation and wait sixty days. After that time, you may file for divorce, annulment, or legal separation.

ARKANSAS

Living together

Cohabitation: considered a misdemeanor; varying fines and sentences, depending on conviction.

Fornication: no penalty

Marriage

Common-law marriage recognized: no

Community-property state: no

Divorce

Grounds:

1. impotency
2. desertion for one year
3. bigamy
4. felony conviction
5. habitual drunkenness and/or cruel and barbarous treatment
6. adultery
7. living separate and apart for three years (without cohabitation)[1]
8. insanity
9. nonsupport

Residency requirements: sixty days or three months

CALIFORNIA

Living together

Cohabitation: no penalty

Fornication: no penalty

---

[1] This is Arkansas' version of no-fault.

Marriage

Common-law marriage recognized: no
Community-property state: yes

Divorce

Grounds:

1. irreconcilable differences
2. insanity

Residency requirement: six months

COLORADO

Living together

Cohabitation: no penalty
Fornication: no penalty

Marriage

Common-law marriage recognized: yes
Community-property state: no

Divorce

Grounds:

1. irretrievable breakdown of marriage

Residency requirement: ninety days

Special note:

A petition for legal separation must state that the marriage is irretrievably broken and must set forth the following data: residence of each party and length of residence in state; date and place of marriage; date on which parties separated; number of children, custody, and child support and alimony (if applicable).

CONNECTICUT

Living together

Cohabitation: no penalty
Fornication: no penalty

Marriage

Common-law marriage recognized: no
Community-property state: no

Divorce

Grounds:

1. irretrievable breakdown of marriage
2. living apart for eighteen months
3. adultery
4. fraudulent contract
5. willful desertion for one year
6. seven years' absence
7. habitual intemperance
8. intolerable cruelty
9. imprisonment for more than one year
10. hospitalization for five years for mental illness

Residency requirement: one year

Special note:

Warning: While Connecticut law requires both partners' agreement to resume a marital relationship after a legal separation, it requires only one partner to file for permanent divorce.

DELAWARE

Living together

Cohabitation: no penalty
Fornication: no penalty

Marriage

Common-law marriage recognized: no
Community-property state: no

Divorce

Grounds:

1. irretrievable breakdown of marriage

Residency requirement: six months

DISTRICT OF COLUMBIA

Living together

Cohabitation: no penalty
Fornication: fine and sentence

Marriage

Common-law marriage recognized: yes
Community-property state: no

Divorce

Grounds:

1. voluntary separation (without cohabitation) for six months
2. involuntary separation (without cohabitation) for one year

Residency requirement: one year

Special note:

Legal separation granted for above reasons, plus adulery and cruelty. A legal separation can be enlarged into a judgment of divorce after one year.

FLORIDA

Living together

Cohabitation: misdemeanor—maximum sixty days sentence
Fornication: misdemeanor—maximum sixty days sentence

Marriage

Common-law marriage recognized: no (recognized before 1968; still valid if started before that date.)
Community-property state: no

Divorce

Grounds:

1. irretrievable breakdown of the marriage
2. mental incompetence

Residency requirement: six months

GEORGIA

Living together

Cohabitation: no penalty
Fornication: misdemeanor

Marriage

Common-law marriage recognized: yes
Community-property state: no

Divorce

Grounds:

1. irretrievable breakdown of marriage
2. incest
3. mental incapacity
4. impotency
5. force or duress in obtaining marriage
6. unknown pregnancy
7. adultery
8. desertion for one year
9. two years' imprisonment
10. habitual intoxication
11. cruel treatment
12. mental illness
13. drug addiction

Residency requirement: six months

Special note:

Parties divorced from bed and board, on subsequent reconciliation, may live together again as husband and wife by first filing in the office of the ordinary of the county where the divorce was granted their written agreement to that effect.

HAWAII

Living together

Cohabitation: no penalty
Fornication: fine and/or sentence

Marriage

Common-law marriage recognized: no
Community-property state: no

Divorce

Grounds:

1. irretrievable breakdown of marriage
2. living separate and apart for two years

Residency requirement: one year

Special note:

A legal separation from bed and board for a period not to exceed two years may be decreed by the family court for any of the causes for which absolute divorce may be granted.

IDAHO

Living together

Cohabitation: misdemeanor—fine and/or sentence
Fornication: fine and/or sentence

Marriage

Common-law marriage recognized: yes
Community-property state: yes

Divorce

Grounds:

1. irreconcilable differences
2. adultery

3. extreme cruelty
4. willful desertion
5. willful neglect
6. habitual intemperance
7. conviction of felony
8. insanity
9. living separate and apart for five years

Residency requirement: six weeks

ILLINOIS

Living together

Cohabitation: misdemeanor—sentence
Fornication: misdemeanor—sentence

Marriage

Common-law marriage recognized: no
Community-property state: no

Divorce

Grounds:

1. bigamy
2. impotency
3. adultery
4. willful desertion for one year
5. habitual drunkenness or excessive use of drugs for two years
6. attempt on the life of other spouse
7. physical and/or mental cruelty
8. felony conviction
9. venereal disease

Residency requirement: one year (six months if offense was committed within state)

INDIANA

Living together

Cohabitation: fine and/or sentence
Fornication: fine and/or sentence

Marriage

Common-law marriage recognized: no (legal before 1958; still in force if contracted before then)
Community-property state: no

Divorce

Grounds:

1. irretrievable breakdown of marriage
2. conviction of an infamous crime
3. impotency (at time of marriage)
4. incurable insanity

Residency requirement: six months

IOWA

Living together

Cohabitation: no penalty
Fornication: no penalty

Marriage

Common-law marriage recognized: yes
Community-property state: no

Divorce

Grounds:

1. breakdown of marriage

Residency requirement: one year

KANSAS

Living together

Cohabitation: misdemeanor—fine and/or sentence
Fornication: no penalty

Marriage

Common-law marriage recognized: yes
Community-property state: no

Divorce

Grounds:

1. incompatibility
2. abandonment for one year
3. adultery
4. extreme cruelty
5. habitual drunkenness
6. gross neglect of duty
7. felony conviction
8. mental illness for three years

Residency requirement: sixty days

Special note:

Decree of Separate Maintenance granted for same grounds as divorce.

KENTUCKY

Living together

Cohabitation: no penalty
Fornication: no penalty

Marriage

Common-law marriage recognized: no
Community-property state: no

Divorce

Grounds:

1. irretrievable breakdown of marriage

Residency requirement: 180 days

LOUISIANA

Cohabitation: no penalty
Fornication: no penalty

Marriage

Common-law marriage recognized: no
Community-property state: yes

Divorce

Grounds:

1. adultery
2. felony conviction
3. living separate and apart for two years (lengthy no-fault)

Residency requirement: one year

Special note:

According to Louisiana law, "a separation from bed and board shall be granted although both spouses are mutually at fault in causing the separation. In such instances alimony *pendente lite* may be allowed but permanent alimony shall not be allowed thereafter following a divorce."

MAINE

Living together

Cohabitation: no penalty
Fornication: no penalty

Marriage

Common-law marriage recognized: no
Community-property state: no

Divorce

Grounds:

1. irreconcilable differences
2. adultery
3. impotence
4. extreme cruelty
5. desertion for three years
6. alcoholism or drug use

7. cruel and abusive treatment
8. neglect

Residency requirement: six months with certain exceptions

Special note:

Maine law provides that when the alleged cause is irreconcilable differences, a divorce shall not be granted unless both parties have received counseling by a professional counselor, and a copy of the counselor's report is made available to the court.

MARYLAND

Living together

Cohabitation: no penalty
Fornication: no penalty

Marriage

Common-law marriage recognized: no
Community-property state: no

Divorce

Grounds:

1. impotency (at time of marriage)
2. any cause by which the laws of the state render the marriage void "*ab initio*" (i.e., from the beginning)
3. adultery
4. abandonment for one year
5. living separate and apart (without cohabitation) for one year (no-fault)
6. felony conviction
7. separation (without cohabitation) for three years
8. incurable insanity

Residency requirement: one year

Special note:

You can get a legal separation for the following causes: cruelty, vicious conduct, abandonment and desertion, and living separate and apart without hope of reconciliation.

MASSACHUSETTS

Living together

Cohabitation: fine and/or sentence
Fornication: fine and/or sentence

Marriage

Common-law marriage recognized: no
Community-property state: no

Divorce

Grounds:

1. irretrievable breakdown of the marriage
2. adultery
3. impotency
4. desertion for one year
5. excessive alcohol or drug use
6. neglect
7. imprisonment for five years
8. cruel and abusive treatment

Residency requirement: one year

Special note:

Section 40 of Massachusetts divorce laws states that "persons divorced from each other cohabitating as husband and wife or living together in the same house shall be guilty of adultery."

MICHIGAN

Living together

Cohabitation: misdemeanor—fine or sentence
Fornication: misdemeanor—fine or sentence

Marriage

Common-law marriage recognized: no
Community-property state: no

Divorce

Grounds:

1. irretrievable breakdown of the marriage[1]

Residency requirement: 180 days

Special note:

An action for separate maintenance may be filed in court in the same manner as an action for divorce. In the complaint, the plaintiff shall make no other explanation of the grounds for separate maintenance than by the use of the statutory language.

MINNESOTA

Living together

Cohabitation: no penalty
Fornication: no penalty

Marriage

Common-law marriage recognized: no
Community-property state: no

Divorce

Grounds:

1. irretrievable breakdown of the marriage

Residency requirement: one year

MISSISSIPPI

Living together

Cohabitation: fine and sentence
Fornication: fine and sentence

---

[1] Person who files this action is known as the "plaintiff," making the other partner the "defendant."

Marriage

Common-law marriage recognized: no
Community-property state: no

Divorce

Grounds:

1. impotency
2. adultery
3. prison sentence
4. willful desertion
5. habitual drunkenness
6. habitual drug use
7. habitual cruel and inhuman treatment
8. insanity (at time of marriage)
9. bigamy
10. pregnancy of wife by another person (at the time of marriage)
11. incest
12. incurable insanity (confinement for three years)

Residency requirement: six months

Special note:

Persons cohabiting after a divorce are committing adultery.

MISSOURI

Living together

Cohabitation: no penalty
Fornication: no penalty

Marriage

Common-law marriage recognized: no
Community-property state: no

Divorce

Grounds:

1. irretrievable breakdown of the marriage[1]

Residency requirement: ninety days

MONTANA

Living together

Cohabitation: no penalty
Fornication: no penalty

Marriage

Common-law marriage recognized: yes
Community-property state: no

Divorce

Grounds:

1. irretrievable breakdown of marriage

Residency requirement: ninety days

NEBRASKA

Living together

Cohabitation: fine and sentence
Fornication: no penalty

Marriage

Common-law marriage recognized: no
Community-property state: no

Divorce

Grounds:

1. irretrievable breakdown of marriage

Residency requirement: one year

---

[1] Missouri's high court has ruled that there must be substantial reasons behind this contention. In other words, you've got to come up with a better reason than just boredom before you can prove that your marriage is irretrievably broken.

NEVADA

Living together

Cohabitation: no penalty
Fornication: no penalty

Marriage

Common-law marriage recognized: no
Community-property state: no

Divorce

Grounds:

1. incompatibility
2. living separate and apart for one year
3. insanity for two years

Residency requirement: six weeks

NEW HAMPSHIRE

Living together

Cohabitation: no penalty
Fornication: no penalty

Marriage

Common-law marriage recognized: no
Community-property state: no

Divorce

Grounds:

1. impotency
2. adultery
3. extreme cruelty
4. imprisonment for one year
5. abuse or ill treatment
6. absence for two years
7. habitual drunkenness
8. religious beliefs
9. abandonment for two years

10. neglect
11. irreconcilable differences

Residency requirement: bona fide resident of the state

Special note:

Legal separations are granted for the same reasons as absolute divorces.

NEW JERSEY

Living together

Cohabitation: no penalty
Fornication: misdemeanor—fine and/or sentence

Marriage

Common-law marriage recognized: no
Community-property state: no

Divorce

Grounds:

1. adultery
2. desertion for one year
3. extreme cruelty
4. living separate and apart for eighteen months (no-fault)
5. drug or alcohol addiction
6. insanity and confinement for two years
7. imprisonment for eighteen months
8. deviant sexual conduct

Residency requirement: bona fide resident of the state

Special note:

Legal separations are granted for the same reasons as absolute divorces.

NEW MEXICO

Living together

Cohabitation: warning by judge

Fornication: no penalty

Marriage

Common-law marriage recognized: no
Community-property state: no

Divorce

Grounds:

1. incompatibility
2. cruel and inhuman treatment
3. adultery
4. abandonment

Residency requirement: six months

NEW YORK

Living together

Cohabitation: no penalty
Fornication: no penalty

Marriage

Common-law marriage recognized: no
Community-property state: no

Divorce

Grounds:

1. cruel and inhuman treatment
2. abandonment for one year
3. imprisonment for three years
4. adultery
5. living separate and apart for one year (no-fault)

Residency requirement: two years with exceptions

Special note:

A legal separation may be granted for cruel treatment, abandonment, neglect, adultery, or imprisonment.

NORTH CAROLINA

Living together

Cohabitation: misdemeanor—fine and/or sentence
Fornication: misdemeanor—fine and/or sentence

Marriage

Common-law marriage recognized: no
Community-proeprty state: no

Divorce

Grounds:

1. adultery
2. impotence (at time of marriage)
3. unknown pregnancy (at time of marriage)
4. living separate and apart for one year (no-fault)
5. unnatural sex acts
6. continuous separation for three years due to insanity

Residency requirement: six months

Special note:

Legal separations are also granted for abandonment, cruel treatment, personal indignities, and excessive use of drugs and/or alcohol.

NORTH DAKOTA

Living together

Cohabitation: no penalty
Fornication: no penalty

Marriage

Common-law marriage recognized: no
Community-property state: no

Divorce

Grounds:

1. adultery
2. extreme cruelty
3. willful desertion
4. willful neglect
5. habitual intemperance
6. felony conviction
7. insanity for five years
8. irreconcilable differences

Residency requirement: one year

Special note:

A legal separation may be granted for the same reasons as absolute divorce.

OHIO

Living together

Cohabitation: no penalty
Fornication: no penalty

Marriage

Common-law marriage recognized: yes
Community-property state: no

Divorce

Grounds:

1. former spouse living
2. absence for one year
3. adultery
4. impotency
5. extreme cruelty
6. fraudulent contract
7. neglect
8. habitual drunkenness
9. imprisonment
10. procuring an out-of-state divorce

11. living separate and apart for two years (no-fault)

Residency requirement: six months

OKLAHOMA

Living together

Cohabitation: no penalty
Fornication: no penalty

Marriage

Common-law marriage recognized: yes
Community-property state: no

Divorce

Grounds:

1. abandonment for one year
2. adultery
3. impotency
4. unknown pregnancy at time of marriage
5. extreme cruelty
6. fraudulent contract
7. incompatibility (no-fault)
8. habitual drunkenness
9. gross neglect of duty
10. imprisonment
11. procuring an out-of-state divorce
12. insanity and confinement for five years

Residency requirement: six months

Special note:

Couples interested in legal separation, please note: Either husband or wife may obtain alimony from the other without a divorce, in an action brought for that purpose in the district court for any of the causes for which a divorce may be granted.

OREGON

Living together

Cohabitation: no penalty
Fornication: no penalty

Marriage

Common-law marriage recognized: no
Community-property state: yes

Divorce

Grounds:

1. irreconcilable differences

Residency requirement: six months

PENNSYLVANIA

Living together

Cohabitation: no penalty
Fornication: no penalty

Marriage

Common-law marriage recognized: yes
Community-property state: no

Divorce

Grounds:

1. impotency
2. previous marriage still in force
3. adultery
4. desertion for two years
5. cruel and barbarous treatment
6. intolerable indignities
7. fraudulent contract
8. imprisonment for two years
9. incest
10. insanity and confinement for three years

Residency requirement: one year

Special note:

A legal separation is available only to the wife and only on these grounds: that her husband abandoned or turned her out of doors, treated her cruelly or visited intolerable indignities upon her, or was an adulterer.

RHODE ISLAND

Living together

Cohabitation: no penalty
Fornication: small fine

Marriage

Common-law marriage recognized: yes
Community-property state: no

Divorce

Grounds:

1. impotency
2. adultery
3. extreme cruelty
4. willful desertion for five years
5. drunkenness
6. drug use
7. neglect for one year
8. gross misbehavior
9. living separate and apart for three years
10. irreconcilable differences

Residency requirement: one year

SOUTH CAROLINA

Living together

Cohabitation: fine and sentence
Fornication: fine and sentence

Marriage

Common-law marriage recognized: yes
Community-property state: no

Divorce

Grounds:

1. adultery
2. desertion—one year
3. physical cruelty
4. habitual drunkenness or drug use
5. living separate and apart for three years (no-fault)

Residency requirement: one year

SOUTH DAKOTA

Living together

Cohabitation: no penalty
Fornication: no penalty

Marriage

Common-law marriage recognized: no
Community-property state: no

Divorce

Grounds:

1. adultery
2. extreme cruelty
3. willful desertion for one year
4. willful neglect for one year
5. habitual intemperance
6. felony conviction
7. incurable insanity

Residency requirement: bona fide resident of state

TENNESSEE

Living together

Cohabitation: no penalty
Fornication: no penalty

Marriage

Common-law marriage recognized: no
Community-property state: no

Divorce

Grounds:

1. impotency
2. previous marriage still in force
3. adultery
4. willful desertion for one year
5. conviction of infamous or felonious crime
6. imprisonment
7. attempt on life of spouse
8. wife's refusal to move with her husband
9. pregnancy at time of marriage by another person
10. habitual drunkenness or drug use
11. irreconcilable differences
12. cruel or inhuman treatment
13. wife beating
14. abandonment by husband

Residency requirement: six months

TEXAS

Living together

Cohabitation: no penalty
Fornication: no penalty

Marriage

Common-law marriage recognized: yes
Community-property state: yes

Divorce

Grounds:

1. marriage insupportable because of discord (no-fault)
2. cruelty
3. adultery
4. felony conviction
5. abandonment
6. living separately and apart for three years
7. insanity and confinement for three years

Residency requirement: six months

UTAH

Living together

Cohabitation: no penalty
Fornication: fine or sentence

Marriage

Common-law marriage recognized: no
Community-property state: no

Divorce

Grounds:

1. impotency
2. adultery
3. willful desertion for one year
4. neglect
5. habitual drunkenness
6. felony conviction
7. cruel treatment
8. living separate and apart for three years (no-fault)
9. insanity

Residency requirement: bona fide resident of the state

VERMONT

Living together

Cohabitation: no penalty
Fornication: no penalty

Marriage

Common-law marriage recognized: no
Community-property state: no

Divorce

Grounds:

1. adultery
2. prison sentence
3. intolerable severity
4. willful desertion for seven years
5. neglect
6. incurable insanity
7. living apart for six months (no-fault)

Residency requirements: six months (to bring action); one year (for final decree)

Special note:

A divorce from bed and board (like Decree of Separate Maintenance) can be granted by the court for any amount of time.

VIRGINIA

Living together

Cohabitation: misdemeanor—fine and/or sentence
Fornication: misdemeanor—fine

Marriage

Common-law marriage recognized: no
Community-property state: no

Divorce

Grounds:

1. adultery (sodomy or buggery committed outside marriage)[1]
2. felony conviction
3. cruelty, willful desertion
4. living separate and apart for one year (without cohabitation)

Residency requirement: six months

WASHINGTON

Living together

Cohabitation: no penalty
Fornication: no penalty

Marriage

Common-law marriage recognized: no
Community-property state: yes

Divorce

Grounds:

1. irretrievable breakdown of marriage

Residency requirement: a bona fide resident of the state

WEST VIRGINIA

Living together

Cohabitation: misdemeanor—fine and/or sentence
Fornication: misdemeanor—fine

Marriage

Common-law marriage recognized: no
Community-property state: no

---

[1] Not granted if there is voluntary cohabitation after the knowledge of the fact.

Divorce

Grounds:

1. adultery
2. felony conviction
3. willful desertion for one year
4. cruel and inhuman treatment
5. habitual drunkenness
6. drug addiction
7. living separate and apart for two years (no-fault)
8. insanity

Residency requirement: bona fide resident of the state

WISCONSIN

Living together

Cohabitation: fine and sentence
Fornication: fine and sentence

Marriage

Common-law marriage recognized: no
Community-property state: no

Divorce

Grounds:

1. adultery
2. imprisonment for three years
3. willful desertion for one year
4. inhuman treatment
5. habitual drunkenness
6. living separate and apart for one year (no-fault)

8. insanity and confinement for one year

Residency requirement: six months

Special note:

No motion for divorce or legal separation, contested

or uncontested, shall be brought to trial until the family court commissioner has, within 120 days after service of the summons upon the family court commissioner or five days after the action is set for trial, whichever is sooner, certified to the court that a reconciliation effort has been made, which certification shall be filed and entered in the court record book.

WYOMING

Living together

Cohabitation: fine and/or penalty
Fornication: no penalty

Marriage

Common-law marriage recognized: no
Community-property state: no

Divorce

Grounds:

1. irreconcilable differences
2. incurable insanity

Residency requirement: sixty days

VIRGIN ISLANDS

Divorce

Grounds for divorce or legal separation: irretrievable breadown of marriage.
Residency requirement: six weeks for nonresidents

PUERTO RICO

Divorce

Grounds:

1. adultery
2. felony conviction

3. habitual drunkenness
4. cruel treatment
5. abandonment
6. impotency
7. corruption to prostitution
8. insanity
9. living separate and apart for two years

Residency requirement: one year